And this is just the beginning...

Wilton. BAKING & DECORATING

4. IDEAS THAT WORK FOR THE WORKING WOMAN.

Two special pages of hints and ideas introduce our new collection of fast and festive desserts.

6. THIRTY-FIVE BIRTHDAY CAKES

Choose your favorite from dozens of distinctive designs. There's one for everyone from infants to seniors!

24. ONE PAN— SO MANY WAYS TO DECORATE!

See the same cake decorated 6 different ways—each so original you'll say "It's Pantastic!"

26. HOLIDAY ENTER-TAINING

A year full of fun times! Our calendar of cakes, cookies and treats takes you from New Year's to Christmas.

54. SPECIAL EVENTS

You'll find special ideas to highlight those once-in-a-lifetime celebrations from baby showers to retirements.

64. ENTERTAINING WITH CHOCOLATE

How sweet it is! These delicious treats are sure to tempt chocoholics and dessert-lovers.

Printed and bound in the U.S.A.

66. WEDDING CAKES

An array of treats to reign at the bridal shower plus traditional tiered cakes that are sure to get a warm reception!

76. AMERICAN REGIONAL DESSERTS

From sea to shining sea... eight hometown desserts we love to serve (and to eat!).

For photography purposes, many cakes in this book were decorated with royal icing.

80. DECORATOR'S GUIDE

99. PRODUCTS

CREDITS

Creative Director **Jack Siegel**
Associate Creative Director **Marc Ross**
Art Director **Diane Pierson**
Cake Designer **Gretchen McCarthy**
Copy Director **Marie De Benedictis**
Copywriters **Jane Mikis,
  Linda Skender**
Senior Decorators **Marie Kason,
  Amy Rohr**
Cake Decorators **Theresa Anderson,
  Nancy Suffolk**
Assistant Decorators **Debbie Kelly,
  Susan Matusiak**
Production/Traffic Coordinator
  Mary Stahulak
Photography **Tom Zamiar**
Illustration **Bobbye Cochran,
  Roger Harvey, Holly Dickens**

COMPLIMENTS

Dear Decorator,

The 1986 Wilton Yearbook, "Baking and Decorating," has something special in store for you!

The wide variety of ideas included in this Yearbook were specifically chosen to reflect today's tastes and your changing lifestyle. In addition to over one hundred unique cake designs, you'll find dozens of new ideas for making and decorating delicious candy, cookies and unusual desserts.

In answer to your requests, we've expanded our wedding section and have designed a new collection of desserts that are fast and delicious. To meet your needs, we've developed many new products, including new licensed character pans, specialty bakeware and dozens of new cake tops and accessory items.

Quite honestly, this Yearbook is our best yet. I hope you'll use it to discover the many pleasures decorating offers—the sense of accomplishment you feel, the joy of giving, the good times you can share with your family and friends. And, in addition, I hope you will personally enjoy decorating through-out 1986 and for many years to come.

Sincerely,

Vince Naccarato

Vincent Naccarato
President, Wilton Enterprises, Inc.

IDEAS THAT WORK FOR THE WORKING WOMAN

DELICIOUS DESSERTS FOR TODAY'S LIFESTYLE!

Whether you're managing an office or managing a home, you'll love our new collection of time-saving desserts.

On these two pages, and throughout this yearbook, you'll find more cakes and desserts specially designed to help you fit "homemade" into your busy schedule.

So next time you're short on time, look for this symbol◆. It'll show you the way to a great new dessert idea that's fast *and* delicious!

◆ Cakes can be baked and frozen up to 3 months before decorating day. Wrap each layer in heavy-duty foil; thaw still-wrapped cake before icing.

◆ Buttercream icing can be made up to 2 weeks in advance and stored in the refrigerator in an airtight container. Bring to room temperature, then rewhip before using.

◆ Royal icing flowers will keep for months at room temperature in an airtight container. It's a good idea to keep a supply on hand for emergencies.

◆ Make a single layer, one-pan cake for easier decorating with less fuss. Ring Mold Pans, Loaf Pans and larger Squares and Rounds each serve 10 or more and hold a standard boxed cake mix.

◆ Shortcakes, tart shells and meringues are easy to bake and store. Add ready-to-use canned pie filling, pudding or fruit and trim with canned whipped cream for a quick dessert.

◆ Making fancy cookies is easier than you think! Use Wilton Cookie Molds to bake cookies, then add extra flavor and color quickly with Cookie Dips and Sprinkle Tops. You'll find hundreds of super ideas in the Wilton "How To Make Great Tasting Fancy Cookies" book.

◆ Cupcakes make great party cakes! Dip and swirl top of each cupcake in bowl of icing, roll in chopped nuts or sprinkle with tinted coconut. Add a Wilton cake pick that fits your party theme. Let the children help—these party-perfect cakes are extra-easy!

◆ Wilton Candy Melts are a sweet way to decorate a plain or frosted cake. Add 1 tsp. solid vegetable shortening for each ounce of melted Candy Melts. Drizzle mixture over cake with a spoon or disposable decorating bag.

◆ Chopped or whole nuts, plain or toasted coconut, drained canned or fresh fruit can add color and flavor to a simple iced cake. And, best of all, you can pick up everything you need ready-to-use at the supermarket!

◆ Homemade candies or shaped cookies come in handy when you need an extra-quick decoration. It just takes a few seconds to arrange the pieces around the sides or on top of your iced cake.

◆ Confectioners' sugar, cinnamon-sugar or powdered cocoa can produce artistic results so easily. Position paper doilies, strips or designs on plain or iced cake, sift sugar over cake top, then carefully remove papers to reveal your design!

◆ Ice cream desserts can be molded weeks ahead of time and frozen until needed. Add sauces, toppings and trims you've made yourself or purchased ready-made.

Wilton Cake Tops, Icing Mixes and ready-to-use toppings can really save the day when you're in a hurry. Here are some more time-saving products:

◆ Wilton Cake Icer Tip (#789) pipes out a 2-in. ribbon of smooth or ribbed icing quickly and evenly. It's sized just right for single layer or character cakes. Just once around, blend with a spatula and you're done!

◆ Triple Star Tip can cut your decorating time in half! One squeeze pipes out three size-17 stars.

◆ Wilton Cookie Cutters, Message Patterns and Pattern Press Sets let you create a fancy cake in a jiffy! Simply press onto iced cake then cover marks with quick-to-pipe letters, outlines and swirls.

◆ Wilton Decorating Comb is the easy way to even out icing. Just pull along cake sides or swirl over cake top for perfectly even ridges just like on bake-shop cakes.

◆ Little Loafers Pans are perfect for single serving desserts. Cover with Quick Pour Icing (see recipe on Candy Wafer & Fondant Mix) and add simple icing flourishes. Or you could personalize each cake with the guest's name!

◇ON-THE-GO GLAZED POUND CAKE

Bake cake in Wilton Fancy Ring Mold. Top with glaze. (Melt 1 cup Candy Melts with 2 tsp. butter; use low heat and stir constantly. Stir in 3 Tbsps. brandy or liqueur.) Drizzle with additional melted Candy Melts. Fill bowl with canned pudding topped with tip 2110 rosette. Spoon a bit onto each serving. *Serves 12.*

◇LICKETY-SPLIT LEMON CAKE

Ice cake top (10-in. Square) with canned lemon pudding. Use Wilton Cake Icer Tip and thawed non-dairy whipped topping to cover lower portion of sides. Use tip 16 to add zigzag sides, criss-cross strings on top and pull-out star border to decorate. Trim with lemon slices and leaves. Refrigerate until serving time. *Serves 24.*

◇READY-SET-GO FRUITED DESSERT

Bake cake in Wilton 9 x 13-in. Sheet Cake Pan. Ice and sprinkle with chopped nuts. Add drained canned peach slices and maraschino cherries. Edge with tip 18 shells. *Serves 15.*

◇SHORTCUT SHORTCAKES

Bake shortcakes using Wilton Shortcakes 'n Treats Pan. Just before serving, add a scoop of ice cream. Spoon on preserves, ready-to-use pie filling or ice cream topping. Trim with tip 2110 whipped cream rosette. *Each serves 1.*

◇QUICK CANDY-GO-ROUNDS

Make candies using Candy Melts and Parisian Cookie Mold. Ice 10-in. Round cake. Press on nuts. Allow icing to crust. Cut paper stars from a sheet of paper; place on cake top. Sift confectioners sugar over cake top then carefully remove stars with a spatula to reveal pattern. Attach candies with dabs of icing. *Serves 12.*

KIDS' BIRTHDAYS...
Lots of Fun For Everyone.

Birthday cakes should be as entertaining for you as they are for the kids.

This year, think big for the small fry...and for yourself.

Put your own hand to one of these cake ideas. And they'll clap for you.

Focus on a theme.

Spotlight a fairy tale, a character, a colorful clown, a toy. Match the birthday child's costume to the cake, and everyone'll do a double take.

Place cards?

Bake cookies and pipe each guest's name on them in icing. Use one design or mix and match.

We've got the cutters, recipes and ideas for the making.

1 OF A KIND!
Decorating Needs
- **Guitar Pan, p. 177**
- **Tips 3, 4, 12, 18, 21, 131, 349, p. 118-121**

1. Make 20 tip 131 drop flowers with tip 4 dot centers. Ice cake sides and lightly ice cake top smooth. With toothpick, mark candle and "cake." Ice background area brown, candle gold and "cake" pink.

2. Outline candle and face with tip 4 strings. Add tip 4 dot eyeballs. Pipe tip 12 bead-motion flame (flatten with finger dipped in cornstarch). Add tip 12 bead melting wax.

3. Print tip 3 and 4 messages. Outline "cake top" with tip 18 shells; "base" with tip 21. With toothpick, mark 1½-in. scallops on "cake." Attach flower garland with dots of icing. Add tip 349 leaves. Edge cake base with tip 21 shell border. *Serves 12.*

For more ways to use
GUITAR PAN
see Pan Index p. 192.

6

LOVABLE LITTLE LAMBY KINS

Decorating Needs

- 10-in. Square Pan, p. 167
- Ball Pan, p. 184
- Egg Minicake Pan, p. 183
- Tips 4, 16, 21, 104, 224, p. 118-120
- 6-in. Cake Circle, p. 162
- 1-in. Filigree Bell, p. 155
- Dowel Rods, p. 160

1. Make 30 tip 224 drop flowers with tip 4 dot centers. Ice 1-layer square cake smooth, pat with spatula for a grassy effect. Push dowel rods (cut to fit) into cake where lamb will go.

2. For Lamb: Position half ball cake on cake circle. Attach mini egg to ball with icing. Position cakes atop square. With toothpick, mark eyes, nose, mouth, ears and legs (lightly ice cakes for easier marking). Cover marks with tip 4. Fill in eyes and add dot pupils with tip 4. Pipe tip 4 zigzag hoofs.

3. Cover face, ears and legs with tip 16 stars. Pipe tip 21 reverse shell "wool" on lamb. Add tip 104 ribbon bow. Print tip 4 message. Attach bell and flowers with dots of icing. Edge square cake top and base with tip 21 shell borders. *Serves 20.*

For more ways to use 10-IN. SQUARE, BALL & EGG MINICAKE PANS see Pan Index p. 192.

PEEP-SQUEAK

Decorating Needs

- Chick•In•Egg Pan, p. 183
- Tips 4, 8, 17, p. 118-119
- '86 Pattern Book, p. 135 (Flyer Pattern)
- 8-in. Tapered Spatula, p. 124
- Decorator's Brush, p. 126
- Piping Gel, p. 125 (Add a small amount to yellow icing, so fluffing is easier.)

1. Ice cake smooth. With toothpick, mark Flyer Pattern on cake top. Cover marks with tip 4 strings.

2. Pipe in goggles, beak and "2" with tip 8 (smooth with dampened brush). Fill in eyes with tip 4. Cover scarf and helmet with tip 17 stars.

3. Cover face and body with tip 8 "C" motion swirls, then fluff with 8-in. tapered spatula to resemble feathers. Add tip 4 message. Edge cake base with tip 17 star border. *Serves 12.*

For more ways to use CHICK•IN•EGG PAN see Pan Index p. 192.

◆ BABY BEAR HUGS

Decorating Needs

- 8-in. Round Pans, p. 166
- Tips 4, 6, 16, 18, p. 118-119
- Honey Bear, p. 136
- Cake Dividing Set, p. 126

1. Ice 2-layer round cake smooth. Using Cake Dividing Set, with toothpick, dot mark sides into 24ths.

2. Outline candles with tip 16 stripes. Fill in with tip 18 zigzags.

3. Edge cake top and base with tip 6 bead borders. Pipe tip 18 pull-out star flames on cake top. Print tip 4 message. Position Honey Bear on cake top. *Serves 12.*

For more ways to use 8-IN. ROUND PANS see Pan Index p. 192.

Dennis is "Bearly" 3 years old

For more ways to use
HUGGABLE TEDDY
BEAR PAN
see Pan Index p. 192.

For more ways to use
8 IN. ROUND PANS
see Pan Index p. 192.

PARTYTIME TEDDY

Decorating Needs
• Huggable Teddy Bear Pan, p. 182
• Tips 3, 4, 21, 127, 233, p. 118-121
• Party hat, candy-coated chocolates

1. Ice belly, inside of ears and bottom of paws smooth.

With toothpick, mark nose. Outline paws, belly, nose, mouth and cheeks with tip 4 strings.

2. Pipe in nose with tip 4 (smooth with finger dipped in cornstarch). Cover snout (build up with stars for dimension) and suit with tip 21 stars.

3. Print tip 3 message; number with tip 4.

To secure hat, push a wooden stick into cake, then position hat. Cover body with tip 233 fur. Pipe tip 127 ruffle collar. Cover head with tip 233 fur.

Attach candy eyes, tongue and polka dots with dots of icing. *Serves 12.*

COOKIE CUTTER MAGIC

Decorating Needs
• 8-in. Round Pans, p. 166
• Tips 3, 18, p. 118-119
• Gingerbread Set, p. 114
• Juggler Clown, p. 136
• Clown Separator Set, p. 136
• Roll-out Cookie Recipe, p. 98
• Lollipops, candy-coated chocolates

1. Out of cookie dough, cut 11 cookie men using Gingerbread Set (allows 2 extra in case of breakage). Bake and cool.

Pipe tip 3 facial features, hair and zigzag trims. Attach candy buttons with dots of icing.

2. Ice 2-layer round cake smooth. Print tip 3 message. Edge cake top and base with tip 18 star borders. Attach 9 cookies to cake sides with dots of icing.

3. Push lollipop balloons into cake sides (angle slightly). Place cake on Clown Separator Set. Add Juggler Clown. *Serves 12.*

**For more helpful hints,
review Decorating Guide, p. 80.**

8

◇ TIP-TOP CLOWN

Decorating Needs
- 10-in. Round Pans, p. 166
- Petite Doll Mold, p. 180
- Tips 2A, 12, 17, 21, p. 118-119
- Cake Dividing Set, p. 126
- Cake Circle, p. 162
- Comical Clowns, p. 136
- Circus Balloons, p. 136
- Sprinkle Tops, p. 112
- Gumdrops

1. Ice 2-layer round cake smooth. Sprinkle with sprinkles. Using Cake Dividing Set, with toothpick, dot mark sides into 16ths. Pipe tip 21 stripes on cake sides. Fill in alternate rows with tip 21 zigzags. Edge cake top and base with tip 21 rosette borders. Position gumdrops.

2. For Clown: Ice petite doll cake on cake circle cut to fit. Pipe tip 12 arms and hands. Place clown on round cake. Pipe tip 2A shoes (shape with finger dipped in cornstarch). Add tip 17 zigzag ruffles and rosette buttons. Push in clown head and balloons. *Serves 24.*

For more ways to use 10 IN. ROUND PAN and PETITE DOLL MOLD see Pan Index p. 192.

TOPSY-TURVY

Decorating Needs
- Stand-Up Snowman Pan Kit, p. 178
- Tips 2A, 4, 17, 104, 224, 352, p. 118-121
- '86 Pattern Book, p. 135 (Clown Pattern)
- Cake Circles, p. 162
- Dowel Rods, p. 160
- Rocking Horse Cake Pick, p. 142
- Pound Cake Recipe, p. 95
- Candles, holders

1. Make 40 tip 224 drop flowers with tip 4 dot centers. On cake board, trace where clown will go, then mark hands. Pipe tip 2A hands. Ice cake halves together. Hint: Push sharpened dowel rods into cake (angle into opposite half).

2. Ice "cake" (build up slightly). With toothpick, mark Clown Pattern on one side. Outline "cake" base, facial features, legs, shoes. Pipe tip 2A dot cheeks, nose and eyes. Add tip 4 dot eyeballs. Trim hands with tip 104 ruffles.

3. Cover shoes, body, face, tie with tip 17 stars. Pipe tip 352 pull-out leaves hair (pipe on cake board and work up). Mark garland on "cake" and cover with tip 17 drop strings. Trim "cake" top and base with tip 17 shell borders. Attach flowers with icing. Trim with tip 352 leaves. Position candles and pick. *Serves 12.*

For more ways to use SNOWMAN PAN KIT see Pan Index p. 192.

9

Back View

For more ways to use
STAND-UP CABBAGE
PATCH KIDS® PAN SET
see Pan Index p. 192.

A SPECIAL TREAT FROM PARTY CABBAGE PATCH KID®

Decorating Needs
• Stand-Up Cabbage Patch Kids® Cake
  Pan Set, p. 187
• Tips 3, 4, 5, 16, 104, p. 118-119
• Decorator's Brush, p. 126
• Pound Cake Recipe, p. 95

1. Allow pound cake to cool completely in back half of pan (at least 4 hours; see pan instructions).

2. Outline hair part, eyes, nose, mouth, hands, package, shoes, and dress sash and bow (on back) with tip 3 strings. Fill in package area with tip 5. Smooth

with dampened brush. Add tip 3 string bow to package.

Cover hair with tip 16 side by side stripes, front and back curls with tip 16 reverse shells. Add tip 3 outline hair yarn ties.

Cover face, dress, legs, hands and shoes with tip 16 stars. Fill in whites of eyes with tip 4. Add tip 4 dot eyes, pupils and shoe buttons. Trim dress with tip 104 ribbon collar and ruffles. Add tip 104 bows to hair.

3. On back of dress, add tip 16 stripe sash and bow. Trim dress with tip 16 star flowers with tip 3 dot centers. Facial features and hands may be overpiped. *Serves 12.*

©1984 Cabbage Patch Kids® is a Registered Trademark of and Licensed from Original Artworks, Inc. Cleveland, Georgia, U.S.A. All rights reserved.

For more ways to use
9-IN. PETAL PAN
see Pan Index p. 192.

For more ways to use
LONG LOAF PAN
see Pan Index p. 192.

For more ways to use
STAND-UP SNOWMAN
CAKE PAN KIT, MINI
LOAF PAN SET and
EGG MINICAKE PANS,
see Pan Index p. 192.

PRETTY PASTEL PETAL

Decorating Needs
- 9-in. Petal Pan, p. 169
- Tips 2, 18, 104, 225, 349, p. 118-121
- Birthday Bear Care Bear™ p. 137

1. Make 50 tip 225 drop flowers with tip 2 dot centers.

2. Ice 2-layer cake smooth. Edge cake top with tip 104 triple ribbon border, starting with bottom row and working up. Pipe tip 18 shell border around cake about two inches down from top. Edge cake base with tip 18 shell border. Attach flowers to cake top and sides with dots of icing. Trim with tip 349 leaves.

Position Birthday Bear Care Bear on cake top. *Serves 12.*

© MCMLXXXLV American Greetings Corp.

◆ CARROT PATCH CULPRITS

Decorating Needs
- Tips 4, 9, 16, 47, p. 118-119 • Long Loaf Pan,
- Bunny Family, p. 140   p. 170
- Carrot Cake (Use 9 cups batter from packaged mix, or your recipe.)

1. With toothpick, mark a double row of holes about 1″ in from the ends of the cake and about 2″ apart, for carrots. With a potato peeler, scoop out cake from holes, making each "carrot" hole about ½″ in diameter and 2″ deep. Pipe tip 9 "carrots," building up icing until about ½″ is sticking out of hole. Add tip 16 green pull-out star carrot tops.

2. Position Bunny Family atop cake. Add tip 47 ribbon fence. Pipe tip 16 pull-out star grass. Write tip 4 message. *Serves 18.*

AT EASE!

Decorating Needs
- Stand-Up Snowman Cake Pan Kit, p. 178
- Mini Loaf Pan Set, p. 170
- Egg Minicake Pan, p. 183
- Tips 4, 12, 17, p. 118-119
- Decorator's Brush, p. 126
- Pound Cake Recipe, p. 95
- Cookies

1. Bake pound cake and join halves together according to pan instructions.

Bake two Mini Loaf cakes. Bake two Egg Minicakes. Cut out one end of each loaf cake to contour around soldier for legs. Cut off one end of each minicake for feet. Position. Build up forearms and shoulders with tip 12.

2. With toothpick, mark hat, chin strap, facial features, belt, chest straps and boots on cake. (For easier marking, lightly ice areas smooth.) With tip 4, outline facial features, chin and chest straps, belt, collar, edges of sleeves and boots. Cover hat, face, uniform, chest straps, belt, boots, and collar with tip 17 stars. Add tip 4 zigzag collar trim.

Fill in eyes, nose, mouth, cheeks, buttons and chin strap with tip 4. Smooth with dampened brush.

Attach cookie epaulets. Pipe tip 17 zigzag fringe. Add tip 12 dot hands. Smooth with dampened brush.

3. Trim hat with tip 17 upright shells and tip 4 buttons. *Serves 18.*

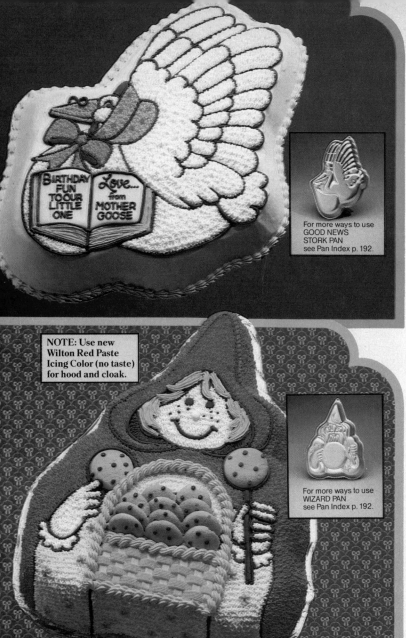

For more ways to use
GOOD NEWS
STORK PAN
see Pan Index p. 192.

NOTE: Use new
Wilton Red Paste
Icing Color (no taste)
for hood and cloak.

For more ways to use
WIZARD PAN
see Pan Index p. 192.

NURSERY SET CELEBRITY

Decorating Needs
- **Good News Stork Pan, p. 182**
- **Tips 4, 17, p. 118-119**
- **Decorator's Brush, p. 126**
- **'86 Pattern Book, p. 135** (Mother Goose Pattern)

1. Ice cake sides, part of top and book area smooth. With toothpick, mark Mother Goose Pattern on cake top. Cover marks with tip 4 strings. Score "pages" of book with tip 17 by lightly running tip across icing in lines.

2. Cover goose, hat, beak and bow with tip 17 stars. Build up cheeks with tip 17 stars. Fill in inside bonnet, inside bow and eyes with tip 4. Smooth with dampened brush. Pipe tip 17 pink stars randomly over bonnet.

3. Add tip 4 glasses. Edge cake base with tip 17 shell border. Print tip 4 message. *Serves 12.*

BASKET OF GOODIES

Decorating Needs
- **Wizard Pan, p. 176**
- **Tips 2, 4, 7, 16, 18, 47, 225, p. 118-121**
- **Decorator's Brush, p. 126**
- **'86 Pattern Book, p. 135** (Red Riding Hood Pattern)
- **Small cookies**

1. Make 20 tip 225 drop flowers with tip 4 dot centers.

2. With toothpick, mark Red Riding Hood Pattern on cake top. (For easier marking, lightly ice cake first.) Position cookie near finger with dot of icing. Cover marks, going over cookie for finger, and outline cookie, forehead and inside basket with tip 4 strings. Cover face, cloak, dress, hands and ruffles with tip 16 stars. Add tip 16 side by side lines hair. Add tip 4 dot eyes and nose (smooth with dampened brush) and outline mouth. Make tip 2 dot freckles. Cover inside hood with tip 4 zigzags. Cover basket with tip 47 basketweave. Make tip 18 rope handle and border. Pipe tip 7 wand. Smooth with dampened brush.

3. Attach cookies with dots of icing. Outline with tip 4. With a spatula, make slits in cake top where cookies will go. Position cookies in basket. Attach flowers with icing. *Serves 12.*

FAIRY TALE COTTAGE

Decorating Needs
- **10-in. Square Pan, p. 167**
- **Holiday House Kit, p. 179**
- **Tips 2, 2B, 4, 7, 18, 47, 129, 234, 349, p. 118-121**
- **'86 Pattern Book, p. 135** (Snow White Pattern)
- **Gingerbread Cutters, p. 114**
- **Cake Boards, p. 162**
- **Dowel Rods, p. 160**
- **Decorator's Brush, p. 126**
- **Roll-Out Cookie Recipe, p. 98**
- **Royal Icing Recipe, p. 83**
- **Pound Cake Recipe, p. 95** (for Holiday House)
- **Cookie wafers, candy, lollipops**

1. Out of royal icing, make 50 tip 129 drop flowers with tip 2 centers. On 16 flowers, pipe tip 7 royal icing stems. Out of cookie dough, using Snow White Pattern, cut 2 cookies. With Gingerbread Cutters, cut out 9 dwarfs. Bake and cool. With royal icing, paint faces, hands, dress, shirts, trousers and feet. Add tip 2 royal icing outline faces, belts and dress trim, dot beards, dwarfs' hair, and Snow White's cheeks, and side by side lines Snow White's hair. Pipe tip 7 hats and cape.

2. Ice sides of 1-layer square cake smooth with brown icing, top fluffy with green. Position dowel rods and push into cake where house will go. With knife, level bottom of house. Position house on cake board cut to fit and place atop dowel rods. Insert another dowel rod through house into cake base. Ice house cake smooth. Outline windows and door with tip 4. Pipe tip 47 door slats, house timbers and window trims. Pipe tip 7 dot window panes. Smooth with brush. Attach wafer shutters with icing. Add tip 18 pull-out stars roof. Sandwich 2 wafers with icing. Position on roof for chimney. Pipe tip 2B ribbon sidewalk. Smooth with brush.

3. Edge cake top with tip 18 shell border, base with tip 21 shell border. Add tip 234 grass blades around house. Attach flowers on stems along walk with icing. Attach other flowers to border. Trim all flowers with tip 349 leaves. Attach red candies to lollipops with icing. Trim with tip 349 leaves. Position in cake. *Serves 24.*

For more ways to use
10-IN. SQUARE PAN and
HOLIDAY HOUSE KIT
see Pan Index p. 192.

TO MARKET...TO MARKET

Decorating Needs
- Stand-up Snowman Pan Kit, p. 178
- Tips 1A, 4, 16, 45, 47, p. 118-119
- '86 Pattern Book, p. 135
  (Farmer Pattern)
- Decorator's Brush, p. 126
- Piping Gel, p. 125
- Pound Cake Recipe, p. 95

1. Ice backs of cake halves and push cakes together. (Hint: Push sharpened dowel rods diagonally into cake.) With toothpick, mark Farmer Pattern on cake. (Hint: For easier marking, lightly frost cake first.) Cover marks with tip 4 strings. Outline sleeves, kerchief, and overalls with tip 4. Build out nose with tip 1A. Shape with fingers dipped in cornstarch. Smooth with dampened brush. Fill in hoofs, mouth and inside ears with tip 4. Smooth with brush. Cover face, body, kerchief and overalls with tip 16 stars. Add tip 4 dot eyes, and nostrils and buttons. Smooth with brush. Add tip 4 outline eyebrows.

2. Pipe tip 47 vertical basket stripes, tip 45 horizontal stripes (smooth side up). Pipe tip 45 (ribbed side up) stripe hat band. Cover hat with tip 16 stars. Fill basket with tip 1A build-up dot apples. Trim with tip 4 stems. *Serves 24.*

Note: For shine on nose and apples, brush with piping gel.

For more ways to use
STAND-UP SNOWMAN
PAN KIT
see Pan Index p. 192.

Back View

13

CLICKS RIGHT IN

Decorating Needs
- Chick • In • Egg Pan, p. 183
- Tips 3, 4, 21, p. 118-119
- '86 Pattern Book, p. 135 (Lock Pattern)
- Small round cookie

1. Ice cake sides and part of top smooth with white icing, lock face area with brown. With toothpick, mark Lock Pattern on cake top. Cover lock outline with tip 4 brown strings, numbers and lines on dial with tip 3 white strings. Cover outer edge of lock with tip 21 stars. Fill in indicator with tip 4. Smooth with finger dipped in cornstarch. Position cookie in center. Edge cake base with tip 21 shell border. Write tip 4 message. *Serves 12.*

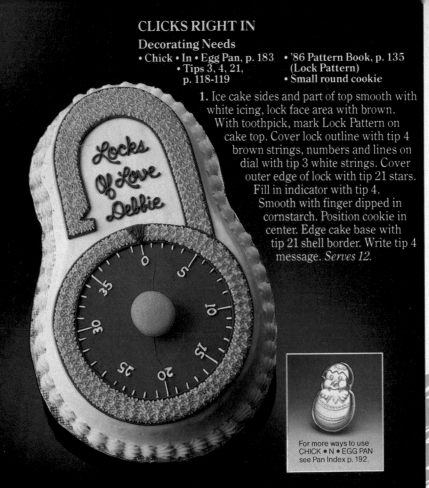

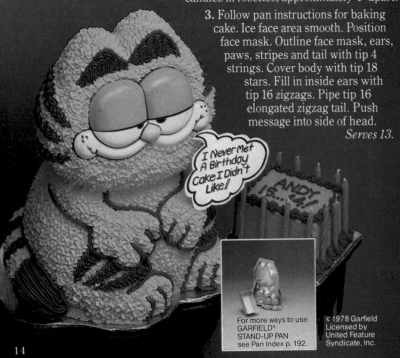

For more ways to use CHICK • N • EGG PAN see Pan Index p. 192.

GARFIELD'S GIFT

Decorating Needs
- Garfield® Stand-Up Cake Pan Set, p. 186
- Mini Loaf Pan Set, p. 170
- Tips 4, 16, 18, p. 118-119
- Cake Board, p. 162
- Pound Cake Recipe, p. 95
- Construction paper, toothpick, tape, candles, plastic straws

1. Make construction paper message. Attach it to a toothpick with tape.

2. For mini birthday cake: On cake board cut to fit, ice cake smooth. Print tip 4 message. Edge cake top with tip 16 shell border, base with rosettes. Stick candles in rosettes, approximately 1" apart.

3. Follow pan instructions for baking cake. Ice face area smooth. Position face mask. Outline face mask, ears, paws, stripes and tail with tip 4 strings. Cover body with tip 18 stars. Fill in inside ears with tip 16 zigzags. Pipe tip 16 elongated zigzag tail. Push message into side of head. *Serves 13.*

I Never Met A Birthday Cake I Didn't Like!

For more ways to use GARFIELD® STAND-UP PAN see Pan Index p. 192.

Everybody loves a party. And Birthdays are the best! But how do you please that teen, so often hard to please? With ideas like these. Delightful ideas. Easy to do. They all say, "You're Special," and "I Love You."

TEEN BIRTHDAYS

Let's

BEEF UP

And here's another suggestion...

Help your teen make any one of these treats for a special friend.

It's a super experience you'll both enjoy.

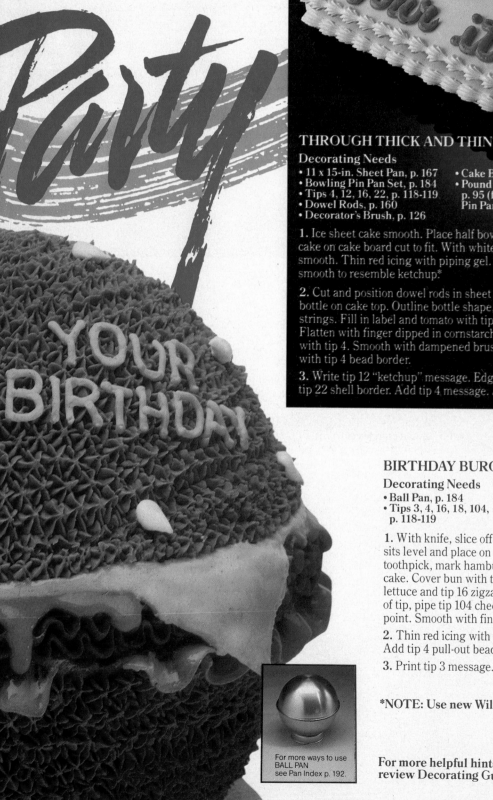

Party

YOUR BIRTHDAY

HAPPY BIRTHDAY... YOU'RE A'CUTE TOMATO"

Pour it on

THROUGH THICK AND THIN

Decorating Needs
- 11 x 15-in. Sheet Pan, p. 167
- Bowling Pin Pan Set, p. 184
- Tips 4, 12, 16, 22, p. 118-119
- Dowel Rods, p. 160
- Decorator's Brush, p. 126
- Cake Board, p. 162
- Pound Cake Recipe, p. 95 (for Bowling Pin Pan)

For more ways to use 11 IN. x 15 IN. SHEETPAN and BOWLING PIN PAN see Pan Index p. 192.

1. Ice sheet cake smooth. Place half bowling pin pound cake on cake board cut to fit. With white icing, ice cake smooth. Thin red icing with piping gel. Ice part of cake smooth to resemble ketchup.*

2. Cut and position dowel rods in sheet cake where bottle will go. Position bottle on cake top. Outline bottle shape, cap, label and tomato with tip 4 strings. Fill in label and tomato with tip 16 stars. Pipe tip 12 bottle cap. Flatten with finger dipped in cornstarch. Fill in tomato's eyes and stem with tip 4. Smooth with dampened brush. Add tip 4 features. Edge bottle with tip 4 bead border.

3. Write tip 12 "ketchup" message. Edge sheet cake top and base with tip 22 shell border. Add tip 4 message. *Serves 28.*

BIRTHDAY BURGER TO GO

Decorating Needs
- Ball Pan, p. 184
- Tips 3, 4, 16, 18, 104, p. 118-119
- Piping Gel, p. 125
- Cake Circles, p. 162
- Pound Cake Recipe, p. 95

1. With knife, slice off one side of cooled ball cake so it sits level and place on a cake circle cut to fit. With toothpick, mark hamburger bun and hamburger on cake. Cover bun with tip 18 stars. Add tip 104 ruffle lettuce and tip 16 zigzag hamburger. With narrow end of tip, pipe tip 104 cheese, bringing each slice to a point. Smooth with finger dipped in cornstarch.

2. Thin red icing with piping gel. Pipe tip 4 ketchup. Add tip 4 pull-out beads for sesame seeds.

3. Print tip 3 message. *Serves 12.*

***NOTE: Use new Wilton Red (no taste) for "Ketchup."**

For more ways to use BALL PAN see Pan Index p. 192.

For more helpful hints, review Decorating Guide, p. 80.

HERE'S A "PIZ-ZA" MY HEART

Decorating Needs
- 12-in. Heart Pan, p. 168
- Tip 7, p. 118
- Bread Dough Pizza Crust Recipe (see below)
- Pizza sauce, sliced mushrooms, olives, pepper rings, mozzarella cheese, Parmesan cheese, cheese spread, oregano, basil

1. Pizza Crust

2 pkgs. active dry yeast
1½ cups warm water
2 Tbsps. sugar
1½ Tbsps. solid vegetable shortening, melted
1 tsp. salt
4-4½ cups flour
oil

Stir yeast into warm water until dissolved. Add sugar, melted shortening and salt. Stir in 3 cups of flour. Gradually add remaining flour to form a soft dough. Turn onto a lightly floured surface; knead until smooth and elastic. Let dough rest 5 minutes in a covered bowl. Brush pan with oil. Roll dough to flatten. Press evenly over bottom and up sides of pan.

2. Arrange topping on pizza. Position olives inside pepper rings. Bake at 425°F. for 20-25 minutes.

3. Write tip 7 message with cheese spread. *Serves 6.*

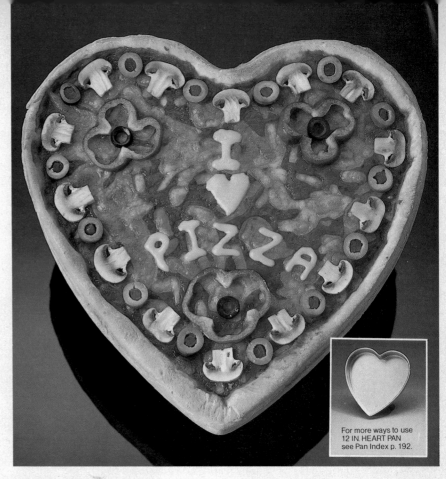

For more ways to use 12 IN. HEART PAN see Pan Index p. 192.

TEEN BIRTHDAYS
(Cont.)

BIRTHDAY HOT-LINE

Decorating Needs
- Petite Doll Pan, p. 180
- Little Loafers, p. 172
- Tips 4, 12, 16, p. 118-119
- Dowel Rods, p. 160
- Cake Circles, p. 162

1. Position 2 little loafer cakes together. (Slice ends off so cakes fit snugly together.) Ice sides smooth.

2. Ice tops of 2 doll cakes smooth on cake circles cut to fit. Position on loaves for phone ends. Push sharpened dowel rods through both doll and loaf cakes to secure. With toothpick, mark phone handles and ear- and mouthpieces on cake. Cover marks with tip 4 strings. Cover phone with tip 16 stars.

3. Edge cake base with tip 4 bead border. Add tip 12 "e" motion wire. Add tip 4 dot "holes" and print tip 4 message. *Serves 8.*

For more ways to use PETITE DOLL PAN and LITTLE LOAFERS see Pan Index p. 192.

16

LICENSED TO GO!

Decorating Needs
- Huggable Teddy Bear Pan, p. 182
- Tips 4, 8, 17, p. 118-119
- '86 Pattern Book, p. 135 (Car Pattern)

1. Ice cake smooth. With toothpick, mark Car Pattern on cake top. Cover marks with tip 4 strings. Cover faces, clothes, auto and license with tip 17 stars. Add tip 4 outline facial features and dot eyes and pupils. Pipe tip 17 stripe hair.

2. Pipe in tip 8 convertible top and bumper. Flatten with finger dipped in cornstarch.

Add tip 4 outline light rims and trunk lock and dot lights. Flatten with finger dipped in cornstarch. Add tip 17 zigzag tires.

3. Edge cake base with tip 17 shell border. Print tip 4 message and license. *Serves 12.*

For more ways to use
HUGGABLE TEDDY BEAR
PAN
see Pan Index p. 192.

PRACTICE MAKES PERFECT

Decorating Needs
- Bunny Pan (stand-up), p. 183
- Tips 4, 7, 18, p. 118-119
- Pound Cake Recipe, p. 95

1. Allow pound cake to cool completely in back half of pan (at least 4 hours—see pan instructions). With knife, cut off part of ears and entire snout. Insert 2 plastic straws down through head and body. Ice instep area smooth.

2. With toothpick, mark slipper on cake. For easier marking, lightly ice cake. Cover marks with tip 4 outlines. Cover top of leg warmer with tip 18 zigzags. Starting with top row, cover middle of leg warmer with alternate green and gold rows of tip 18 upright shells. Complete warmers with tip 18 zigzags.

Cover shoe with tip 18 stars.
Pipe tip 7 sole.

3. Write and print tip 4 message.
Serves 12.

For more ways to use
STAND-UP BUNNY PAN
see Pan Index p. 192.

ADULT BIRTHDAYS...

◇ A REAL CHARMER

Decorating Needs
- 10-in. Round Pan, p. 166
- Tip 18, p. 118
- Poster board, cocoa powder, sliced almonds, candied cherries, chopped nuts

1. Ice 1-layer cake white. Pat sides with chopped nuts.

2. To make stencil: Cut six 10-in. x ¾-in. poster board strips. Lattice strips (1⅝-in. apart) and tape. Place on cake top. Sprinkle squares with cocoa powder.

3. Pipe tip 18 star border on top and base. Attach cherry and almonds with dots of icing to resemble flowers. *Serves 12.*

For more ways to use 10 IN. ROUND PAN see Pan Index p. 192.

For more ways to use 10 IN. SQUARE PAN see Pan Index p. 192.

For more ways to use MINI LOAF PAN see Pan Index p. 192.

TINY TORTES

Decorating Needs
- Mini Loaf Pan, p. 170
- Cookie Pan, p. 175
- Tip 18, p. 119
- Candy Melts™*, p. 106
- Pound Cake Recipe, p. 95
- Assorted nuts, candied cherries

1. Place cakes on cooling rack over Cookie Pan. When cakes are cool, torte and fill. Pour melted Candy Melts over cakes. For marbelized effect: Melt light cocoa and white Candy Melts separately. Pour cocoa into a shallow dish. Then pour or use a disposable decorating bag, to drizzle lines of the white into the dish. Use end of a

2. To decorate: Pat with chopped nuts before coating sets. Let coating set at room temperature. Add tip 18 icing scrolls, shells, rosettes or attach nuts and fruits with dots of melted coating. For eye-catching contrast, dip marbelized cakes into dark cocoa Candy Melts.

THE BEST IS YET TO COME

Accentuate the positive.
Eliminate the negative.
That's what this world needs now.

TULIPS IN THE SQUARE

Decorating Needs
• 10-in. Square Pan, p. 167
• Tips 3, 18, p. 118-119

1. Ice 1-layer cake smooth. With spatula, score cake top into nine 3-in. squares.

2. With toothpick, mark tulips in squares. Pipe tip 18 outline stems, triple shell flower petals (pipe 2 outside shells first) and elongated shell leaves.

3. Add tip 18 stars on cake top. Edge cake top and base with tip 18 shell borders. Print tip 3 message. *Serves 12.*

WHAT A SHARP COOKIE!

Decorating Needs
• Fancy Cookie Making & Pastry Kit, p. 113
• Cookie Dips , p. 112
• Sprinkle Tops, p. 112
• Candied cherries

1. With cookie dough, pipe a delightful assortment of bars, stars and flowers following instructions in the Fancy Cookie Making & Pastry Kit. Bake and cool.

2. Dip into melted Cookie Dips, pat with Sprinkle Tops or garnish with candied cherries.

19

ADULT BIRTHDAYS...

Show someone special just how great turning another year older can be. Present a lovely or clever creation and you'll make their day!

Attention, you men... what could win her heart more than a cake you decorated? You know she'd be thrilled!

PRETTY SPECIAL

Decorating Needs
- 8-in. Round Pans, p. 166
- Tips 3, 16, 21, 225, 352, p. 118-121
- Cake Dividing Set, p. 126

1. Make 110 tip 225 drop flowers with tip 3 dot centers. Ice 2-layer cake smooth; top white, sides chocolate.

2. Using Cake Dividing Set, with toothpick, dot mark cake top into 6ths; cake base into 12ths. With toothpick, mark "C" and "S" Scrolls on cake top between marks. Cover marks with tip 21 scrolls.

3. Edge cake base with tip 16 five-shell clusters. Add tip 16 center stars and attach flowers. Attach flower sprays to cake sides. Pipe tip 352 leaves. Write tip 3 message on cake top. *Serves 12.*

For more ways to use 8-IN. ROUND PANS see Pan Index p. 192.

SHE CAN'T BE BEAT!

Decorating Needs
- Cupid's Heart Pan, p. 181
- Tips 4, 17, 104, 352, p. 118-121
- Flower Nail No. 7, p. 121
- In-Step Jogger, p. 138
- Finely chopped nuts

1. Make three tip 104 roses. Ice background area on cake top and sides smooth. Pat sides with chopped nuts.

2. Outline arrow and banner with tip 4 strings and fill in with tip 17 stars.

3. Edge cake top with tip 104 ruffle. Trim ruffle edge and cake base with tip 17 shell border. Print tip 4 message on cake top. Pipe two tip 104 sweet peas and attach roses to cake top with dots of icing. Add tip 352 leaves. Position In-Step Jogger. *Serves 12.*

For more ways to use

It's Still Fun To Celebrate!

GROWIN' BETTER

Decorating Needs
- Round Mini-Tier Set, p. 168
- Tips 4, 17, 131, p. 118-120
- Tennis Star, p. 138

1. Make 50 tip 131 drop flowers with tip 4 dot centers. Ice cakes smooth. Position 5 and 6½-in. cakes together on cake board cut to fit to form 3. With toothpick, mark 3 and 0 on cake tops. (Mark about 1¾-in. from edge.)

2. Cover marks with tip 4 strings and fill in numbers with tip 17 stars.

3. Add tip 4 messages. Edge bases of cakes with tip 17 star borders. Attach flowers with dots of icing. Position cake together and add Tennis Star. *Serves 12.*

For more ways to use ROUND MINI-TIER SET see Pan Index p. 192.

For more ways to use 8-IN. SQUARE PANS see Pan Index p. 192.

◇ YELLOW RIBBONS

Decorating Needs
- 8-in. Square Pans, p. 167
- Tips 1D, 16, 18, p. 118-119
- Coconut flakes

1. Ice 2-layer cake sides smooth. Pat sides with coconut flakes.

2. Pipe tip 1D stripes on cake top, alternating ribbed and smooth stripes. With toothpick, dot mark 1⅝-in. wide vertical lines on cake top. Draw a spatula or skewer along dot marks.

3. Edge cake top and base with tip 18 rosette border. Trim cake top with tip 16 stars. *Serves 12.*

For more helpful hints, review Decorating Guide, p. 80.

GLAMOUR GUPPY

Decorating Needs
- Big Fish Pan, p. 177
- Tips 4, 8, 17, p. 118-119
- Decorator's Brush, p. 126
- Gone Fishin' Singboard, p. 138

1. Lightly ice face smooth. With toothpick, mark sunglasses and lips.

2. Outline sunglasses, lips, scales, fins and tail with tip 4 strings. Pipe in sunglasses with tip 8 (smooth with dampened brush).

3. Cover lips, face, fins, scales and tail on cake top and sides (except water area) with tip 17 stars. Add tip 8 "C" motion wave caps. Generously ice water area and fluff with spatula to resemble waves. Add tip 4 dot beauty mark. Print tip 4 message on Gone Fishin' Signboard. Push into cake. *Serves 12.*

For more ways to use
BIG FISH PAN
see Pan Index p. 192.

For more ways to use
CHICK • IN • EGG PAN
see Pan Index p. 192.

ADULT BIRTHDAYS
(Continued)

PUTTIN' ON THE DOG!

Decorating Needs
- Chick • In • Egg Pan, p. 183
- Tips 3, 4, 8, 16, 17, p. 118-119
- '86 Pattern Book, p. 135
  (Puppy Pattern)

1. Ice cake smooth; book area orange, the rest brown. With toothpick, mark Puppy Pattern.

2. Cover marks with tip 4 strings. Pipe in eyes, snout, nose and tongue with tip 8; small areas around eyes with tip 4 (smooth with finger dipped in cornstarch). Add tip 8 dot eyeballs and pads of feet (flatten with finger).

3. Cover ears with tip 17 stripes. Pipe tip 17 stars on face, paws and body (use tip 16 for smaller areas around face and paws). Print tip 3 message. Add tip 4 dot freckles on cheeks. Add tip 17 shell border on cake base. *Serves 12.*

THIS IS THE LIFE!

Decorating Needs

- 10-in. Square Pan, p. 167
- Holiday House Kit, p. 179
- Tips 2A, 3, 4, 7, 10, 16, 17, 45, 104, 131, 233, 349, p. 118-121
- Lazy Bones, p. 141
- Dowel Rods, p. 160
- Pound Cake Recipe (for house), p. 95
- Wafer cookies

1. Make 45 tip 131 drop flowers with tip 3 dot centers. Ice 1-layer square cake smooth. Write tip 3 message.

With toothpick, mark five 2 in. wide X's on each side. Cover marks with tip 45 smooth stripe latticework. Edge cake top and base with tip 17 shell borders.

For more ways to use 10-IN. SQUARE & HOLIDAY HOUSE KIT see Pan Index p. 192.

2. For house: Ice cake front and side walls only smooth (for easier decorating, lay cake down—back can be iced later).

With toothpick, mark scalloped siding. Outline windows, shutters, door and siding with tip 4 strings. Pipe in windows with tip 7; door with tip 10 (smooth with finger dipped in cornstarch). Add tip 4 dot doorknob. Cover siding with tip 16 stars. Pipe tip 2A smooth stripe eaves on front and sides.

3. Upright cake on cake board cut to fit and place on square cake. Push sharpened dowel rod through house into square for support. Ice back smooth.

Cover roof with rows of tip 104 ruffles (work up from bottom, slightly overlapping rows).

Attach wafer cookies together with icing for chimney. With knife, cut cookie ends at an angle and attach to roof with icing. Pipe tip 233 grass around house. Attach flowers to cake top and sides with dots of icing. Trim with tip 349 leaves. Place Lazy Bones atop cake. *Serves 24.*

For more ways to use CANDLELIT TREE PAN see Pan Index p. 192.

SOME BIRTHDAYS ARE FOR THE BIRDS!

Decorating Needs

- Candlelit Tree Pan, p. 178
- Tips 4, 16, 70, 113, p. 118-121
- Pound Cake Recipe, p. 95
- Royal Icing Recipe, p. 83
- Licorice sticks, ice cream sugar cones, candy-coated chocolates

1. While cake bakes, cover 2 sugar cones with royal icing. For beak: Outline halves with tip 4 and cover with tip 16 stars. For hat: Outline rows with tip 4 and cover with tip 16 stars, alternating colors. Let dry.

2. Ice belly area smooth. Outline with tip 4. For claws: Cut licorice sticks into six 3-inch long pieces. Push under cake.

Working up from the bottom, cover body and wings with tip 113 pull-out leaf feathers; face and head with tip 70 feathers.

3. Push a sharpened dowel rod into cake where beak goes (let 3 in. extend). Attach beak and hat with icing. Add candy-coated chocolate eyes with dots of icing. Pipe tip 4 dot pupils on candy. Print tip 4 message. *Serves 12.*

23

One Pan...So Many

Get the most from your Wilton Shaped Pans. They're unique, but versatile!

The Panda Pan

For best results, bake cake and assemble, following pan instructions. Position cakes on doubled cake circles and use icing to "anchor" to surface.

PANDA PAN Serves 12.

see Pan Index p. 192.

BOUNCING BABY DOLL

With toothpick, mark facial features, hands and dress on cake. Ice shoe soles smooth. Outline eyes, mouth, hands, arms, shoes with tip 4. Cover face, dress, arms, hands, diaper and shoes with tip 17 stars. Fill in tip 4 whites of eyes and collar. Smooth with finger dipped in cornstarch. Add tip 4 dot eyes. Smooth with finger. Add tip 2 dot pupils and freckles, outline mouth and eyelashes. Make tip 21 reverse shell hair. Add tip 12 dot cheeks and nose. Smooth with finger. Trim dress with tip 126 ruffle, sleeve with tip 103 ruffle. Trim dress ruffle with tip 4 bead border.

GRR! I'M NO PUSSYCAT

Color spaghetti for whiskers. Build up front paws with tip 12. With toothpick, mark facial features and stripes. Outline face, snout, ears, nose, mouth, legs and stripes with tip 4. Make tip 4 fill-in nose and mouth. Smooth with finger dipped in cornstarch. Cover face and body with tip 17 stars. Add tip 4 dot eyes. Smooth with finger. Make tip 12 dot toes and tip 4 pull-out dot claws. Push spaghetti whiskers into snout.

CUTE AND CUDDLY

Ice snout, stomach and feet smooth. Outline ears, snout, stomach, paws, nose, mouth, feet with tip 4. Pipe in tip 4 ears and nose. Smooth with finger dipped in cornstarch. Cover body with tip 233 "hair." Attach candy-coated chocolate eyes with icing. Pipe tip 4 dot pupils. Make bow with real ribbon. Attach to neck with icing. Pipe tip 4 message.

The Petal Pan

9 IN. PETAL PAN Serves 12.

see Pan Index p. 192.

TULIP FANTASY

Drain canned peaches and pears. Slice pear halves into petal shapes, and slice sliced peaches in half. Quarter 2 green maraschino cherry halves. Ice cake sides and top smooth. Score top at petal indentations with spatula. Press chopped nuts around sides. Position pears and peaches into tulip shapes between scored lines. Position green cherry "stems" at base of tulips. Edge cake top and border with tip 16 shells. Trim middle with tip 16 rosette. Place cherry on rosette.

HEARTS AND LACE

Ice cake smooth. Using small heart cookie cutter from Heart Set (p. 114), cut out 8 cardboard hearts. Position on cake top at petal curves. Pipe tip 3 "e" motion border around hearts. Pipe tip 18 shells down curved sides of cake. Add tip 3 "e" motion borders. Press silver dragées between shells on cake sides. Sprinkle confectioners' sugar over cake top. With spatula, remove cardboard hearts. Press silver dots (dragées) in rows towards cake center. Edge cake top and base border with tip 18 shells.

CLASSIC ELEGANCE

Ice cake smooth, sides brown, top white. Lightly press three circles of varying sizes on cake top. (We used margarine tub covers.) With tip 2, pipe fudge topping along circles. With spatula, score every other petal indentation from the outside in; score alternate petal indentations from the inside out. Position slivered almonds along edges of cake top and base border. Attach slivered almond flowers with green maraschino cherry "stems" (cut maraschino cherry into eighths) and red maraschino cherry half centers along sides and on center top of cake with dots of icing.

24

Ways To Decorate!

It's fun to change the design to suit the occasion. Below are suggestions.

BASHFUL CUT-UP

Make 1 tip 131 flower with tip 4 dot center. Let dry and attach to florist's wire with dab of icing. Set aside. With toothpick, mark hands; outline with tip 4. Pipe in tip 12 hands. Smooth with finger dipped in cornstarch. Push white Candy Melts™ "ears" into sides of head. Make two Egg Minicake feet. Cover head, ears, body and feet with tip 18 stars. Add tip 18 reverse shell hair and tip 21 zigzag ruffles. Attach candy-coated chocolate eyes with icing. Make tip 4 string mouth. Pipe tip 8 dot nose and cheeks. Smooth with finger. Add tip 21 rosette button and tip 4 dot polka dots. Place small party hat on head. Attach flower on stem to hat.

You'll find even more great ideas for these pans throughout this book.

WHAT A JOKER!

With toothpick, mark hat, outfit and hands. Build up front part of hat tails with tip 12. Outline mouth, nose, hands, suit belt design, hat and shoes with tip 4. Cover hat, face and body with tip 17 stars. Trim shirt with tip 18 zigzag. Make tip 4 dot eyes. Smooth with finger dipped in cornstarch. Attach gum ball nose and bells on hat and toes with dots of icing.

READY TO RUN

Build up feet area with tip 2A. With toothpick, mark facial features, stomach and paws. Outline eyes, nose, mouth, markings, legs, paws and stomach with tip 4. Cover head, ears and body with tip 18 stars. Add tip 4 fill-in nose. Smooth with finger dipped in cornstarch. Make tip 4 dot eyeballs and freckles. Add gum drop tongue with dab of icing. Overpipe outlines with tip 4. Attach cardboard tail.

NOTE: All these designs use 2 layer cakes; they can also be made on round cakes.

FLOWER CASCADE

Make 75 tip 224 flowers with tip 3 dot centers. Ice cake smooth, sides white, top brown. Using scroll press from 15-Pc. Pattern Press Set (p. 126), mark pattern on cake top. Cover marks with tip 17 "C" scrolls and reverse scrolls down sides. Attach flowers with dots of icing. Trim with tip 349 leaves. Edge cake base with tip 18 reverse shell border.

STRAWBERRIES 'N CREAM

With a brush, glaze cake top with strawberry glaze. Position fresh strawberry halves in triangle pattern on each of petal sections of cake top. Glaze strawberries. Pipe tip 21 stabilized whipped cream shells on cake top at petal indentations, tip 21 side-by-side scrolls along edge of each petal. Pipe tip 21 rosette in center. Place whole strawberry on rosette and position sliced strawberry "petals" around center strawberry. Pipe tip 21 zigzag around center of cake sides.

RIBBONS OF SUNSHINE

Make approximately 35 tip 224 flowers with tip 3 dot centers. Ice cake smooth. Starting at the outer edge and working towards the center, pipe 4 tip 104 ribbon borders, alternating colors. Edge cake base with tip 104 ribbon border. Attach flowers with dots of icing. Trim with tip 349 leaves. Print tip 4 message.

a toast to all that's good!

A. CUPS OF CHEER

Decorating Needs
- **10-in. Round Pan, p. 166**
- **Tips 3, 14, 16, 32, 224, 349, p. 118-121**
- **Cordial Glasses Candy Mold, p. 100**
- **Candy Melts™* p. 106**
- **Cake Dividing Set, p. 126**
- **Orange Liqueur, orange peel**

1. Mold 8 cordial cups out of Candy Melts. See p. 94.

2. Make 75 tip 224 drop flowers with tip 3 dot centers. Ice 2-layer cake smooth, top pink, sides brown.

With cake dividing set, dot mark cake top into eighths and sides into sixteenths. Connect cake top marks with tip 14 zigzag garlands and sides with stringwork.

For more ways to use 10 IN. ROUND PAN see Pan Index p. 192.

With toothpick, mark second row of strings between first row on cake sides. Connect marks with tip 14 strings. Pipe tip 32 upright shells at cake base border at points of second row of strings. Edge cake top and base with tip 16 shell border. Attach flowers with dots of icing. Trim with tip 349 leaves.

3. Write tip 3 message on cake top. Put cordial cups on cake top. Fill with orange liqueur. Garnish with orange peel. *Serves 24.*

A.

B.

C.

B. CAVIAR CUT-UPS

Make no more than 1 day ahead.

Decorating Needs
- **Playing Card Set Cookie Cutters, p. 114**
- **Sliced white bread**
- **Softened cream cheese, red and black caviar**

Using cookie cutters, cut shapes out of bread. Spread with softened cream cheese, then with caviar.

C. MIDNIGHT MUNCHIES

Decorating Needs
- Tartlet Mold Set, p. 173
- Mini Muffin Pan, p. 174
- Tip 2110, p. 119
- Pie crust recipe, quiche recipe, liver pâté recipe, little shrimp, dill weed, sliced olives, bacon pieces

Prepare pastry dough. Line pans with dough. Fill to slightly under top with quiche. Bake and cool.

For patê canapés, prick dough with fork and bake shell only. Cool shell and pipe tip 2110 patê into shell. Garnish canapés with olive slices, bacon pieces, shrimp and dill weed.

D. THE SANDS OF TIME

Decorating Needs
- 10-in. Round Pan, p. 166
- Tips 3, 5, 16, 17, 224, 349, p. 118-121
- '86 Pattern Book, p. 135 (Swirls and Hourglass Pattern)
- Cake Dividing Set, p. 126
- Father Time and Baby New Year, p. 141

1. Make 50 tip 224 drop flowers with tip 3 dot centers.

2. Ice 2-layer cake smooth, sides ivory, top brown. Using cake dividing set, divide cake into twelfths. With toothpick, mark Swirls and Hourglass pattern on cake top and sides. Cover marks with tip 5 outlines. Fill hourglasses with tip 16 stars. Edge cake top with tip 17 rope border.

3. Attach flowers with dots of icing. Trim with tip 349 leaves.

Position Father Time and Baby New Year on cake top. *Serves 24.*

E. BEAR'S NIGHT OUT

Decorating Needs
- Panda Pan, p. 180
- Tips 4, 10, 17, 233, p. 118-119
- Cordial Glasses Candy Mold, p. 100
- Candy Melts™*, p. 106
- Candy-coated chocolates, 2¼" round cookie, noisemaker

1. To Make Hat: Mold 1 cordial cup out of Candy Melts. See p. 94 for technique. Dip cookie into melted Candy Melts. Let set until firm. Attach cookie "rim" to cordial cup "crown" with melted Candy Melts.

2. Ice stomach area smooth. Pipe tip 10 snout and feet. Flatten with finger dipped in cornstarch. Fill in ears and nose with tip 4. Smooth with finger dipped in cornstarch. Cover coat and trousers with tip 17 stars. Pipe tip 10 shirt and sleeves. Flatten with finger dipped in cornstarch. Pipe tip 17 stripe tie band around neck and zigzag bow tie. Cover bear with tip 233 pull-out "fur."

3. Attach candy-coated chocolate eyes and cuff links with dots of icing. Attach hat to head with icing.

Print tip 4 message. *Serves 12.*

E.

For more ways to use
PANDA PAN
see Pan Index p. 192.

D.

For more ways to use
10 IN. ROUND PAN
see Pan Index p. 192.

*brand confectionery coating

27

VALENTINE'S DAY

It's Time For Some Heart To Heart Talk.

This is the day, in the midst of a winter wet and weary, when you want to do something that comes straight from the heart.

This is the day to serve up a sweet and tender confection.

This is the day to send that certain message— it's love and affection.

ROSE RHAPSODY

Decorating Needs
- Cupid's Heart Pan, p. 181
- Tips 3, 4, 16, 21, 113, 125, p. 118-121
- 2-in. Flower Nail, p. 121

1. Use 2-in. Flower Nail and tip 125 to make large rose and rosebud. Freeze.

2. Ice cake top and sides smooth. Outline banner with tip 4, cover with tip 16 stars and add tip 3 message.

Use tip 125 to add double row of ruffles. Edge inside with tip 16 shells. Add tip 21 shell border to base of cake.

3. Pipe tip 8 main stems. Position roses. Trim with tip 3 sepals, thorns and stems for leaves. Add tip 113 ruffled leaves. *Serves 12.*

For more ways to use HAPPINESS HEART PANS see Pan Index p. 192.

For more ways to use CUPID'S HEART PAN see Pan Index p. 192.

◇ PIE FOR YOUR GUY

Decorating Needs
- Happiness Heart Pan Set, p. 181
- Cookie Sheet, p. 175
- Tip 3, p. 118
- Heart Set Cookie Cutters, p. 114
- Packaged pie crust mix
- 30 oz. can cherry pie filling

1. Prepare pastry for a double crust pie following package directions. Roll out to ⅛-in. thickness. Place Happiness Heart pan on crust; use knife to cut pastry 1½ in. larger than pan. Transfer crust to pan and trim edges.

Reserve ¼ cup juice from pie filling. Pour remaining filling into crust. Bake and cool according to filling instructions.

2. Roll out additional pastry. Use Heart Set cutters to cut one 4⅛ in. and about twenty 1¼ in. hearts. Bake on cookie sheet at 450° for 5-7 minutes; cool.

3. Position hearts around rim of pie pan and in center. Use tip 3 and reserved juice to outline and fill-in small hearts; decorate large heart with dots, C-scrolls and message. *Serves 8.*

HONEY BUNNY

Decorating Needs
- Holiday Bunny Pan, p. 183
- Tips 3, 4, 16, 17, 101, 103, p. 118, 119
- Decorator's Brush, p. 126
- Pound Cake Recipe, p. 95
- Uncooked spaghetti

1. Use decorator's brush to paint spaghetti with icing color. Bake and cool cake according to pan instructions. Use toothpick to mark large heart. Ice message area smooth with spatula.

2. Use tip 3 to outline heart and all of bunny's features. Use tip 3 to fill in eyes, ears and teeth; smooth with dampened brush.

Cover bunny's cheeks with tip 16 stars. Cover bow tie and body with tip 17 stars, tail with tip 17 rosettes.

3. Add tip 101 bow and tip 103 ruffle around heart. Make tip 4 bead heart nose, decorations and pupils; flatten with finger (for shine, brush with piping gel). Make tip 4 pull-out dot lashes and print messages. Use tip 4 dots and outlines for funny face. Position spaghetti whiskers. *Serves 12.*

WINGS OF LOVE

Decorating Needs
- Book Pan, p. 176
- Tips 2, 4, 16, 21, 103, 224, 352, p. 118-121
- Flower Nail #7, p. 121
- '86 Pattern Book (Lace Hearts Pattern), p. 135
- Royal Icing Recipe, p. 83

1. Make 50 Lace Hearts. Cover pattern with waxed paper and trace hearts with tip 2 royal icing strings. Dry thoroughly.

Make about 55 tip 224 drop flowers with tip 4 dot centers. Use tip 103 to make roses on flower nail #7.

2. Ice cake top and sides smooth. Mark hearts with a toothpick. Cover marks with tip 16 shells. Position drop flowers around shells. Add roses and pipe tip 103 sweet peas; trim with tip 352 leaves. Print tip 4 message.

3. Edge cake top with tip 16 shells; edge base with tip 21 shells. Carefully position royal icing lace points in icing shells. *Serves 12.*

For more ways to use HOLIDAY BUNNY PAN see Pan Index p. 192.

For more ways to use BOOK PAN see Pan Index p. 192.

VALENTINE'S DAY (CONT.)

on page 94). After unmolding, use tip 3 to add contrasting swirl of coating.

2. Use spatula to ice top of cake smooth with pink icing. Ice lower heart top and sides with second color. Cover tiered heart sides with tip 16 zigzag.

3. Add tip 104 ruffle around tiered heart. Trim with tip 104 ribbon and bow. Add tip 16 shell border to edge and base of cake. Add tip 3 message; position Bon Bons. *Serves 12.*

A. VALENTINE CLASSIC
Decorating Needs
- 10-in. Square Pan, p. 167
- Tips 16 and 104, p. 119

1. Use a spatula to ice cake top and sides smooth. Use a toothpick to mark scallops, top rows of hearts and side hearts.

2. Pipe tip 104 bead hearts on cake top and sides. Add tip 104 ribbon scallops to cake top. Finish with tip 16 shell border on cake top and base. *Serves 24.*

B. DOUBLE YOUR PLEASURES
Decorating Needs
- Double Tier Heart Pan, p. 181
- Tips 3, 16 and 104, p. 118, 119
- Bon Bons Candy Mold, p. 101
- Candy Melts,™* p. 106
- Creme Center Mix (optional), p. 106

1. Prepare Bon Bons using Candy Melts and Creme Center Mix (follow directions on packages or see candymaking instructions

C. HEARTS AND KISSES
Decorating Needs
- Heart Minicake Pan, p. 181
- Classic Truffle Candy Kit, p. 107
- Candy Melts,™* p. 106
- Tip 3, p. 118
- Liqueur (or flavoring) and whipping cream
- Ribbon

1. FOR HEART BOXES: Melt Candy Melts according to package directions. Pour melted coating into Minicake pan, filling to the brim. Refrigerate for no more than 5 minutes until coating has hardened just on the outside.

Remove from refrigerator and pour out soft coating centers (this coating can be re-used later). Refrigerate candy "shells" until coating is completely hardened, about 30 minutes. Unmold onto a soft cloth and trim any rough edges with a sharp knife.

* brand confectionery coating.

A. For more ways to use 10-IN. SQUARE PAN see Pan Index p. 192.

B. For more ways to use DOUBLE TIER HEART PAN see Pan Index p. 192.

SWEETS FOR....

30

2. FOR CANDIES: Prepare Classic Truffle recipe (page 8 of instruction booklet) flavoring mixture with your favorite liqueur or brandy. Roll truffle mixture into round centers and dip in additional melted coating. Use tip 3 to decorate candies with lines, zigzags and spirals.

3. Fill your completed candy hearts with truffles. Top with another candy heart, secure with ribbon and tie in a bow. Use dots of melted coating to keep ribbon in place.

D. VALENTINE VARIETY COOKIES

Decorating Needs
- Cookie Sheet, p. 175
- Tips 3, 5, 16, 225, 349, p. 118-121
- Heart Set Cookie Cutters, p. 114
- Cookie Dips, p. 112
- Cookie Icing Mix, p. 112
- Roll-Out Cookie Recipe, p. 98
- Jam, candied cherries, silver dots (dragees)

1. Roll chilled dough and cut heart shapes in assorted sizes. Cut open heart center with a small cutter. Bake and cool cookies.

2. Use melted Cookie Dips to coat whole, half or just edges of cookies. Make sandwich cookies using Cookie Icing or jam.

3. Add finishing touches following our examples or using your imagination. Pipe tip 5 bead hearts, tip 16 zigzag, stars and reverse shells, and tip 3 lines. Cut cherries and attach to cookies with dots of icing. Trim with silver dots or tip 225 drop flowers with tip 3 dot centers; add tip 349 leaves.

E. MY HEART'S DELIGHT

Decorating Needs
- Loaf Pan, p. 170
- Tips 2A, 4, 17, 21, p. 118, 119
- Candy Melts,™* p. 106
- Heart Set Cookie Cutters, p. 114
- Toothpicks, aluminum foil

1. Melt Candy Melts according to package directions. Line cookie sheet or cake pan with foil. Set Heart Cookie Cutter on foil; use spoon to fill center with melted Candy Melts until coating reaches thickness you want. Tap lightly to release air bubbles. Refrigerate to harden, then pop out your candy heart. Repeat to make about 4 medium hearts and 8 large hearts.

Attach toothpicks to backs of medium hearts. Dip toothpicks in melted coating then place flat against heart. For extra strength, spoon a little coating over toothpick. Let set.

2. Cut two "V" shaped grooves into top of cake with a long knife. Remove cake. Fill to level of cake using tip 2A or spatula. Top each filled groove with two parallel outlines using tip 2A.

3. Edge outside of each groove with tip 4 scallops. Trim top edges with tip 17 shells, base of cake with tip 21 shells.

Attach large hearts to sides and ends of cake with dabs of icing or melted Candy Melts. Position medium hearts on cake top, inserting toothpicks at an angle so they won't show. *Serves 12.*

For more ways to use HEART MINICAKE PAN see Pan Index p. 192.

C.

E.

For more ways to use LOAF PAN see Pan Index p. 192.

D.

For more ways to use COOKIE SHEET see Pan Index p. 192.

Rejoice in a Glorious Springtime

A. COOKIE BASKET AND COOKIES

Decorating Needs
- Easter Basket Cookie Kit, p. 116
- Cookie Sheets, p. 175
- Tips 3 and 16, p. 118, 119
- Decorator's Brush, p. 126
- Royal Icing Recipe, p. 83
- Roll-Out Cookie Recipe, p. 98
- Ribbon, artificial grass, gumdrops

1. Follow Easter Basket Cookie Kit instructions for cutting and baking your Easter Basket. Use open end of decorating tip to cut 6 holes in each panel before baking. Use sharp knife to cut oval-shaped "leaves" from cookie scraps; press with knife blade to mark veins. Attach cookie leaves and circles to panels with a little water before baking.

2. Assemble Easter Basket according to kit instructions. Trim with ribbon laced through holes and bow tied to handle. Use painting technique to brush color onto leaves and circles.

3. Cut and bake animal cookies following kit instructions. Follow our examples or use your imagination to decorate cookies with gumdrops, tip 3 dots, lines and zigzags and tip 16 stars. Fill Easter Basket with "grass" and position your homemade cookies for a lovely centerpiece.

◇ B. SUBLIME LEMON AND LIME

Decorating Needs
- 11-in. Continental Flan Pan, p. 171
- Tip 21, p. 119
- Stabilized Whipped Cream Recipe, p. 82
- Ingredients for Lemon Cake (see recipe in Flan Pan recipe booklet)
- Fresh lime, maraschino cherry

1. Bake cake and add lemon filling as directed in Flan Pan recipe booklet.

2. Slice lime and quarter pieces. Position on cake top. Pipe tip 21 shells and center rosette. Top rosette with cherry and additional lime pieces. Refrigerate until serving time. *Serves 8.*

C. GREAT EGGS!™ EGG-CITEMENT

Decorating Needs
- Great Eggs! Kit, p. 107
- Candy Melts™*, p. 106
- Easter Bunnies, Egg and Chick In Egg Candy Molds, p. 102
- Fancy Candy Wrappers, p. 107
- Ribbon

1. Prepare candies using Easter molds and Candy Melts. Unmold. Attach egg halves together with a dab of melted coating; let set, then wrap in Fancy Wrappers.

2. Use Great Eggs! large egg and instructions to make hollow Candy Melts egg. Drizzle top of egg with parallel lines, then cross with a different color.

3. Attach bow with coating. Position candies inside egg.

D. EGG-STRAVAGANZA

Decorating Needs
- Egg Pan Set, p. 183
- Tips 4, 14, 21, 68, 225 and 352, p. 118 -121
- Lily Nail Set, p. 121
- Stamens, p. 122
- '86 Pattern Book (Egg) p. 135
- Royal Icing Recipe, p. 83
- Pound Cake Recipe, p. 95

1. Make about 7 royal icing lilies using lily nail and tip 68 (see decorating instructions, p. 93). Add tip 14 centers and insert stamens. Set aside to air dry.

Make about 72 tip 225 royal icing drop flowers. Dot centers with tip 4. Air dry.

2. Slice a bit off bottom of cake so it will sit level. Join cake halves together and ice cake smooth.

With a toothpick, mark Egg Pattern around middle of cake. Cover marks with tip 21 "s" shaped outlines in alternating colors.

With a toothpick, mark scallops and vertical lines. Cover with tip 4 strings.

3. Add tip 4 dot designs; flatten with finger dipped in cornstarch.

Attach lilies and drop flowers with dots of icing. Trim with tip 352 leaves. *Serves 12.*

A.

* brand confectionery coating

B.

For more ways to use
CONTINENTAL
FLAN PAN
see Pan Index p. 192.

Happy Easter

C.

D.

For more ways to use
EGG PAN SET
see Pan Index p. 192.

For more ways to use CROSS PAN see Pan Index p. 192.

A.

For more ways to use 9-IN. PETAL PAN see Pan Index p. 192.

B.

A. SING HALLELUJAH!

Decorating Needs
• Cross Pan, p. 183
• Tips 4, 14, 16, 47, 68, 172, 349, p. 118-121
• Lily Nail Set, p. 121
• Stamens, p. 122
• Royal Icing Recipe, p. 83

1. Use tip 68 and Lily Nail Set to make 8 or more royal icing lilies (see instructions, p. 93). Add tip 14 center and insert stamens. Let dry.

2. Ice cake smooth. Use tip 47 (ribbed side up) to pipe angled ribbons in alternating colors around cake sides.

Pipe tip 172 rope cross in center of cross. Add tip 16 shell borders to bevels and base.

3. Pipe tip 4 vine down center of rope cross and trim with tip 349 leaves. Position royal icing lilies and your Easter cake is ready! *Serves 12.*

B. EGG-CEPTIONAL COMBINATION

Decorating Needs
• 9-in. Petal Pan, p. 169
• Tips 18 and 47, p. 118, 120
• Candy Melts™* p. 106
• Stand-Up Lamb Candy Mold, p. 103
• Large Eggs Candy Mold, p. 102
• Gelatin in assorted colors, coconut

1. Use Candy Melts and Lamb Mold to make centerpiece. Mold assorted colors of gelatin (use half the amount of water package directs) in lightly oiled Large Eggs Mold. Refrigerate until serving time.

2. Ice cake smooth with thinned icing. Sprinkle top with tinted coconut.**

3. Use tip 47 (ribbed side up) to cover cake sides with basket-weave. Edge cake with tip 18 rope borders.

Position candy lamb and gelatin eggs just before serving time. *Serves 12.*

◇ ONE FOR THE BUNNY…

Decorating Needs
• 6-Cup Muffin Pan, p. 174
• Easter Bunny Picks, p. 140
• Cupcake papers, jelly beans, coconut, red licorice whips and ribbons

1. Use spatula to ice tops of cupcakes; sprinkle with tinted coconut.**

2. Position jelly beans on coconut "grass" and insert

Easter Bunny Pick. Cut licorice whip and insert ends into cupcakes to form handles. Attach ribbon bow with small dot of icing or tie around licorice.

***Hint: To tint shredded coconut place in a plastic sandwich bag. Add a few drops of diluted Wilton Paste Icing Color. Shake bag until color is evenly distributed.*

For more ways to use 6-CUP MUFFIN PAN & 8-IN. ROUND PAN see Pan Index p. 192.

*brand confectionery coating.

34

◇ FOLLOW THE JELLY BEAN ROAD

Decorating Needs
• 8-in. Round Pan, p. 166
• Tip 2A, p. 118
• Stabilized Whipped Cream Recipe, p.82
• Jelly beans and coconut

1. Use spatula to ice cake top and sides. Gently press tinted coconut** onto cake sides.

2. Use toothpick to mark coil on cake top, leaving room for jelly beans in between rows.† Beginning in center of cake, pipe tip 2A outline over marks. Add jelly beans, beginning at center of cake and working toward outer edge. *Serves 12.*

†*Circular motion is easy with a rotating cake stand! See page 163.*

C. LITTLE CHICK-A-DEE

Decorating Needs
• Chick•In•Egg Pan, p. 183
• Tips 4, 16, 21, 224, 352, p. 118-121
• '86 Pattern Book (Chick Pattern), p. 135
• Decorator's Brush, p. 126

1. Make about 14 tip 224 swirl drop flowers with tip 4 dot centers. Freeze until needed.

2. Ice sides and bottom half of cake top smooth. Transfer Chick Pattern to cake. Use tip 4 to outline details. Fill shadow area of bow with tip 4 zigzag.

Cover bow and hat with tip 16 stars. Fill in eyes, irises and built-up beak with tip 4; smooth with dampened brush. Add tip 4 dot pupils and nostrils.

Cover chick's face and body with tip 352 feathers using pull-out star technique.

3. Attach drop flowers. Trim with tip 352 leaves. Print tip 4 message. Add tip 21 star border. *Serves 12.*

D. SIGN OF SPRING

Decorating Needs
• Egg Pan Set, p. 183
• Tips 3, 16, 18, 129, 225 and 349, p. 118-121
• Pound Cake Recipe, p. 95
• Plastic drinking straws

1. Pipe assorted flowers: 80 with tip 225, 25 with tip 129 and 25 with tip 16. Dot all centers with tip 3.

Bake and cool pound cake according to Egg Pan Set instructions. Ice cake halves together; slice off part of end. Insert straws diagonally. Ice cake smooth.

2. Use a toothpick to mark patterns. Pipe tip 18 inverted C-scrolls around middle, C-scrolls around top and bottom. Add tip 18 shell border.

3. Attach flowers with dots of icing. Trim with tip 349 leaves. *Serves 12.*

For more ways to use CHICK•IN•EGG PAN see Pan Index p. 192.

For more ways to use EGG PAN SET p. 192. see Pan Index p. 192.

C.

D.

MOTHER'S DAY

There are so many good reasons to tell her she's "ma"velous. Because of the nice things she does, because she's always there when you need her, because you love her. Decorate one of these loving lovelies and she'll get the message!

HATCHIN' UP A GREAT DAY

Decorating Needs
- Chick•In•Egg Pan, p. 183
- Tips 4, 17, 352, p. 118-121
- Candy-coated chocolates

1. Ice background area on cake top and sides smooth. Outline eggshell, eyes and beak with tip 4 strings. Pipe in eyes and beak with tip 4 (shape and flatten with finger dipped in cornstarch). Add tip 4 dot nostrils.

2. Cover egg with tip 17 stars; chick with tip 352 pull-out leaf feathers.

3. Print tip 4 message. Edge background area on cake base with tip 17 stars. Attach candy eyeballs with dots of icing. *Serves 12.*

Present-perfect! If she loves to bake, give her the pan her cake was baked in, a Decorating Set, Icing Mix, Color Kit and more! See all we have to offer starting on p. 117.

HAPPY MOTHER'S DAY

I'M YOUR FAVORITE CHICK

For more ways to use CHICK•IN•EGG PAN see Pan Index p. 192.

◆ WORKING WOMAN'S SUNSHINE PETAL

Decorating Needs
- 9-in. Petal Pan, p. 169
- Tips 4, 12, 18, 352, p. 118-121
- Chopped nuts, sliced almonds

1. Ice 2-layer cake smooth. Pat sides with chopped nuts. With spatula, score top into 8ths.

2. Pipe tip 12 dot flower faces (flatten with finger dipped in cornstarch). They should be approximately 1-inch in diameter. Add tip 4 outline stems, smiles and dot eyes. Pipe tip 352 leaves.

3. Push almond flower petals into cake around icing dots. Edge cake top and base with tip 18 shell border. *Serves 12.*

Hint: To make this cake even faster, use Candy Melts™* (p. 106) right out of the bag for flower faces.

*brand confectionery coating

For more ways to use 9-IN. PETAL PANS see Pan Index p. 192.

FATHER'S DAY

Applause! Applause! He deserves a hand for being so grand! This year and every year, give him the V.I.P. treatment Make one of these V.I.P. (very important pop) cakes and he'll know he really rates.

For more ways to use 6-IN. ROUND PANS see Pan Index p. 192.

"POP" CAN

Decorating Needs
- 6-in. Round Pans, p. 166
- Tips 2B, 3, 10, 17, p. 118-119
- '86 Pattern Book, p. 135 (Label Pattern)
- Number 1 Dad, p. 141
- Dowel Rod, p. 160

1. Ice 4-layer cake smooth. Push a sharpened dowel rod through all layers for support.

With toothpick, mark Label Pattern on side and pop-top on cake top. Outline label, pop-top, bottom and top rim with tip 3 strings.

2. Cover tab of pop-top with tip 3 zigzags. Fill in can top, label and bottom rim of can with tip 17 stars. Pipe tip 2B smooth stripe on top rim.

3. Pipe tip 10 dots randomly on cake sides (flatten with finger dipped in cornstarch). Print tip 3 words on can. Attach Number 1 Dad with icing. *Serves 16.*

ARGYLE ATTENTION-GETTER

Decorating Needs
- 10-in. Square Pan, p. 167
- Tips 16, 18, p. 119
- '86 Pattern Book, p. 135 (Argyle Pattern)

1. Ice 2-layer cake smooth. With toothpick, mark Argyle Pattern on cake top. Cover X and large diamond with tip 18 stripe. Fill in small diamonds with tip 16 stars.

2. With toothpick, dot mark cake sides in half and draw X's. Cover marks with tip 18 stripes. To mark diamonds, divide each X in half and connect marks. Fill in diamond shapes with tip 16 stars.

3. Edge cake top and base with tip 18 star borders. *Serves 24.*

For more helpful hints, review Decorating Guide p. 80.

For more ways to use 10-IN. SQUARE PANS, see Pan Index p. 192.

Dazzle 'Em...
on the 4th of July!

*Let Uncle Sam add his special sparkle to
your festivities.
Make it the most glorious Fourth of all.
It's the grandest day
for a grand family reunion!*

UNCLE SAM'S CHOICE

Decorating Needs
- 8-in. Round Pan, p. 166
- Tips 3, 16, p. 118-119
- Star Cookie Cutters, p. 114
- '86 Pattern Book, p. 135 (Star Pattern)
- Candy Melts™®, p. 106
- Candy Colors, p. 106
- Lollipops II Candy Mold, p. 101
- Cake Dividing Set, p. 126
- Lollipop Sticks, p. 105
- White cake batter

1. Mold red, white and blue Candy Melts lollipops.

2. Divide cake batter into thirds. Color 1/3 red, 1/3 blue, leave 1/3 white. Bake individually. Fill and stack. Ice 3-layer cake smooth with white icing. Using Cake Dividing Set, with toothpick, dot mark cake top into twelfths; dot mark Star Pattern on cake top. Lightly press cookie cutters onto sides of cake to mark pattern. Cover all marks with tip 3 outlines. Cover red stars with tip 16 stars. Cover area around white stars with tip 16 blue stars. Add tip 3 beads on center. Trim white section of cake edge and base with tip 16 white stars.

3. Add tip 16 rosette. Position lollipops in center of cake. *Serves 12.*

For more ways to use
8-IN. ROUND PAN
see Pan Index p. 192.

38

*brand confectionery coating

AMERICA'S FAVORITE FARE

Decorating Needs

- Good Cheer Mug Pan, p. 184
- Tips 2A, 3, 4, 9, 12, 16, 18, p. 118-119
- '86 Pattern Book, p. 135 (Hat and Hot Dog Pattern)
- Piping Gel, p. 125

1. Ice cake smooth, sides and part of top brown, top yellow. With toothpick, mark Hat and Hot Dog pattern on cake top. Cover marks with tip 4 strings. Add foam by icing top part of cake fluffy with white icing.

2. Cover bottom of glass, handle, cuff, fist, and hat with tip 16 stars. Pipe tip 2A front of bun, tip 9 back of bun, tip 12 hot dog. Fill in tip 4 mustard. Smooth with finger. Fill in mouth, tongue and eyebrows with tip 4. Add tip 4 fill-in whites of eyes, tip 4 dot eyeballs, cuff button. Trim hat with tip 4 fill-in band.

3. With piping gel and tip 4, add droplets to glass. Add tip 18 star cake base border. Print tip 3 message. *Serves 12.*

These cakes will sparkle at other occasions, such as Mother's Day, Father's Day, birthdays, too!

For more ways to use GOOD CHEER MUG PAN see Pan Index p. 192.

JUST PEACHY ROSE

Decorating Needs

- 11-in. Continental Flan Pan, p. 171
- Vanilla pudding, one 29 oz. can sliced peaches, one 16 oz. can pear halves, light corn syrup, liquid icing color

1. To blush fruits: Add 1 or 2 drops of light corn syrup to food color. Drain fruits, pat dry with paper towels and dip into color to coat. Remove and even color with finger tip. Place on paper towel.

2. Fill baked flan cake with vanilla pudding. Arrange blushed pear half "leaves" around edges. Fill in peach slices for "rose," working from the outside in. *Serves 8.*

For more ways to use CONTINENTAL FLAN PAN see Pan Index p. 192.

For more ways to use SHOWER UMBRELLA PAN see Pan Index p. 192.

PICNIC SURPRISE

Decorating Needs

- Shower Umbrella Pan, p. 182
- Tips 1A, 4, 16, 46, p. 118-119
- '86 Pattern Book, p. 135 (Glass Pattern)
- Piping Gel, p. 125

1. Ice cake top and sides smooth with white icing. With toothpick, dot mark cloth and Glass Pattern on cake top. Cover cloth marks with tip 46 smooth lines. Pipe tip 1A dot bottom of glass. Flatten with finger dipped in cornstarch. Cover Glass Pattern marks and glass bottom (on dot) with tip 4 outlines. Outline basket and bow with tip 4.

2. Cover basket, bow and inside bow with tip 16 stars. Fill in glass with tip 4. Smooth with finger. Fill in liquid with tip 4 tinted piping gel. Smooth with spatula.

3. Print tip 4 message. *Serves 12.*

HALLOWEEN—IT'S A

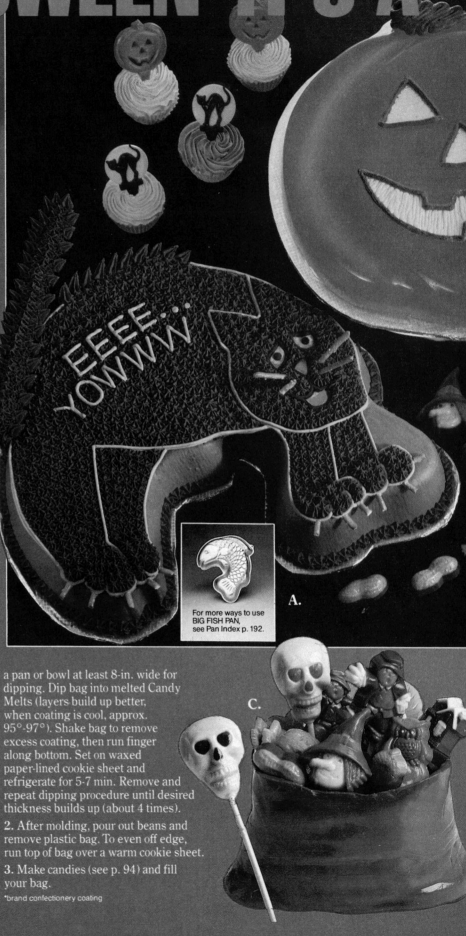

Scary things that make us laugh. Creaking doors and haunted houses. Little ghosts and witches scampering about. When glowing pumpkins beckon merry masqueraders, it's time to get those gobblin' goodies ready!

A. SCARY SCAREDY-CAT

Decorating Needs
- Big Fish Pan, p. 177
- Tips 4, 16, 18, p. 118-119
- '86 Pattern Book, p. 135 (Cat Pattern)
- Pretzel sticks, pretzel rod, large jelly candy

1. Ice top and sides smooth (build up side and top where face and belly will go with extra icing). With toothpick, mark Cat Pattern.

2. Outline face, body and legs with tip 4. Add tip 4 fill-in eyes and dot pupils.

Cover cat with tip 16 stars. Add tip 18 pull-out stars along back. Print tip 4 message.

3. Slice jelly candy to fill mouth and nose areas. Push pretzel stick whiskers and claws into cake. Push pretzel rod into cake side (sharpen end with knife). Add tip 18 pull-out stars. Edge cake base with tip 18 star border. *Serves 12.*

◇ B. ALL SMILES

Decorating Needs
- Jack-O-Lantern Pan, p. 176
- Tip 6, p. 118
- 2-6 oz. packages orange flavored gelatin, 3 oz. cream cheese (whipped and sweetened with confectioners sugar)

1. Lightly oil pan with vegetable oil. Follow recipe and molding instructions on gelatin package. Pour into pan and chill until set.

2. Unmold gelatin on serving plate.

3. With whipped cream cheese and tip 6, outline facial features and fill-in with zigzags. Add tip 6 zigzag stem. Refrigerate until serving time. Decorate no more than 3 hours before serving. *Makes 16 one-half cup servings.*

C. TRICKY TREAT BAG

Decorating Needs
- Candy Melts™© (approx. 2 lbs. for bag), p. 106
- Halloween Lollipops Candy Molds, p. 105
- Lollipop Sticks, p. 105
- Dried beans and popcorn kernels (about 1¼ lb.), plastic lock-top sandwich bag

1. For bag: Fill sandwich bag with dried beans and popcorn kernels. Seal lock-top. Push in bottom corners to round off. Use a pan or bowl at least 8-in. wide for dipping. Dip bag into melted Candy Melts (layers build up better, when coating is cool, approx. 95°-97°). Shake bag to remove excess coating, then run finger along bottom. Set on waxed paper-lined cookie sheet and refrigerate for 5-7 min. Remove and repeat dipping procedure until desired thickness builds up (about 4 times).

2. After molding, pour out beans and remove plastic bag. To even off edge, run top of bag over a warm cookie sheet.

3. Make candies (see p. 94) and fill your bag.

*brand confectionery coating

For more ways to use BIG FISH PAN, see Pan Index p. 192.

A.

C.

SCREAM!

For more ways to use
JACK-O-LANTERN PAN
see Pan Index p. 192.

B.

HAPPY HALLOWEEN

For more ways to use
WIZARD PAN
see Pan Index p. 192

E.

E. BEWITCHING BEAUTY

Decorating Needs
• Wizard Pan, p. 176
• Tips 4, 7, 16, 18, p. 118-119
• Piping Gel, p. 125
• Decorator's Brush, p. 126

1. Ice cake sides brown and cauldron gold. With toothpick, mark hat, face and shawl (lightly ice for easier marking) and cauldron. Outline witch and cauldron with tip 4 string.

2. Pipe in hatband, buckle, eyes, nose, stirrer and star with tip 7 (smooth with finger dipped in cornstarch). Cover hat, face, shawl, body and hands with tip 16 stars.

3. Pipe tip 7 cauldron rim. Add tip 18 stripe hair. Trim shawl with tip 4 outline fringe. Pipe tip 4 dot eyes and moles (smooth with dampened brush). Print tip 4 message. Pipe tip 7 tinted piping gel balls in cauldron. Overpipe with clear piping gel for a bubbly effect. Edge cake base with tip 18 shell border. *Serves 12.*

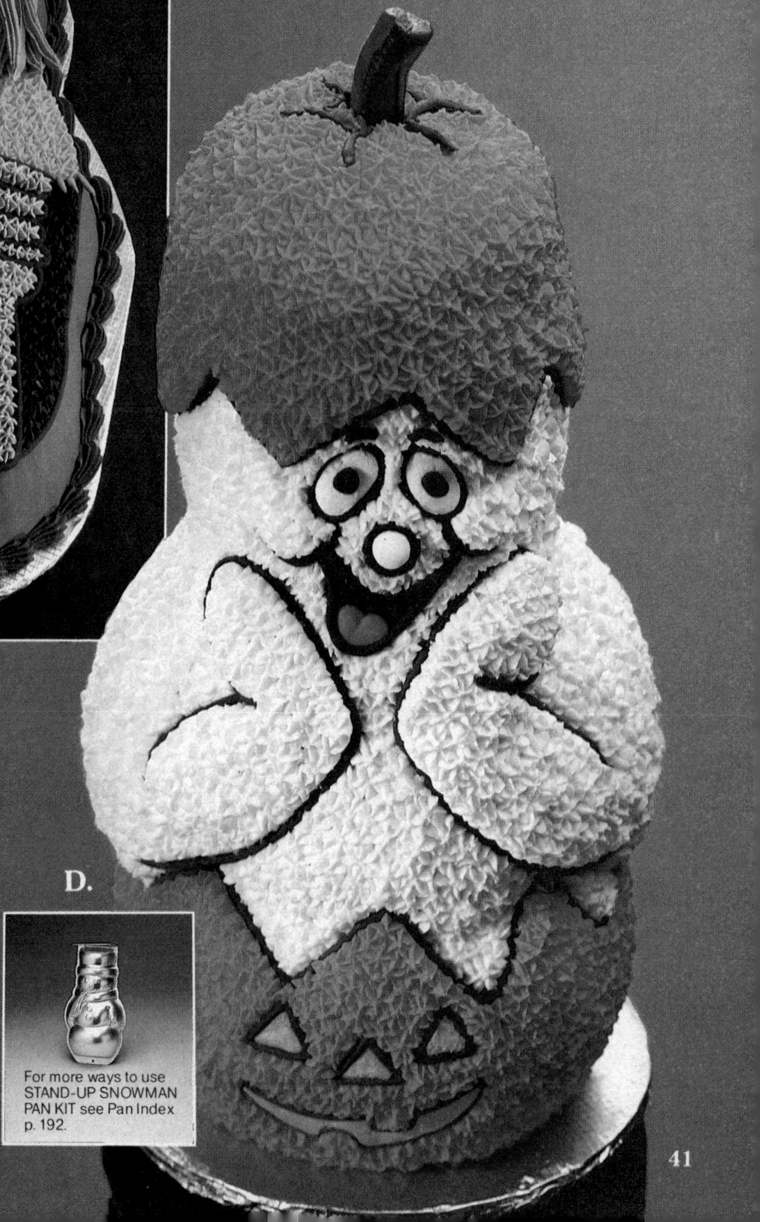

D. PUMPKIN SURPRISE

Decorating Needs
• Stand-Up Snowman Pan Kit, p. 178
• Tips 4, 17, p.118-119
• '86 Pattern Book, p. 135 (Ghost Pattern)
• Decorator's Brush, p. 126
• Dowel Rods, p. 160
• Pound Cake Recipe, p. 95
• Chocolate roll candy

1. Ice backs of cake halves and push together. Hint: Push sharpened dowels diagonally into cake. With a knife, trim scarf area off cake. Lightly ice cake smooth. With toothpick, mark Ghost Pattern on cake.

2. Outline ghost and pumpkin with tip 4 strings. Pipe in ghost's eyes and mouth. Add tip 4 dot nose, eyeballs and tongue (smooth with dampened brush). Fill in pumpkin's eyes, nose and mouth with tip 4 (smooth with dampened brush).

3. Cover pumpkin and ghost with tip 17 stars. Attach chocolate roll candy stem with dots of icing. *Serves 24.*

D.

For more ways to use
STAND-UP SNOWMAN
PAN KIT see Pan Index
p. 192.

FAIRY GOOD

Decorating Needs
- Treeliteful Pan, p. 179
- Tips 4, 16, 18, 127, 131, p. 118-121
- '86 Pattern Book, p. 135 (Witch Pattern)
- Tinted coconut flakes

1. To tint coconut for hair: Place coconut flakes in a small plastic bag. Add a few drops of Violet Paste color and a little water. Squeeze bag to blend color. Let dry on paper towel. Make 2 tip 131 drop flowers with tip 4 dot centers. Ice cake smooth. With toothpick, mark Witch Pattern on cake top. Cover marks with tip 4 strings. Add tip 4 dot eyes.

2. Cover hat, face, shawl, arms, hands, skirt, petticoat, broom handle and legs with tip 16 stars. Edge cake base with tip 18 star border. Add tip 4 dot mole.

3. Pipe broom bristles with tip 18 stripes. Trim bristles with tip 4 strings. Add tip 127 ruffle to skirt. Pat coconut hair on cake. *Serves 12.*

For more ways to use TREELITEFUL PAN see Pan Index p. 192.

FUNNY FACE PUMPKIN PATCH

Decorating Needs
- 10-in. Round Pan, p. 166
- Mini Pumpkin Pan, p. 176
- Tips 4, 6, 16, 17, 233, 352, p. 118-121
- Little Trickers, p. 140
- Cake Circles, p. 162
- Decorator's Brushes, p. 126
- Chopped Nuts

1. Ice one-layer round cake smooth. Pat side with chopped nuts.

2. Lightly ice 6 mini pumpkin cakes smooth on cake circles cut to fit. With toothpick, mark funny faces.

Cover marks with tip 4 strings. Fill in eyes, noses and mouths with tip 4 (smooth with dampened brush). Cover faces with tip 16 stars.

For more ways to use 10 IN. ROUND & MINI PUMPKIN PANS see Pan Index p. 192.

HAPPY HOBGOBLINS

Decorating Needs
• Muffin or Square Pan, p. 167, 174
• Tip 3, p. 118
• Candy Melts™*, p. 106
• Pumpkin candy molds, p. 103
• Ice cream cones

1. Fill ice cream cones no more than half full of cake batter. Place in muffin or square pan for support and bake at 350° for 15-20 minutes or until cake tests done. Let cool completely on wire rack.

2. See p. 94 for all candy making techniques…molding, dipping and decorating. Mold hollow, multi-colored pumpkin candy and dip cake-filled cones using melted Candy Melts. Let set completely.

3. Outline pumpkin facial features, add dot eyes and print names on cones with tip 3 or cut bag filled with melted Candy Melts. Let set. Attach pumpkins to cones with melted coating and let set.

*brand confectionery coating

3. Position mini cakes atop round cake. Edge cake top with tip 233 straw border; base with tip 17 shell border. Pipe tip 6 string vine and add tip 352 leaves. Position Little Trickers. *Serves 18.*

COOKIE KIDS & CRITTERS

Decorating Needs
• Cookie Sheet, p. 175
• Tips 2C, 2D, 3, 16, p. 118-120
• Round Cookie Cutter Set, p. 114
• Cookie Dips, p. 112
• Roll-out Cookie Recipe, p. 98
• Candy-coated chocolates, almonds

1. You'll need to use 4-in. cutter for kids; 2-in. for mouse, pig and owl. 1½-in. for mouse ears. 2½-in. for lion, dog and cat.

2. Use the round ends of decorating tips 2C, 2D and 16 to cut out noses, cheeks, lion's mane and mouth, bear ears and inside of mouse ears. Cut triangles for cat, owl and pig ears with knife. Attach dough shapes with a little water (except bear snout, bake separately). Push in almond whiskers and teeth. Bake and cool.

3. To Decorate: Dip pig and bear snout into melted Cookie Dips. Let set. Attach snout with dots of melted coating. With icing, pipe tip 3 facial features, bows and boy's hair or use tip 16 stripes for pigtails and bangs. Attach candy eyes and almond beak with dots of icing.

For more helpful hints, review Decorating Guide, p. 80

Thanksgiving...
a time to count our Blessings.

There's so much to be grateful for. Freedom, family, friendship, good fortune.

These are the best reasons To gather together.

To celebrate.

To give thanks.

C.

A. MINI MINCEMEAT AND PETITE PUMPKIN TREATS

Decorating Needs
- Tartlet Mold Set, p. 173
- Petite Fancy Ring Mold, p. 172
- Tips 19, 2110, p. 119
- Pumpkin Spice Cake Recipe, p. 95
- Dough for 1 pie crust, one jar mincemeat filling, stabilized whipped cream, maraschino cherries, chopped nuts

1. Prepare pie crust and place in prepared tartlet molds. Pour mincemeat filling in crust and bake 15 min. at 450° or according to directions on jar. Cool completely and remove from pan. Pipe tip 19 whipped cream rosettes in center; top with maraschino cherry.

For more ways to use TARTLET MOLD SET and PETITE FANCY RING MOLD see Pan Index p. 192.

2. Bake Pumpkin Spice cakes; cool. Fill centers with tip 2110 whipped cream flavored with cinnamon. Sprinkle with chopped nuts and chopped maraschino cherries.

Hint: You can also use the New Petit Fours/Pastry Mold Set (p. 170) for your Mincemeat Treats. The eight lovely shapes are perfect for pastries!

For more helpful hints, review Decorating Guide, p. 80.

B. CREAMY PUMPKIN ROLL

Decorating Needs
- Jelly Roll Pan, p. 175
- Tip 17, p. 119
- Pumpkin Roll and Cream Cheese Icing & Filling Recipes, p. 95

For more ways to use JELLY ROLL PAN see Pan Index p. 192.

1. Prepare Pumpkin Roll and Cream Cheese Icing & Filling according to recipes.

2. To Decorate: With toothpick, dot mark center top of cake into eighths, starting about ½-in. from edge. Dot mark center sides into ninths, starting at edge. Dot mark lower sides into eighths to correspond with center top marks. With tip 17 stripes, connect center top marks to center sides and center sides to lower side to form diamonds. Pipe tip 17 stars at points of diamonds, and tip 17 upright shells between diamonds and at bottom points. Pipe tip 17 rosettes within diamonds. *Serves 12.*

C. AUTUMN CASCADE

Decorating Needs
- 12½ x 16½-in. Cookie Sheet, p. 175
- Cookie Holly Wreath Kit, p. 116
- Tip 4, p. 118
- Candy Melts™*, p. 106
- Candy Wafer & Fondant Mix, p. 106
- Rectangular Cake Board, p. 162
- Real ribbon bow, candy mold with acorns

For more ways to use 12½-in. x 16½-in. COOKIE SHEET see Pan Index p. 192.

1. Mold 9 Candy Melts acorns.

2. Following instructions and recipes in Cookie Holly Wreath Kit, bake and ice 20 leaves, using Quick Pour Icing recipe on Fondant Mix canister, some gold and some yellow. Outline veins with tip 4 strings.

Note: Cookies may also be dipped in melted Candy Melts.

3. Arrange cookies on board; attach acorns with melted Candy Melts. Position bow and attach with melted Candy Melts.

*brand confectionery coating

D. HARVEST BOUQUET

Decorating Needs
- Shower Umbrella Pan, p. 182
- Tips 4, 16, 18, p. 118-119
- '86 Pattern Book, p. 135 (Wheat Pattern)
- Decorator's Brush, p. 126

For more ways to use SHOWER UMBRELLA PAN see Pan Index p. 192.

1. Ice cake smooth. With toothpick, mark Wheat Pattern on cake top. Cover marks, outline bow and make stems with tip 4 strings. With thinned icing, fill in blossoms with tip 4. Smooth with dampened brush.

2. Cover inside ribbon with tip 4 zigzags. Cover ribbon with tip 16 stars. Make tip 4 fill-in ribbon pleats.

3. Edge cake base with tip 18 shell border. *Serves 12.*

CHRISTMAS CANDLE

Decorating Needs

- 6-in. Round Pan, p. 166
- Tips 1A, 2, 3, 8, 22, p. 118, 119
- Cookie Holly Wreath Kit, p. 116
- '86 Pattern Book (Flame Pattern), p. 135
- Candy Wafer & Fondant Mix, p. 106
- 10-in. Cake Circle, p. 162
- Fanci-Foil Wrap, p. 163
- Lollipop Stick, p. 105
- Dowel Rod, p. 160
- Piping Gel, p. 125
- Roll-Out Cookie Recipe, p. 98

1. Prepare and roll cookie dough. Use Leaf Cutter from Holly Wreath Kit to cut 12 leaves. Use toothpick to transfer Flame pattern onto dough. Cut with a sharp knife; place lollipop stick on cookie sheet, cover with "Flame" cookie and press lightly. Use dough to make 12 berries, ½ in. diameter. Bake, cool and ice cookies with *Quick Pour Icing* (see recipe on label of Candy Wafer & Fondant Mix). When dry, add tip 3 lines to leaves. For cookie flame, pipe tip 22 stripes.

2. For candle, fill and stack four 6-in. Rounds on foil-covered cake board. Insert dowel rod (cut to fit). Ice smooth. Use toothpick to mark wax and snowflakes. Add tip 1A wax and drips; build up then shape with finger. Add tip 8 bead border. Pipe snowflakes with tip 2 lines and dots and tip 2 beads and dots.

3. Attach leaves and berries with icing; glaze berries with piping gel. Position "Flame." *Serves 16.*

For more ways to use
BALL PAN
see Pan Index p. 192.

HOLIDAY BAUBLE

Decorating Needs

- Ball Pan, p. 184
- Tips 2, 4, 13, 16, 18, 46 and 224, p. 118-120
- Dowel Rod, p. 160
- 6-in. Cake Circles, p. 162
- Fanci-Foil Wrap, p. 163
- Pound Cake Recipe, p. 95
- Ribbon, posterboard

1. Cover cake circle with foil; secure with tape. Cut strip of posterboard 2 x 6 in. long with one scalloped edge. Tape to form circle and cover sides and top with Fanci-Foil. Allow pound cake to cool completely. Take slice off one end so cake will sit level. Join 2 halves with icing or filling; insert dowel rod (cut to fit) through center of cake. Ice cake smooth and position on cake circle. Pipe tip 224 drop flowers with tip 2 dot centers. Freeze.

2. Use toothpick to mark Ornament design on cake. Cover marks with tip 4 outlines. Cover center band with tip 16 stars. Use tip 46 (flat side up) to fill "V" designs with icing stripes; edge with tip 2 outlines. Fill small sections of design with tip 13 stars. Cover rest of ball with tip 18 stars.

3. Trim center band with tip 4 bead border and tip 16 "S" scrolls; attach drop flowers with dots of icing. Position cap on top of ornament. Attach bow with icing. *Serves 12.*

For more ways to use
6-IN. ROUND PAN
see Pan Index p. 192.

MAGIC ELF & HIS DEER FRIEND

Decorating Needs
- Rocking Horse Pan, p. 182
- Cookie Sheet, p. 175
- Tips 2, 4, 6, 14, 16, 17, p. 118, 119
- '86 Pattern Book, p. 135 (Reindeer and Antler patterns)
- Lollipop Stick, p. 105
- Cookie dough

1. Roll out cookie dough on cookie sheet. Use toothpick to transfer Antler Pattern, then cut with a knife and remove excess dough. Slip lollipop stick under antler; press lightly. Bake and cool. Ice cake smooth. Use a toothpick to transfer Reindeer Pattern to cake top. Cover marks with tip 4 outlines.

2. Use tip 6 to fill-in reindeer's hoofs, saddle, eye, harness and elf's face, glove and shoe. Decorate elf's face with tip 2. Add line mouth and outline eyes, then add dot centers and pupils. Add tip 14 stripes for hair. Pipe tip 6 dots for reindeer's nose, bells and tassle on elf's hat. Pipe tip 16 pull-out stars for tail. Cover reindeer's body with tip 17 stars, elf's body with tip 16 stars.

3. Add tip 2 pull-out dot eye lashes; trim bells with tip 2 dots and lines. Position antlers on cake. Pipe tip 4 message and tip 17 shell border. *Serves 12.*

For more ways to use ROCKING HORSE PAN see Pan Index p. 192.

'Tis the season of trees and tinsel. Twinkling lights and tinkling bells. Letters to Santa, gifts for the children. Good cheer and warm wishes. A time for prayers. A time for Peace on Earth.

BAG OF GOODIES

Decorating Needs
- Santa's Sleigh Pan, p. 178
- Tips 3, 4, 12, and 16, p. 118, 119
- Candy dots

1. Ice cake sides smooth. Use toothpick to mark bear and presents. Outline Santa, sleigh, bear, presents and all details with tip 4 strings.

2. Use tip 16 stars for Santa's face and suit, bag, sleigh and presents. Cover belt and area between runners with tip 4 zigzags. Pipe tip 16 zigzag for hat brim, cuffs and jacket bottom. Use tip 16 reverse shells for beard and stripes for hair and mustache.

3. Use tip 4 to pipe-in belt buckle, tip 12 to pipe-in bear, edges of sleigh and runners. Pipe bear's features with tip 3 dots (flatten with finger) and lines. Add candy dots to package and Santa's nose. Decorate sleigh with tip 16 "S" scrolls and presents with tip 16 stripes and bows. Trim bag with tip 16 zigzag. Add tip 16 shell border at base of cake. *Serves 12.*

For more ways to use SANTA'S SLEIGH PAN see Pan Index p. 192.

BEST-EVER HOLIDAY COOKIES

Decorating Needs
- Cookie Molds, p. 111
- Cookie Dips, p. 112
- Tip 2, p. 118
- Sprinkle Tops, p. 112
- Mouthwatering Butter Cookie Recipe, p. 98
- Candy dots (red and silver), confectioners sugar, unsweetened baking chocolate

1. Prepare cookie dough according to recipe instructions. Tint some of the dough with Pink Paste Icing Color; for brown, add melted baking chocolate to dough and mix well. Mix multicolor sprinkles or colored sugar into dough before molding.*

Press in cookie dough, using different colors to highlight the designs as we did (for example, pink dough for Angel's gown). Prick with fork to prevent puffing. Bake and cool according to cookie mold instructions.

2. Decorate cooled cookies following our examples or using your imagination. COOKIE DIPS can be colored with Cookie Color and used to decorate cookies. Dip cookie (or brush on melted coating) for large areas like Snowman's hat and star. Use tip 2 to pipe on outlines shown on Soldier, Tree and Wreath. Use a toothpick to add fine details like dot eyes and line mouths.

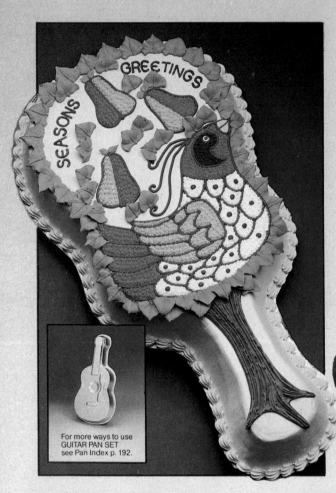

For more ways to use GUITAR PAN SET see Pan Index p. 192.

PARTRIDGE IN A PEAR TREE

Decorating Needs
- Guitar Pan Set, p. 177
- Tips 3, 4, 16 and 112, p. 118-121
- '86 Pattern Book, p. 135 (Partridge Pattern)
- Decorator's Brush, p. 126

1. Ice cake top and sides smooth with a spatula. Use toothpick to mark tree trunk, pears and Partridge Pattern on cake top. Cover marks with tip 4 outlines.

2. Cover partridge and pears with tip 16 stars. Cover tree trunk with tip 16 stripes. Fill beak with tip 3 and smooth with dampened brush.

3. Add tip 16 shell border and tip 112 leaves. Pipe tip 3 dots for eye, pupil and onto body. Finish with tip 3 printed message and your cake is ready. *Serves 12.*

3. Add the finishing touches. Attach red candy dots and silver dots with dots of melted coating. Sprinkle cookie with confectioners sugar to resemble snow.

*You can also add multicolor sprinkles and colored sugar to cookies after they are baked. Brush cooled cookies with glaze of confectioners sugar and water, then sprinkle on trims.

For more ways to use STAND-UP SANTA PAN see Pan Index p. 192.

STAND-UP SANTA CLAUS

Decorating Needs
• Stand-Up Santa Pan, p. 179
• Tips 4, 14, 16, 17, 349, p. 118-121
• Plastic drinking straws

1. Prepare Stand-Up Santa as directed in pan instructions; push straws (cut to fit) diagonally through cake halves. Outline details with tip 4 strings. Cover hat and coat with tip 17 stars; face, mittens, bag and presents with tip 16 stars. Use tip 4 to fill-in eyes and mouth (smooth with finger dipped in cornstarch). Add tip 17 stripe smile and tip 4 dot pupils (flatten with finger dipped in cornstarch).

2. Use tip 17 zigzags for hat brim and cuffs. Add tip 17 rosette for hat tassle. Pipe tip 17 reverse shells for beard and coat trim, stripes for hair and mustache.

3. Trim cake with tip 14 shell eyebrows and stripe ribbons. Use tip 14 bows, stars and pull-out stars to decorate packages. Add tip 349 leaves and tip 4 berries to hat. Finish with tip 4 outlines on patch and cake is ready. *Serves 24.*

◇ PERSONABLE GINGERBREAD COOKIES

Decorating Needs
- Cookie Sheet, p. 175
- Gingerbread Set Cookie Cutters, p. 114
- Tip 2, p. 118
- 1 lb. Candy Box, p. 107
- Rectangle Doily, p. 162
- Gingerbread Cookie Recipe, p. 98
- Wrapping paper, ribbon, artificial holly

1. Prepare cookie dough according to recipe. Roll out and cut with 2½-in. high cutters from set. Bake and cool before decorating.

2. Pipe on features with tip 2. We've decorated our little people with dots, lines, strings, bows, zigzags and "e" motion curls.

3. Cover lid of candy box with wrapping paper. Trim with ribbon and holly. Line bottom of box with folded rectangle doily.

For more ways to use FANCY RING MOLD see Pan Index p. 192.

DECKED OUT RING

Decorating Needs
- Fancy Ring Mold/Pan, p. 172
- Tips 14, 16 and 18, p. 119
- Red and green candied cherries (cut into quarters), apricot preserves

1. Ridges baked into cake are built-in guidelines! Glaze cake with thinned, warmed apricot preserves. Let set. Pipe row of tip 14 shells on crest of each curve on cake top.

2. Trim sides with tip 16 fleur-de-lis, lining up center shell on ridge. Trim base with tip 18 elongated upright shells, centering one shell in each indentation. Pipe tip 16 star where tails of shells meet.

3. Attach cherries with dots of icing. For extra shine, brush fruit with apricot glaze. *Serves 16.*

EGGNOG GELATIN FLAN

Decorating Needs
- 11-in. Continental Flan Pan, p. 171
- Tip 21, p. 119
- Eggnog Gelatin Recipe (below): 1 tsp. un-flavored gelatin, 29 oz. can pear halves, 6 oz. pkg. lemon flavor gelatin, 1 cup sour cream, ¾ cup eggnog, 11 oz. can mandarin oranges
- Stabilized Whipped Cream Recipe, p. 82
- Grapes, strawberries

1. Prepare Eggnog Gelatin Recipe (below). Pour into lightly oiled Continental Flan Pan. Chill until firm, about 2 hours.

EGGNOG GELATIN: Soften unflavored gelatin in ¼ cup cold water. Drain pears and oranges, reserving juice. Set aside 6 pear halves and 20 oranges; dice remaining fruit. Add water to reserved juice to make 2 cups. Bring to a boil; stir in lemon gelatin and unflavored gelatin mixture. Cool to room temperature.

Blend eggnog into sour cream; stir into gelatin mixture. Chill until partially set (consistency of egg whites). Fold in diced fruit. Pour into lightly oiled mold.

2. Unmold gelatin onto serving plate. (HINT: Dip Flan Pan in warm water for a few seconds for easier unmolding. Do not let water go over edge onto gelatin. Wet serving plate with water to make centering gelatin easier.) Smooth a layer of whipped cream into center depression. Arrange reserved pear halves and oranges; add grape halves and strawberry slices on top. Trim with tip 21 rosette. Refrigerate until serving time. *Serves 8.*

GIFT-WRAPPED FRUITCAKES

Decorating Needs
- 6-Cup Muffin Pan, p. 174
- Decorator's Brush, p. 126
- Applesauce Fruitcake Recipe, p. 95
- Candied fruits, slivered almonds, pecans, apricot preserves
- Cupcake papers, ribbon

1. Prepare batter according to recipe instructions. Chop candied fruit and nuts into pea-sized pieces. Fold into batter.

2. Line Muffin Pan with cupcake papers. Fill (no more than ⅔'s full) and bake according to recipe instructions. While fruitcakes cool on wire rack, wash and dry pan.

3. Brush tops with thinned, warmed apricot preserve glaze. Cut fruit and brush with glaze. Position fruit pieces and nuts on tops. Replace cakes in pan.

Trim pan with pretty ribbon and bow. Muffin Pan with decorated cakes makes a tasty gift!

For more ways to use CONTINENTAL FLAN PAN see Pan Index p. 192.

For more ways to use 6-CUP MUFFIN PAN see Pan Index p. 192.

51

CROWD-PLEASING SNOWMAN

Decorating Needs
- **Round Mini Tier Set, p. 168**
- **Tips 3, 4, 17, p. 118, 119**
- **Lollipop Sticks, p. 105**
- **Rectangle Cake Boards, p. 162**
- **Fanci-Foil Wrap, p. 163**
- **Toasted coconut, marshmallow, chocolate chips, candy canes and assorted candies**

1. Position cakes on covered cake boards (or serving platter). Ice fluffy with a spatula. Ice lollipop stick for pipe stem; set aside. Use a toothpick to mark hat, face, mitten, scarf. Outline mitten and scarf and add fringe with tip 4 strings.

2. Pipe tip 17 zigzag hat. Add tip 17 pull-out stars pom-pon. Cover scarf with tip 17 shells. Add tip 17 zigzag around neck.

Position candy canes over mitten outline. Use spatula to ice over candy and build up mitten. Reinforce outline. Cover mitten with tip 17 shells.

3. Use assorted candy pieces to make snowman's face. Push iced lollipop stick into marshmallow; position "pipe" in cake. Add tip 3 message. *Serves 12.*

HAVE A... FROSTY CHRISTMAS

For more ways to use ROUND MINI TIER SET see Pan Index p. 192.

CHRISTMAS COTTAGE

Decorating Needs
- **Holiday House Kit, p. 179**
- **Tip 17, p. 119**
- **Dowel Rods, p. 160**
- **Cake Boards, p. 162**
- **Candy Melts™*, p. 106**
- **Edible Glitter, p. 122**
- **Santa 'N Tree, p. 140**
- **Christmas Carollers, p. 140**
- **Royal Icing Recipe, p. 83**
- **Gingerbread Cake Recipe, p. 95**
- **Assorted candies and candy canes, wafer cookies, sugar ice cream cone**
- **Toothpicks, ribbon**

1. Secure cake board (about 10 x 11-in.) to serving tray or plate with royal icing. Ice fluffy with a spatula using royal icing; sprinkle with Edible Glitter. Ice two cakes together back to back with buttercream. Position "cottage" on iced cake board. Push dowel rods (cut to fit) diagonally through both cakes.

2. Make candy rectangles for windows and rounded rectangle for door. See p. 94 for how to make Candy Cut-Outs.

3. Trim roof with tip 17 buttercream scalloped outlines and shells. Attach Candy Melts door and windows, assorted candies and cookies with dots of buttercream icing. Trim and ice cookies together to form chimney; attach to roof with buttercream icing. Push candy canes through chimney into cake.

Cover ice cream cone with royal icing or Candy Melts. Position on cake board and attach candy "ornaments" with icing. Position Christmas Carollers and attach Santa to roof using buttercream icing (lean against toothpicks). Trim board with ribbon. *Serves 24.*

For more ways to use HOLIDAY HOUSE KIT see Pan Index p. 192.

CHRISTMAS

(CONTINUED)

CHANUKAH

The Festival of Lights. The Feast of Dedication.

A celebration of victory.

A time to rejoice because a great miracle happened.

The Covenant was preserved.

TINY TEMPLE

Decorating Needs

- Holiday House Kit, p. 179
- Tips 1D, 2B, 3, 4, 5, 12, 14 and 47, p. 118, 119
- '86 Pattern Book, p. 135 (Candles Pattern)
- Decorator's Brush, p. 126
- Pound Cake Recipe, p. 95

1. Bake pound cake as directed in kit instructions. Ice front and back smooth. Use toothpick to transfer Candles Pattern to front of cake. Outline all details (except candles) with tip 3 strings.

Pipe stripes with bar tips (smooth side up). Use tip 47 for bar under candles, tip 2B for message area and tip 1D for sides (pipe 3 vertical stripes side-by-side).

2. Pipe tip 12 stripes for candles; add tip 4 drips (blend with dampened brush). Top with tip 14 zigzag flames. Add tip 5 dot below each candle (flatten with finger dipped in cornstarch).

3. Use tip 2B (flat side up) to pipe shingles. Edge front first, then cover roof. Begin at peak and add 1 horizontal row at a time, working front to back and top to bottom.

Use spatula to add snow to eaves (thin with corn syrup for easier handling and extra shine). Add your special message with tip 3.
Serves 12.

For more ways to use HOLIDAY HOUSE KIT see Pan Index p. 192.

DANDY DREIDEL

Decorating Needs

- Shower Umbrella Pan, p. 182
- Tips 2A, 4 and 17, p. 118, 119
- '86 Pattern Book, p. 135 (Dreidel Pattern)
- Decorator's Brush, p. 126

1. Use spatula to ice cake smooth. With a toothpick, transfer Dreidel Pattern to cake top. Cover marks with tip 4 outlines.

2. Fill in tip 2A stem, bottom of Dreidel and shadow of bow; smooth with finger. Pipe large tip 2A dot for ball handle; let icing build up for dimension. Smooth with finger.

Fill in letters with tip 4 and thinned icing; smooth with dampened brush.

3. Cover remainder of Dreidel and bow with tip 17 stars. Add tip 17 shell border to base of cake. For extra dimension, overpipe edges of Dreidel with tip 4.
Serves 12.

For more ways to use SHOWER UMBRELLA PAN see Pan Index p. 192.

*brand confectionery coating.

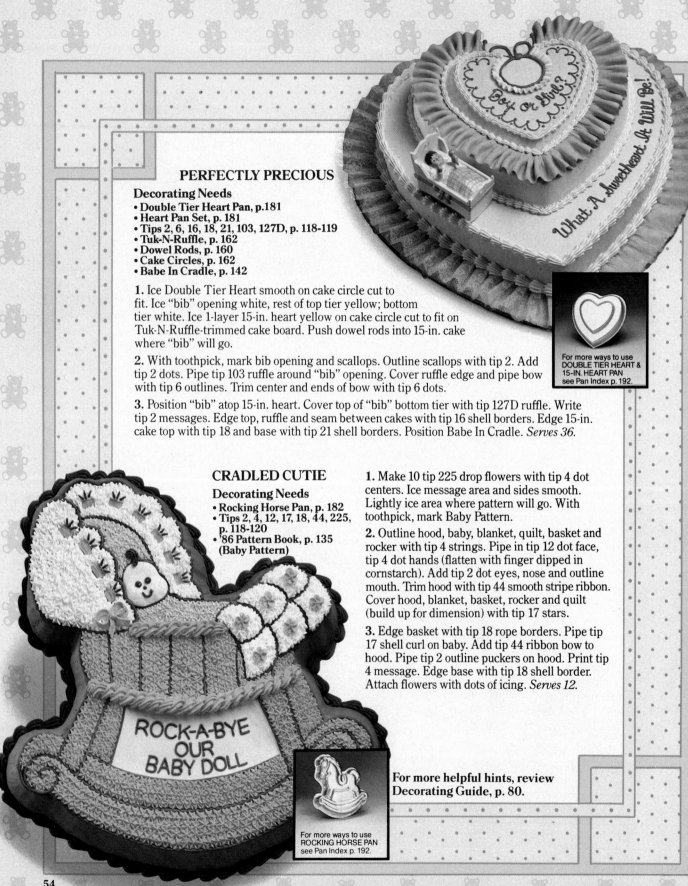

PERFECTLY PRECIOUS

Decorating Needs
- **Double Tier Heart Pan, p.181**
- **Heart Pan Set, p. 181**
- **Tips 2, 6, 16, 18, 21, 103, 127D, p. 118-119**
- **Tuk-N-Ruffle, p. 162**
- **Dowel Rods, p. 160**
- **Cake Circles, p. 162**
- **Babe In Cradle, p. 142**

1. Ice Double Tier Heart smooth on cake circle cut to fit. Ice "bib" opening white, rest of top tier yellow; bottom tier white. Ice 1-layer 15-in. heart yellow on cake circle cut to fit on Tuk-N-Ruffle-trimmed cake board. Push dowel rods into 15-in. cake where "bib" will go.

2. With toothpick, mark bib opening and scallops. Outline scallops with tip 2. Add tip 2 dots. Pipe tip 103 ruffle around "bib" opening. Cover ruffle edge and pipe bow with tip 6 outlines. Trim center and ends of bow with tip 6 dots.

3. Position "bib" atop 15-in. heart. Cover top of "bib" bottom tier with tip 127D ruffle. Write tip 2 messages. Edge top, ruffle and seam between cakes with tip 16 shell borders. Edge 15-in. cake top with tip 18 and base with tip 21 shell borders. Position Babe In Cradle. *Serves 36.*

For more ways to use DOUBLE TIER HEART & 15-IN. HEART PAN see Pan Index p. 192.

CRADLED CUTIE

Decorating Needs
- **Rocking Horse Pan, p. 182**
- **Tips 2, 4, 12, 17, 18, 44, 225, p. 118-120**
- **'86 Pattern Book, p. 135 (Baby Pattern)**

1. Make 10 tip 225 drop flowers with tip 4 dot centers. Ice message area and sides smooth. Lightly ice area where pattern will go. With toothpick, mark Baby Pattern.

2. Outline hood, baby, blanket, quilt, basket and rocker with tip 4 strings. Pipe in tip 12 dot face, tip 4 dot hands (flatten with finger dipped in cornstarch). Add tip 2 dot eyes, nose and outline mouth. Trim hood with tip 44 smooth stripe ribbon. Cover hood, blanket, basket, rocker and quilt (build up for dimension) with tip 17 stars.

3. Edge basket with tip 18 rope borders. Pipe tip 17 shell curl on baby. Add tip 44 ribbon bow to hood. Pipe tip 2 outline puckers on hood. Print tip 4 message. Edge base with tip 18 shell border. Attach flowers with dots of icing. *Serves 12.*

ROCK-A-BYE OUR BABY DOLL

For more ways to use ROCKING HORSE PAN see Pan Index p. 192.

For more helpful hints, review Decorating Guide, p. 80.

BABY'S CUP

Decorating Needs
• **Good Cheer Mug Pan, p. 184**
• **Tips, 3, 8, 16, 21, 103, 129, 352, p. 118-121**
• **Baby Rattles, p. 142**

1. Make 25 tip 129 drop flowers with tip 3 dot centers. Ice background area, inside of cup and sides smooth.

2. Outline cup with tip 8 strings. Cover outside of cup with tip 16 stars. Pipe tip 103 ribbon scallops around rim of cup. Add tip 103 ribbon bows.

3. Print tip 3 message. Attach flowers with dots of icing. Trim with tip 352 leaves. Position Baby Rattles. Edge cake base with tip 21 star border. *Serves 12.*

For more ways to use GOOD CHEER MUG PAN see Pan Index p. 192.

OH, HEAVENLY DAY

Decorating Needs
• **Cross Pan, p. 183**
• **Tips 3, 14, 16, 18, 224, 352, p. 118-121**
• **Sleeping Angels, p. 142**

1. Make 40 tip 224 drop flowers with tip 3 dot centers. Ice cake smooth; top gold, beveled area and sides white. With toothpick, mark tree and cascade.

2. Outline top branches with tip 14 stripes. Cover trunk and side branches with tip 16 short, wavy stripes. Edge cake top and sides with tip 16 and base with tip 18 shell borders.

3. Pipe tip 16 reverse shell cascade on cake top and sides. Print tip 3 message. Trim branches with tip 352 leaves. Attach flowers to beveled area with dot of icing. Position Sleeping Angel. *Serves 12.*

For more ways to use CROSS PAN see Pan Index p. 192.

A.

B.

C.

For more ways to use
10-IN. ROUND PAN
see Pan Index p. 192.

5

Congratulations
Harry & Marie

3

SCOOPER
DUPER
YEARS

HAPPY
ANNIVERSARY

For more ways to use
TREELITEFUL PAN
see Pan Index p. 192.

Anniversary
Happiness

For more ways to use
ROCKING HORSE PAN
see Pan Index p. 192.

Anniversaries

Together.

*Through good times
And bad.*

*Through ruffled feathers
And smooth sailing.*

Two people

*Who treasure old memories
And look forward to
making new ones.*

*Who understand the true
meaning of the word,*

Together.

A. LAVISHED WITH LOVE

Decorating Needs
- 10-in. Round Pan, p. 166
- Tips 3, 4, 16, 21, 103, 104, 224, 349, 352, p. 118-121
- Flower Nail No. 7, p. 121
- '86 Pattern Book, p. 135 (Heart Scroll Pattern)
- Anniversary Years, p. 150

1. Make 24 tip 104 roses; 3 tip 103 roses and 6 sweet peas; and 50 tip 224 drop flowers with tip 3 centers.

2. Ice 2-layer cake smooth. With toothpick, mark Heart Scroll pattern along cake sides, and an 8-in. circle on cake top.

Cover heart marks on cake side with tip 16 scroll outlines. Pipe tip 21 yellow reverse shells on 8-in. circle marks on cake top. Pipe tip 21 white reverse shells in reverse direction next to yellow reverse shells.

3. Attach large roses along cake base with dots of icing. Trim with tip 352 leaves. Position Anniversary Years on cake top. With dots of icing, attach small roses and sweet peas on cake top. Trim with tip 349 leaves. Attach drop flowers to cake top edge and at points of hearts with dots of icing. Trim with tip 349 leaves. Write tip 4 message. *Serves 24.*

B. IT'S BEEN SUPER SPECIAL

Decorating Needs
- Treeliteful Pan, p. 179
- Tips 1A, 3, 7, 18, p. 118-119
- Piping Gel, p. 125
- Red hard candy pieces, cherry stem

1. Ice cake smooth, side white, top light gold. With spatula, mark waffle cone on cake top. Cover marks with tip 3 strings. With spatula swirl icing to resemble ice cream scoops. Add tip 1A cherry. Brush with piping gel. Press candy pieces into pink icing to resemble strawberry pieces.

2. Print tips 3 and 7 messages. Push cherry stem into "cherry." Edge cake with tip 18 shell base border. *Serves 12.*

C. FOREVER HAPPY

Decorating Needs
- Rocking Horse Pan, p. 182
- Tips 2, 4, 10, 18, 21, 224, 349, p. 118-121
- Royal Icing Recipe, p. 83
- Decorator's Brush, p. 126
- Lollipop Stick, p. 105

1. Make 50 tip 224 drop flowers with tip 4 centers. To Make Horn: On waxed paper, with royal icing, pipe 3½-in. long, tip 10 rope (wide at bottom, narrowing at the top). Let dry. Attach lollipop stick to flat side with icing, letting about 3-in. of stick extend at wide end.

2. Ice part of cake top and sides smooth. Outline body, mouth, mane, tail, eye and hoofs with tip 4 strings. Fill in eye, ear and hoofs with tip 4. Smooth with dampened brush. Cover body with tip 18 stars. Pipe tip 21 reverse shell hair and stripe tail, pulling tip up for ends of tail. Add tip 4 dot nose and tip 2 outline lashes.

3. Write tip 4 message. Attach flowers with icing. Trim with tip 349 leaves. Edge cake base with tip 18 shell border. Push horn into head. *Serves 12.*

D. TRUE LOVE AND DEVOTION

Decorating Needs
- 10½-in. Ring Mold Pan, p. 173
- Heart Mini-Tier Set, p. 168
- Tips 3, 12, 14, 16, 101, 102, 352, p. 118-121
- Flower Nail No. 7, p. 121
- Cake Circles, p. 162
- Anniversary Couple, 50th Golden, p. 154
- Golden Moments, p. 150

1. Make 30 each, tips 101 and 102 roses.

2. Ice two 10½-in. ring cakes smooth, sides gold, top white. On cake circles cut to fit, ice one 1-layer 9-in. heart cake and one 1-layer 7½-in. heart cake smooth. With toothpick, lightly mark 2-in. scrolls on sides of ring cakes. Cover marks with tip 16. With toothpick, lightly mark 1-in. double scrolls on ring cakes' top and bottom edges. Cover marks with tip 12. Overpipe with tip 14.

Attach separator plates to pillars and position 7½-in. and 9-in. heart cakes on top.

3. With toothpick, lightly mark 1-in. swirled shell pairs on heart cake bottom edges and reverse swirled shell pairs on top edges. Cover with tip 16. Position 9-in. heart cake on ring cake and 7½-in. heart cake within ring cake. Position small roses on heart cakes and large roses on ring cakes. Trim roses with tip 352 leaves. Position Anniversary Couple and Golden Moments on cake tops. Print tip 3 message. *Serves 34.*

For more ways to use 10½-IN. RING MOLD PAN and HEART MINI-TIER SET see Pan Index p. 192.

GOOD FISHING

A.

For more ways to use
BIG FISH PAN
see Pan Index p. 192.

SAILING
TOWARDS
NEW
HORIZONS

For more ways to use
SAILBOAT PAN
see Pan Index p. 192

B.

*The chance to do
what you've always wanted.
Hobbies to pursue.
Vacations to plan.
Gardens to plant.
Easels to fill.
The great beginning to a new chapter.*

C.

For more ways to use
11-IN. x 15-IN. SHEET PAN
and 6-IN. x 2-IN. ROUND
PAN see Pan Index, p. 192

C. ENJOY! ENJOY!

Decorating Needs
- **11-in. x 15-in. Sheet Pan, p. 167**
- **6-in. x 2-in. Round Pan, p. 166**
- **Tips 3, 16, 21 p. 118-119**
- **Cake circle, p. 162**
- **In-Step Jogger, p. 138**
- **Golf Pro, p. 138**
- **Baseball Topper Set, p. 138**
- **Two vanilla wafer cookies**

1. Leave sheet cake in pan. Ice top smooth.

2. Position one-layer round cake on cake circle cut to fit. Ice top smooth. Position on sheet cake. Cover sides and part of top with tip 16 stars. Pipe tip 21 zigzags watchband.

3. Sandwich cookies together with icing. Position as "winder" at top of round cake. Pipe tip 3 shell watch face and outline hands. Edge cake with tip 21 shell border. Print and write tip 3 message. Position In-Step Jogger, Golf Pro and Baseball Topper Set on cake top. *Serves 30*

A. BEST CATCH OF THE YEAR

Decorating Needs
- **Big Fish Pan, p. 177**
- **Tips 4, 17, 126, p. 118-119**
- **Decorator's Brush, p. 126**

1. Ice sides of cake smooth. Outline fish, mouth, cheek, eye, and fins with tip 4. Cover face, fins, stomach and tail with tip 17 stars. Fill in mouth and eye with tip 4. Smooth with dampened brush.

2. Starting at bottom end, cover back and neck with tip 126 scallop "scales." Add tip 4 outline eyelashes, fins and eyebrow.

3. Print tip 4 message. Edge cake with tip 17 shell border. *Serves 12.*

B. THIS IS THE LIFE

Decorating Needs
- **Sailboat Pan, p. 184**
- **Tips 4, 12, 18, p. 118-119**
- **Decorator's Brush, p. 126**

1. Ice cake sides smooth. Outline sail, mast, boom, cabin and hull with tip 4 strings. Flow in sky area and windows with tip 4 thinned icing (smooth with dampened brush.)

2. Pipe tip 12 smooth stripe mast and boom. Add tip 18 stripe trim on hull. Cover sail, spinnaker, cabin and hull with tip 18 stars.

3. Ice water area generously and pat with spatula to resemble waves. Pipe tip 18 swirled shell white caps. Edge base with tip 18 shell border. Print tip 4 message. *Serves 12.*

For more ways to use
8-IN. SQUARE PAN
see Pan Index p. 192

D.

For more helpful hints, review **Decorating Guide, p. 80.**

D. KEEPING UP

Decorating Needs
- **8-in. Square Pan, p. 167**
- **Tips 4, 16, 18, p. 118-119**
- **Gone Fishin' Signboard, p. 138**
- **Bunny Family, p. 140**
- **Backyard Gardener, p. 141**
- **Sprinkle Tops, p. 112**
- **Pretzels**

1. Ice two-layer cake smooth. Press Sprinkle Tops around sides of cake. With toothpick, mark cake top into 7 rows, each 1⅛" wide. Pipe tip 18 zigzags down each row. Pipe tip 16 pull-out stars "carrot tops" randomly down each row.

2. Position pretzels along top edge as fence. Edge cake base with tip 18 shell border.

3. Print tip 4 message on Gone Fishin' Signboard. Position cake tops on cake. *Serves 16.*

59

◆ A TEXTBOOK CASE

Decorating Needs
- 8-in. Square Pan, p. 167
- Tips 3, 9 and 789, p. 118, 120
- Decorator's Brush, p. 126
- Glad Graduate, p. 143
- Cake board and paper to cover

1. Ice 2-layer cake top smooth. Pipe tip 789 stripes for edges of books. Use ribbed side up for "pages"; smooth side up for "backbones."

2. Outline and build-up edges with tip 9. Blend with dampened brush. Print tip 3 message and book titles.

3. Position Graduate on cake. Add covered cake board "cover," resting it on Graduate. Blend icing over edge with dampened brush. *Serves 16.*

For more ways to use 8-IN. SQUARE PAN see Pan Index p. 192.

FRECKLE-FACED GRADUATE

Decorating Needs
- Wonder Mold Pan, p. 180
- Tips 4, 12, 17 and 103, p. 118, 119
- Freckle-Faced Little Girl, p. 180
- Posterboard, paper, gold cord

1. For hat, make a posterboard ring, about 1-in. diameter. Attach 2-in. square. Paint or ice to match gown. Trim with gold cord.

Push doll pick into cake. Pipe over arms and around waist with tip 12; use finger dipped in cornstarch to smooth and shape built-up icing. Ice front skirt area smooth.

2. Outline gown details with tip 4. Pipe tip 103 ruffles on skirt. Fill-in collar with tip 4; smooth with finger. Cover graduation gown with tip 17 stars.

3. Roll paper for diploma; tie with cord and position in hand. Secure hat with icing. Pipe tip 4 message and your graduate is complete. *Serves 12.*

For more ways to use WONDER MOLD PAN see Pan Index p. 192.

MICKEY MADE THE GRADE

Decorating Needs
- Mickey Mouse® Pan, p. 187
- Tips 3, 14, 16 and 18, p. 118, 119

1. Ice cake top and sides smooth. Use toothpick to mark hat, gown, diploma and "!" Outline details with tip 3.

2. Fill in eyes, nose and pencil tip with tip 3; smooth with finger. Add tip 3 dot pupils; flatten with finger dipped in cornstarch.

Pipe tip 16 stripes below eraser. Cover mouth and shadow with tip 14 stars.

3. Cover remainder of design with tip 16 stars. Use tip 3 dot and strings to make tassel on hat. Print tip 3 message and add tip 18 star border. *Serves 12.*

MICKEY MOUSE © Walt Disney Productions. Wilton Enterprises, Inc. authorized user.

For more ways to use MICKEY MOUSE® PAN see Pan Index p. 192.

◆ BEST OF LUCK

Decorating Needs
- Happiness Heart Pan Set, p. 181
- Mini Shamrock Pan, p. 184
- Tips 3, 4 and 16, p. 118, 119
- Glowing Grad, p. 143
- Mortarboard & Diploma Cake Picks, p. 143
- Posterboard, serving board, ice cream

1. Bake and cool 4 heart cakes. Position cakes in clover shape on cakeboard or serving tray. Ice seams smooth.

Cut stem from posterboard. Place in position. Outline with tip 4 and cover with tip 16 stars.

2. Use toothpick to mark center lines. Outline outer edge of each heart with tip 4 strings. Cover cake top and sides with tip 16 stars.

Print tip 3 graduation message and position Glowing Grad. *Serves 24.*

3. For ice cream shamrocks, soften ice cream at room temperature until just softened, about 30 minutes. Stir with a spoon then pack firmly into Mini Shamrock Pan. Cover with foil and freeze until firm, about 5 hours. Unmold just before serving time and trim with tip 4 outlines. Insert Mortarboard and Diploma cake picks. *Each serves 1.*

For more ways to use HAPPINESS HEART PANS & MINI SHAMROCKS see Pan Index p. 192.

DAYS OF *B*LESSINGS

Very special days. Sure to be remembered the rest of their lives.

TAKE THIS BREAD AND WINE...

Decorating Needs
- Cross Pan, p. 183
- Tips 1, 4, 5, 8, 10, 103, 225, 349, p. 118-121
- Communion Girl (or Communion Boy), p. 142
- Cookie (2-in. diameter)

1. Make about 35 tip 225 drop flowers with tip 4 dot centers. Freeze until needed. Ice cake top, bevel and sides smooth (use three colors for extra dimension). Edge top with tip 8 bead border.

2. Use toothpick to mark vine around sides of cake, and vine and wheat on cake top. Use tip 4 strings to pipe wheat stems and both vines. Trim vines with tip 349 leaves. Add drop flowers to cake sides.

3. Pipe tip 5 grape clusters (see instructions, p. 93). Trim base of each cluster with tip 349 leaves. Add tip 1 "e" motion tendrils. Pipe tip 4 wheat stalks (see instructions, p. 93). Add tip 103 bow.

Edge lower bevel with tip 8 bead border. Add tip 10 bead border to base of cake.

Ice cookie (2-in. diameter). Position "Host" and Communion Girl on cake top. *Serves 12.*

(For larger gatherings, set Cross cake on top of iced 2-layer 12 x 18-in. sheet cake. Decorate sides with additional vines, flowers and beads. Trim with tip 21 bead border. Combination cake serves 68.)

For more ways to use CROSS PAN see Pan Index p. 192.

RECEIVE THE SPIRIT

Decorating Needs
- Guitar Pan, p. 177
- Tips 2, 2A, 3, 12, 17, 18, 21, p. 118-121
- Shining Cross, p. 142
- '86 Pattern Book, p. 135 (Chalice Pattern)
- Decorator's Brush, p. 126
- Cookie, maraschino cherries

1. Ice 3-in. diameter cookie. Attach Shining Cross with icing; set aside until needed. Ice cake sides and background areas of cake top smooth. Use toothpick to transfer Chalice Pattern to cake top. Outline chalice rims and wine with tip 3 strings.

2. Fill in wine with tip 3; smooth with dampened brush.

Pipe-in chalice rim and horizontal details with tip 12. Fill-in and build-up chalice stem with tip 2A; pat with finger to smooth.

Pipe chalice outline and details with tip 17 shells. Cover remainder of chalice with tip 17 stars.

3. Trim base of chalice with tip 18 elongated shells. Edge cake top with tip 18 shells; trim base of cake with tip 21 shell border.

Position cherry halves, cookie and cross. Print tip 2 message and rejoice! *Serves 12.*

(For larger gatherings, set Guitar Cake on top of iced 2-layer 12 x 18-in. sheet cake. Trim with tip 21 shell border. Combination cake serves 68.)

For more ways to use GUITAR PAN see Pan Index p. 192.

DAYS OF ACHIEVEMENT

With new found strengths, they face the future with the knowledge of eternal truths.

BAT MITZVAH BEAUTY

Decorating Needs
- 6-in. Square Pan (bake 3), p. 167
- 15-in. Hexagon Pan, p. 169
- Tips 4, 5, 17, 21, 32, 103, 104 and 352, p. 118-121
- Cake Icer Tip 789, p. 119
- Flower Nail No. 7, p. 121
- '86 Pattern Book, p. 135 (Medium Star Pattern)
- Candles

1. Make and freeze flowers until needed: about 24 tip 104 sweet peas and 3 tip 103 rosebuds on waxed paper; 8 tip 103 roses and 9 tip 104 roses using Flower Nail #7.

Cut each 6-in. cake in half diagonally. Position 1-layer hexagon cake on cake board or large serving platter; ice sides with tip 789. Attach one 6-in. half to each side of hexagon to form 6 points of star. Ice cake smooth.

2. Use toothpick to mark bouquet on cake top and to transfer star pattern to cake top. Outline stars with tip 4 strings; cover with tip 17 stars.

3. Reserve 5 roses and 10 sweet peas for points of cake. Pipe tip 5 vines; attach roses, rosebuds and sweet peas with dots of icing. Position roses and sweet peas on cake points. Trim flowers with tip 352 leaves and tip 104 bow and streamers. Add tip 4 message, candles, tip 21 shell top border and tip 32 shell bottom border. *Serves 34.*

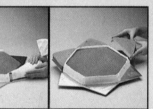

For more ways to use 6-IN. SQUARE and 15-IN. HEXAGON PAN see Pan Index p. 192.

BAR MITZVAH TRIBUTE

Decorating Needs
- 12x18-in. Sheet Pan, p. 167
- Tips 1D, 3, 4, 17, 18, 21 and 126, p. 118-121
- '86 Pattern Book, p. 135 (Star and Letters Patterns)

1. Ice 1-layer cake smooth. Use toothpick to transfer Star and Letters Patterns to cake sides and top. Outline stars with tip 4 strings. Outline letters with tip 3 strings; fill with tip 17 stars.

2. Use tip 1D (smooth side up) to pipe ribbon across cake top and sides. Add tip 126 bow and streamers.

3. Edge cake top with tip 18 shells. Add tip 21 shell border to base of cake. Add your good-luck message with tip 3. *Serves 28.*

For more ways to use 12x18-IN. SHEET PAN see Pan Index p. 192.

B. For more ways to use SPRINGFORM PAN see Pan Index p. 192.

C. For more ways to use 9-IN. PIE PAN see Pan Index p. 192.

A. For more ways to use CONTINENTAL FLAN PAN see Pan Index p. 192.

D.

Temptations, smooth and creamy.
Desserts, devilishly delightful.
Sweet confections to entice a queen.
Culinary creations to enchant a king.
Royally rich.
Princely morsels.
Chocolate, the crowning touch.

A. COCOA-FLAN SUPREME

Decorating Needs
• 11-in. Continental Flan Pan, p. 171
• Tip 17, p. 119
• Candy Melts™❋ p. 106
• Stabilized Whipped Cream Recipe, p. 82
• Pudding, bananas, maraschino cherry, lemon juice

1. Bake 3 cups of chocolate cake batter in greased and floured Continental Flan Pan. Slice bananas and dip in lemon juice to prevent browning. Drain on paper towel.

Melt Candy Melts according to package directions. Dip about 18 banana slices for outer ring. Set aside on waxed paper until coating sets.

2. Fill center of cooled cake with pudding (we chose butterscotch-flavored). Position outer ring of dipped banana slices and inner ring of plain slices.

3. Trim with tip 17 whipped cream zigzag. Top with cherry. Refrigerate until serving time. *Serves 8.*

B. CHOCOLATE CHEESECAKE CLASSIC

Decorating Needs
• Springform Pan, p. 171
• Little Loafers Pan, p. 172
• Candy Melts™❋ p. 106
• Chocolate Cheesecake Recipe, p. 95
• Mandarin oranges, confectioners sugar, maraschino cherry

1. Prepare Chocolate Cheesecake according to recipe instructions; cool completely. Mold about 2 cups of Candy Melts in Little Loafers Pan; refrigerate until needed.

Drain mandarin oranges and blot dry with paper towel. Dip one end in melted coating; set aside on waxed paper until needed.

2. Cut 3½-in. diameter paper circle. Place in center of cake. Sift confectioners sugar over cake then carefully remove paper. Arrange oranges on cake top.

3. Unmold block of coating. Use sharp knife to shave off curls of coating about 1½-in. long (for best results coating should be just slightly cooler than room temperature). Position curls and cherry on cake. Add additional shavings around cake. *Serves 12.*

C. CHERRIES AND CUSTARD

Decorating Needs
• 9-in. Pie Pan, p. 172
• Little Loafers Pan, p. 172
• Tip 19, p. 119
• Candy Melts™❋ p. 106
• Stabilized Whipped Cream Recipe, p. 82
• Pastry for single crust pie, chocolate and vanilla flavored puddings, maraschino cherries (drained)

1. Bake and cool pie shell in 9-in. Pie Pan according to directions for unfilled crust. Prepare chocolate pudding and pour into cooled pie shell; refrigerate until firm. Prepare vanilla pudding and pour over chocolate pudding; refrigerate until firm.

2. Melt 1 lb. Candy Melts. Dip 12 cherries to coat about three quarters; set aside on waxed paper to set. Pour remaining coating into Little Loafers Pan; refrigerate until hardened, then unmold.

3. Pipe tip 19 whipped cream zigzags and rosettes across top of pie. Position candy-coated cherries. Use a sharp knife or vegetable peeler to make candy curls; place on pie. Refrigerate until serving time. *Serves 8.*

D. SWEET CONFECTIONS

Decorating Needs
• Assorted Wilton Candy Molds, p. 100-103
• Candy Melts™❋ p. 106
• Decorator's Brush, p. 126
• Tip 3, p. 118

1. Candies pictured were made using Wilton molds and Candy Melts in assorted colors. Roses and "X" designs were "painted" into the mold with coating before filling mold with another color of coating (see candymaking instructions, p. 94). Spirals were added to Bon Bons with tip 3 and coating after unmolding candies.

E. DOUBLE DUTCH

Decorating Needs
• 8-in. Square Pan, p. 167
• Tips 12, 17, 19 and 104, p. 118, 119
• Flower Nail No. 7, p. 121

1. Use tips 12 and 104 and Flower Nail #7 to make one chocolate icing rose. Make about 6 tip 104 sweet peas on waxed paper. Freeze flowers until needed.

2. Ice 2-layer cake smooth. Use toothpick to mark C-scroll designs on cake top and sides. Cover marks with tip 19 C-scrolls and reverse C-scrolls. Trim tails with tip 19 stars.

3. Position rose and sweet peas on cake center. Trim top cake edge with tip 17 shell border. Trim bottom with tip 19 shells. *Serves 16.*

❋brand confectionery coating.

For more ways to use
8-IN. SQUARE PAN
see Pan Index p. 192.

E.

Bridal Showers

Brightly wrapped packages. Curled ribbons and bows.

Warm wishes and love from family and friends. A toast to the bride and groom.

Two hearts, one love. Forever and ever.

HEAVENLY TIERS

Decorating Needs
- 6-in. & 10-in. Round Pans, p. 166
- Tips 14, 17, 18, 45, 103, 352, p. 118-121
- Flower Nail No. 7, p. 121
- Cake Dividing Set, p. 126
- Dowel Rods, p. 160
- Cake Circles, p. 162
- Angelinos, p. 155
- Petite Elegance, p. 151

1. Pipe flowers with tip 103 and freeze until needed. Make about 8 small and 4 medium roses using flower nail #7. Make about 32 sweet peas on waxed paper.

Place two filled 6-in. layers on 6-in. cake circle; ice 6-in. and filled 10-in. cakes smooth. Cut dowel rods to fit flush with depth of 10-in. cake; insert where 6-in. tier will rest. Position 6-in. tier.

2. Use Cake Dividing Set to mark tiers into fourths. Pipe tip 45 ribbons along cake tops and sides. Edge ribbons with tip 14 swirled shells; pipe small shells at base of each ribbon, rosettes at top. Add tip 18 swirled shells to cake base; tip 17 to all edges.

3. Position Petite Elegance on cake top. Attach Angelinos to cake sides with icing. Position flowers on icing dots; trim with tip 352 leaves. *Serves 32.*

For more ways to use 6-IN. & 10-IN. ROUND PANS see Pan Index p. 192.

For more ways to use PETIT FOURS AND PASTRY SET see Pan Index p. 192.

WINSOME FLORAL

Decorating Needs
- 10-in. Round Pan, p. 166
- Tips 4, 18, 21, 104, 124 and 352, p. 118-121
- Flower Nail No. 7, p. 121
- 15-Pc. Decorator Pattern Press Set, p. 126
- Cake Dividing Set, p. 126

1. Use tip 124 and flower nail #7 to make rose. Use tip 104 to make about 15 sweet peas on waxed paper. Freeze until needed.

Ice 2-layer cake smooth. Use Cake Divider and Pattern Press to create center design. Use toothpick and Cake Divider Set to mark 16 equal divisions for stringwork.

2. Cover center "double-e" design with tip 18 scrolls that end in center with an "e-motion" curl. Position center rose and sweet peas. Trim with tip 352 leaves.

Decorate sides with two rows of tip 4 drop strings. Add top row first; second row connects midpoints of top row. Edge cake top with tip 18 shells. Pipe inner ring of tip 18 "e-motion" curls. Add tip 21 shell border to base of cake. *Serves 24.*

For more ways to use 10-IN. ROUND PAN see Pan Index p. 192.

WITH THIS RING...

Decorating Needs
- 9-in. Hexagon Pan, p. 169
- Tips 12, 18, 44, 104, 352, p. 118-121
- Flower Nail No. 7, p. 121
- 15-Pc. Decorator Pattern Press Set, p. 126
- Bridal Shower Delight, p. 142

1. Make 6 roses on waxed paper covered flower nail using tip 12 to pipe base and tip 104 to pipe petals. Freeze until needed.

2. Ice 2-layer cake smooth. Use "C"-scroll Pattern Press to mark designs on sides. Cover marks with tip 18 "C"-scrolls; add tip 18 drop strings.

Pipe tip 44 ribbons along cake top and sides. Add tip 18 star border to cake top. Use spatula to position roses; trim with tip 352 leaves.

3. Finish cake base with tip 18 shell border. Top cake with Bridal Shower Delight. *Serves 12.*

For more ways to use 9-IN. HEXAGON PAN see Pan Index p. 192.

BITE-SIZED DELIGHTS

Decorating Needs
- Petit Fours and Pastry Mold Set, p. 170
- Tips 2, 21, 129, 225 and 349, p. 118-121
- Candy Wafer & Fondant Mix, p. 106
- Sprinkle Tops, p.112
- Apricot preserves, pudding or pie filling, cherries, nuts, lemon and lime peel

1. FOR PETIT FOURS: Bake mini-cakes in Petit Fours and Pastry Molds. Glaze with warm, thinned apricot preserves. Let set.

Prepare Quick Pour Icing following directions on Candy Wafer & Fondant Mix label. Place mini-cakes on wire rack; spoon icing over cakes to coat. Let set. Decorate with tip 2 lines, scallops, "e" motion curls, bead hearts and fleur de lis.

Trim with tip 129 and tip 225 drop flowers with tip 2 dot centers; add tip 349 leaves. Add candy sprinkles.

2. FOR TARTS: Bake pastry in Petit Fours and Pastry Molds. Fill with pudding or pie filling. Or pipe in tip 21 truffle mixture or whipped cream zigzags.

Trim with tip 21 rosettes, chopped cherries, pistachios, lemon and lime peels.

Bridal Showers
(CONTINUED)

SHOWER SHOW-OFF

Decorating Needs
• Shower Umbrella Pan, p. 182
• Tips 3, 16, 17, 103, 225 and 349, p. 118-121

1. Pipe about 17 tip 225 drop flowers with tip 3 dot centers. Freeze until needed.

Ice center of umbrella, cake sides and background areas of cake top smooth. Outline bow, shaft and umbrella ribs with tip 3. Cover shadow above bow with tip 3 zigzags.

2. Cover umbrella and bow with tip 17 stars. Cover shaft with tip 16 stars.

Edge umbrella with tip 103 ruffle. Trim with tip 16 shells. Cover ball handle and tip with tip 16 rosettes.

3. Attach drop flowers with dots of icing. Trim with tip 349 leaves.

Finish with tip 3 message and tip 17 shell border and you're ready to surprise the bridal couple. *Serves 12.*

For more ways to use
SHOWER
UMBRELLA PAN
see Pan Index p. 192.

WHEEL-BARREL OF FUN

Decorating Needs
• Piano Kit, p. 180
• Tips 2, 16, 103, 104 and 352, p. 118-121
• Flower Nail No. 7, p. 121
• Cookie (2-in. diameter), pretzel rods (3-in. long)

1. Pipe about 20 tip 104 sweet peas on waxed paper. Pipe two tip 103 roses and two tip 104 roses on Flower Nail. Freeze flowers until needed.

Ice cookie for wheel and two pretzels for handles. Set aside.

2. Snap legs onto base according to kit instructions. Position first cake layer on kit base, top with filling, then add second cake layer. Ice cake smooth. Edge cake top and base with tip 16 shell borders.

Position sweet peas and roses. Trim with tip 352 leaves. Add tip 2 message.

3. Attach cookie to front leg with icing. Push toothpick into one end of each pretzel; wedge toothpicks between cake and base to position handles. *Serves 12.*

For more ways to use
PIANO KIT
see Pan Index p. 192.

ELEGANT CHEESECAKE

Decorating Needs
- **Springform Pan, p. 171**
- **Tip 21, p.119**
- **Stabilized Whipped Cream Recipe, p. 82**
- **Pecan halves, drained cherries, canned peach slices (drained), cheese cake recipe**

1. Prepare your favorite cheesecake recipe for a 9-in. Springform Pan (or use box mix). Bake and cool according to instructions. Release from pan.

2. Use toothpick to mark triangles; fill with tip 21 whipped cream zigzags. Position peach slices around edge. Trim base with tip 21 shells.

Decorate center with cherry, cherry slices and pecan halves. Refrigerate until serving time. *Serves 12.*

For more ways to use SPRINGFORM PAN see Pan Index p. 192.

FLOWERS AND CANDY

Decorating Needs
- **10½-in. Ring Mold/Pan, p. 173**
- **Tips 3 and 21, p.118, 119**
- **Baroque Gum Paste Molds, p. 122**
- **Candy Melts™*, p. 106**
- **Candy Wafer & Fondant Mix, p. 106**
- **Flowers, apricot preserves**

1. Prepare Candy Melts decorations using lightly oiled Baroque Gum Paste Molds. Pipe in melted coating using tip 3 (do not fill side curls). Refrigerate (do not freeze) until set. To unmold, run tip of knife along edges of mold, then flex slightly to release candy. Trim any rough edges with a sharp knife or vegetable peeler. (If candy breaks, rejoin pieces with dots of coating.)

2. Glaze cake with thinned, warmed preserves. Use Candy Wafer & Fondant Mix to prepare Quick Pour Icing Recipe on label. Add 1 Tbsp. water. After heating, stir in 1 or 2 oz. melted unsweetened chocolate, then add vegetable oil and flavoring. Add brown color, if necessary. Cover cake with icing; let set.

3. Edge base of cake with tip 21 shells. Attach candy pieces to sides of cake with dabs of coating. Arrange flowers in cake center (use bride's favorite fresh or artificial flowers). *Serves 14.*

For more ways to use 10½-IN. RING MOLD see Pan Index p. 192.

*brand confectionery coating.

Wedding Bliss

*You're cordially invited
to fall in love
with six
dramatic romantics.
They're easier
to decorate
than you might think.
Each is a tribute
to true love.*

LOVE STORY

Decorating Needs
- 6, 10, 14-in. Round Pans, p. 165
- Tips 4, 18, 129, 224, 349, 352, p. 118-12
- 15-Pc. Pattern Press, p. 126
- 4½ & 6½-in. Arched Pillars, p. 161
- 7 & 11-in. Round Separator Plates, p. 16
- Dowel Rods, p. 160
- Cake Dividing Set, p. 126
- Tuk-N-Ruffle, p. 162
- Cake Circles, p. 162
- Devotion, p. 144
- Fresh flowers

1. Make 40 tip 131, 30 tip 129 and 30 tip 224 drop flowers with tip 4 dot centers. Read Tiered Cake Assembly, p. 86. Ice 2-layer cakes smooth on cake circles (14-in. on Tuk-N-Ruffle trimmed cake board) and separator plates.

2. To mark scrolls: Using Cake Dividing Set, with toothpick, dot mark 6-in. and 10-in. cake sides into 12ths, 14-in. cake into 24ths. Using pattern press scroll, imprint designs at marks. Cover marks with tip 18 "C" scrolls.

3. Edge separator plates with tip 18 scallops. Edge cake tops with tip 18 reverse shells; bases with tip 18 shells. Attach flowers to cakes sides with dots of icing. Trim with tip 349 and 352 (on 14-in. cake) leaves. Assemble tiers with separator plates on pillars at reception. Arrange fresh flowers on separator plates and position Devotion. **Serves 116.**

1. Make 80 tip 103 daisies (see p. 93) with tip 4 dot centers. (Pat centers with Edible Glitter.) Let dry on flower formers. With melted Candy Melts, mold 60 candies (see p. 94) in the Barcelona (diamond-shaped) Cookie Molds. Let set. Ice 2-layer round cakes smooth (on cake circles with precut center holes using Cake Corer as a guide.) Core out cake centers for Tall Tier Stand column. Using Cake Dividing Set, with toothpick, mark 6-in. cake into 8ths, 8-in. into 10ths, 12-in. in 16ths, 16-in. into 18ths.

2. Place cakes atop separator plates (smaller plates will not sit securely, so place over pan or bowl). Attach candies to cake sides and with toothpick, mark triangles ¼-in. from candy. Outline candy and cover marks with tip 16 shells.

3. Edge cake tops and bases with tip 17 shell borders. Attach daisies to candy with dots of icing. Add tip 352 leaves. At reception, assemble tiers (before adding each tier, position column section, attach center daisies on 8 and 12-in. cakes and rim with tip 352 leaves). Position Captivation.
Serves 181.

*brand confectionery coating.

KISS 'N TELL
Decorating Needs
- 6, 8, 12, 16-in. Round Pans, p. 166
- Tips 4, 16, 17, 103, 352, p. 118-121
- Flower Nail No. 7, p. 121
- Tall Tier Stand Set, p. 156
- Cake Corer Tube, p. 156
- Flower Formers, p. 122
- Edible Glitter, p. 122
- Barcelona Cookie Molds, p. 108
- Candy Melts.™* p. 106
- Cake Circles, p. 162
- Captivation, p. 145

RADIANT ROMANTIC

Decorating Needs
- 8, 10, 12-in. Round Pans, p. 165, 166
- Beveled Pan Set (8, 10, 12, 16-in.), p. 168
- Tips 2, 16, 17, 18, 224, 225, 349, p. 118-121
- Cake Dividing Set, p. 126
- 9 & 11-in. Round Separator Plates, p. 160
- Expandable Pillars (5 & 7-in. tall), p. 161
- Cake Circles, p. 162
- Dowel Rods, p. 160
- Tuk-N-Ruffle, p. 162
- Chapel Bells, p. 149
- Petite Elegance, p. 151

1. Make 475 tip 224 and 500 tip 225 drop flowers with tip 2 dot centers. Read Tiered Cake Assembly, p. 86. Ice 2-layer round cakes with beveled tops and bases smooth on cake circles and separator plates (12 & 16-in. atop Tuk-N-Ruffle trimmed cake board).

2. Using Cake Dividing Set, with toothpick, dot mark 8, 10, 12-in. cake sides into 16ths. Mark ovals (approximately 1¼-in. wide) by connecting dots. Outline ovals with tip 16 stripes.

3. Edge separator plates with tip 17 scallops. Trim beveled tops with tip 16 rosettes. Edge 8, 10, 12-in. bases with tip 17 zigzag puffs. Add tip 16 rosettes between puffs. Edge 16-in. beveled base with tip 18 reverse shell border. Attach flowers to cake sides with dots of icing. Trim with tip 349 leaves. Assemble tiers with separator plates on pillars at reception. Position Petite Elegance on 12-in. cake and Chapel Bells on 8-in. cake top.
Serves 110.*

*Serving size is 1 x 2 x 4-in. high. By tradition, the top tier is saved for the couple's first wedding anniversary. We do not figure it in with the number of servings.

FOREVER YOURS

Decorating Needs

- **Hexagon Pan Set**, p. 169
- **Tips 5, 17, 19, 20, 21, 190, 352**, p. 118-121
- **10-in. Hexagon Separator Plates**, p. 160
- **5-in. Square Filigree Pillars**, p. 161
- **Cake Dividing Set** (Triangle marker), p. 126
- **Dowel Rods**, p. 160
- **Cake Circles**, p. 162
- **Petite Tender Heart**, p. 152
- **Fresh flowers**

1. Make 90 tip 190 drop flowers with tip 5 dot centers. Read Tiered Cake Assembly, p. 86. Ice 2-layer cakes smooth on cake circles cut to fit and separator plates. Position 6-in. cake atop 9-in.,12-in. atop 15-in.

2. With toothpick, mark 1¼-in. high triangles in the following widths (for easier measuring, use Triangle Marker); 3-in. on 6-in., 2-in. on 9 and 12-in. and 1½-in. on 15-in. cake sides. Fill in triangles with tip 17 zigzags and edge with tip 5 bead borders.

3. Edge cake tops and bases with shell borders (tip 19 on 6 and 9-in., tip 20 on 12-in. and tip 21 on 15-in.). Attach flowers with dots of icing and add tip 352 leaves. At reception, assemble tiers with separator plates on pillars. Arrange fresh flowers on separator plate and position Petite Tender Heart.
Serves 144.

PROMENADE OF LOVE

Decorating Needs

- 8, 10, 12, 16-in. Round Pans, p. 165,166
- Tips 20, 22, 103, 104, 352, p. 119-121
- Flower Nail No. 7, p. 121
- Crystal-Look Tier Set, p. 157
- 5-in. Crystal-Look Pillars, p. 161
- 9-in. Crystal-Look Separator Plates, p. 160
- Filigree Stairways, p. 157
- Kolor-Flo Fountain (base only), p. 158
- Crystal-Look Fountain Cascade Set, p. 158
- Cake Dividing Set, p. 126
- Decorator's Brush, p. 126
- Dowel Rods, p. 160
- Cake Circles, Boards, p. 162
- Flower Holder Ring, p. 158
- Scrolls, p. 154
- Bridesmaid & Groomsmen, p. 154
  - Rhapsody, p. 144
  - Fresh flowers, ferns, acrylic paint, ribbon bows

1. Make 65 tip 103 roses, 350 tip 104 rosebuds, 50 tip 104 sweet peas. Paint bridal parties with acrylic paint. Read Tiered Cake Assembly, p. 86. Ice two 8-in., three 10-in., one 12- and 16-in. 2-layer cakes smooth on cake circles, plates and foil-covered cake boards. Using Cake Dividing Set, with toothpick, dot mark 8-in. cake sides into 8ths, 10-in. into 10ths, 12- and 16-in. into 12ths. Position 12-in. cake atop 16-in.

2. Mark drapes (approximately 1½-in. deep) by connecting dot marks. Mark bottom in between each curve. Cover marks with tip 104 drapes (pipe bottom row first). Edge cake tops with tip 20 reverse shell borders; bases with tip 22 shells.

3. Push Scrolls into cake sides. Attach flowers to sides, bows to stairway railings with dots of icing and trim with tip 352 leaves. At reception, assemble fountain with cascade and flower holder ring on separator plate. Assemble tiers with plates on pillars. Push Stairways into cakes. Arrange flower sprays and scrolls on 9-in. separator plates (build up with mounds of icing). Attach flowers to 8 and 10-in. cake tops. Trim flowers with tip 352 leaves. Position Bridesmaids, Groomsmen and Rhapsody. Arrange fresh flowers and ferns in flower holder ring. **Serves 298.**

ENDLESS LOVE

Decorating Needs
- 6 & 14-in. Round Pans, p. 165, 166
- 8 & 16-in. Square Pans, p. 167
- Tips 16, 18, 21, 103, 104, p. 119
- Flower Nail No. 7, p. 121
- Cake Dividing Set, p. 126
- 7-in. Round, 9-in. Square Separator Plates, p. 160
- 5 & 7½-in. Corinthian Pillars, p. 161
- Dowel Rods, p. 160
- Cake Circles, Boards, Tuk-N-Ruffle, p. 162
- Harmony, p. 147
- Fresh flowers, waxed paper

1. Make 170 tip 104 sweet peas; 40 each tip 103 and 104 two-tone roses. Read Tiered Cake Assembly, p. 86. Ice 2-layer cakes smooth on cake circles and separator plates (16-in. on Tuk-N-Ruffle trimmed cake board).

2. For diamonds: Cut a 1½-in. square out of waxed paper. Using Cake Dividing Set, with toothpick (approximately 1-in. from top), dot mark 6-in. cake into 6ths, 8 and 14-in. sides into 8ths and 16-in. into 12ths. Position 14-in. round atop 16-in. square. Make diamonds on cake sides. Outline with tip 18 scrolls.

3. Edge cake tops with tip 18 shell borders; bases with tip 18 "S" scrolls. Edge separator plates with tip 16 scallops. Attach flowers to cake sides with dots of icing. At reception assemble tiers with separator plates on pillars.

Position Harmony and arrange flowers on separator plates.
Serves 237.

American
REGIONAL DESSERTS

Every region of our blessed land boasts of several outstanding desserts...each one more appealing than the other.

We're delighted to present this luscious collection of America's favorite desserts. Why not try one tonight. You'll love it.

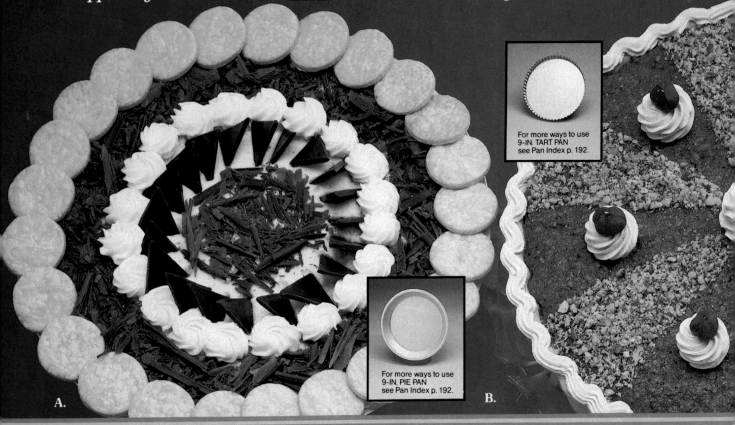

For more ways to use 9-IN. TART PAN see Pan Index p. 192.

For more ways to use 9-IN. PIE PAN see Pan Index p. 192.

A.

B.

A. BLACK BOTTOM PIE
Though credited to the Deep South, this luscious pie is a favorite everywhere.
Recipe, p. 96

Decorating Needs
• 9-in. Pie Pan, p. 172
• Tip 21, p. 119
• Round Cookie Cutter Set, p. 114
• Candy Melts™❋ p. 106
• Stabilized Whipped Cream, recipe p. 82
• Grated chocolate

Make 24 candy triangles. (About 1" long.) See Candy Making, p. 94, Candy Cut-Outs.

With smallest cutter and half of the pastry dough, cut out 24 circles from pie crust dough. Bake and cool. After cooling prepared pie as per recipe, sprinkle grated chocolate around pie edge, about 1" wide.

Pipe tip 21 whipped cream rosettes around inner rim of chocolate. Position candy triangles on pie top and pastry circles along pie plate rim. Sprinkle grated chocolate in center. *Serves 12.*

B. DATE AND FIG TART
Dessert tarts, especially popular in the south Texas area, often have a custard and/or fresh fruit base. The unusual combination of dried fruit, nuts and spices in this recipe creates a delicious chewy tart that is a special Southwestern favorite.
Recipe, p. 96

Decorating Needs
• 9-in. Tart Pan, p. 171
• Tip 16, p. 119
• Cake Dividing Set, p. 126
• Stabilized Whipped Cream with cinnamon, recipe p. 82
• Chopped nuts, whole hazelnuts, waxed paper

For more ways to use
9-IN. SPRINGFORM PAN
see Pan Index p. 192.

For more ways to use
8-IN. ROUND PAN
AND BEVEL PAN SET
see Pan Index p. 192.

C.

D.

Cut out a 9-in. circle of waxed paper. With cake dividing set, divide paper into 12 triangles. Cut out every other triangle and a circle in the center. Place paper pattern on top of tart. Sprinkle chopped nuts on top where triangles have been cut out: Carefully remove pattern.

Pipe tip 16 whipped cream rosettes on triangles without nuts and on circle in center. Edge top of tart with tip 16 scallops. Position hazelnuts on rosettes, *Serves 12.*

C. NEW YORK CHEESECAKE
New Yorkers go wild for this rich creamy cheesecake. Make it and see why!
Recipe, p. 97

Decorating Needs
- **9-in. Springform Pan, p. 171**
- **Tip 21, p. 119**
- **Currant Jelly Glaze, p. 95**
- **Stabilized Whipped Cream, p. 82**
- **Fresh strawberries**

Glaze strawberries with Currant Jelly Glaze (see p. 98). Position sliced strawberries on cake center. Pipe tip 21 whipped cream rosette. Position whole strawberry on rosette. Garnish bottom edge with whole strawberries. *Serves 12.*

D. BOSTON CREAM PIE
You'll find many variations of this popular dessert in Boston alone. Try this one. It's as pretty as it's delicious. **Recipe, p. 97**

Decorating Needs
- **8-in. Round Pan, p. 166**
- **Bevel Pan Set, p. 168**
- **Tip 7, p. 118**
- **Candy Melts,™* p. 106**

Slice off bottom section of 8-in. bevel cake and place on cake rack over drip pan. Pour chocolate glaze over cake. Let cool and set. Split 8-in. round cake into two layers and spread a generous amount of cream filling between layers and on top of cake. Place glazed bevel cake on top of round cake. Pipe tip 7 melted Candy Melts "C" scrolls around top of cake. *Serves 12.*

77

*brand confectionery coating

A. MARY TODD LINCOLN'S VANILLA-ALMOND CAKE

This delicious cake is said to have been President Lincoln's favorite dessert. When you try it, you'll see why.
Recipe, p. 96

Decorating Needs
- 8-in. Round Pans, p. 166
- Tips 18, 103, p. 119
- Flower Nail No. 7, p. 121
- Candy Melts,™* p. 106
- **Whole almonds, ground almonds**

Dip about 12 whole almonds into melted Candy Melts. Make one tip 103 rose. Ice two-layer cake smooth. Press ground almonds around sides and on top. Pipe tip 18 rosettes around top and bottom cake edges. Position uncoated whole almonds in a circle around inner top of cake. Position coated almonds next, leaning them on circle of uncoated almonds. Position rose in center. Position whole almonds inside rosettes on top and bottom cake edges. *Serves 12.*

*brand confectionery coating.

B. LADY BALTIMORE CAKE

No one knows for sure whether Lady Baltimore really originated this famous Maryland cake. There are now many variations of it, all delicious!
Recipe, p. 97

Decorating Needs
- 8-in. Square Pans, p. 167
- Tip 32, p. 119
- **Pecan and cherry halves, ground nuts**

Level three one-inch layers. Cool and fill with filling (see recipe). Ice smooth with plain frosting. Press ground nuts around sides and sprinkle on top along outer edges. Pipe tip 32 shell top and bottom borders. Position cherry and pecan halves on cake top. *Serves 16.*

AMERICAN REGIONAL DESSERTS

B.

For more ways to use 8-IN. SQUARE PAN see Pan Index p. 192.

A.

For more ways to use 8-IN. ROUND PANS see Pan Index p. 192.

For more ways to use
8-IN. ROUND PANS
see Pan Index p. 192.

C.

For more ways to use
ANGEL FOOD PAN
see Pan Index p. 192.

D.

D. HAWAIIAN PINEAPPLE RING

Here is a beautiful, delicious cake anyone can decorate. It salutes our island state by using two of Hawaii's most popular products, pineapple and coconut.
Recipe, p. 97

Decorating Needs
- Angel Food Pan, p. 171
- Stabilized Whipped Cream, p. 82 (2 recipes)
- One 20-oz. and one 8-oz. can of sliced pineapple, shredded coconut, candied cherries, fresh pineapple top.

Ice cake. Press shredded coconut onto cake top and sides.

Cut 11 pineapple slices in half. Position halves along bottom edge of cake, pressing into sides. Position halves along top edge of cake, as shown, between slices at bottom. Press cherries along bottom edge. Pull off some leaves at bottom of pineapple top, so top fits into center ring. Position. Refrigerate until serving time. *Serves 12.*

desserts. We've used a Pennsylvania Dutch favorite, chocolate, to create this luscious dessert. It's beautiful as well as tasty.
Recipe, p. 96

Decorating Needs
- 8-in. Round Pans, p. 166
- Tips 7, 16, 21, 32, p. 118-119
- 15-Pc. Decorator Pattern Press Set, p. 126

Ice two-layer cake smooth. Using Pattern Press Set, imprint tulip design on cake top, letting outer petals touch; on cake sides, imprint tulip design between cake top tulips. Pipe tip 7 outline stems and zigzag leaves. Fill in tulips with tip 32. Edge cake top with tip 16 stars, bottom with tip 21 shells. *Serves 12.*

C. PENNSYLVANIA DUTCH CHOCOLATE CAKE

It is said that George Washington first learned about Pennsylvania Dutch cooking at Valley Forge and was among the first to sing the praises of this hearty cuisine. These colorful people are famous for all types of foods, from breakfast scrapple to rich

The Decorator's Guide
BAKING, DECORATING & CANDY MAKING

Now that you've got the ideas, here are the HOWS that will lead to WOWS!

Learn the basics of cake decorating, then advance to the challenges of flower making. Ideally, practice makes perfect! But often, even first tries are good enough to impress. After you've mastered these techniques, don't stop there… expand your knowledge with the Wilton Home Study Courses (pp. 127-129) or Wilton Method Classes in a store near your home.

You'll want to try all of our taste-tempting desserts and cake recipes including luscious regional favorites.

Find out how sweet it can be…our "fun"-damental candy making instructions will have you molding luscious treats in no time.

Behind every successful cake decorator/baker/candy/cookie maker are Wilton quality products. We've added many new, exciting products to our extensive line-up—they start on page 99!

BAKING YOUR CAKE

The First Step To Success

A properly baked cake makes the best foundation for your icing and the decorations that follow, so it's important to carefully follow these step-by-step instructions. Remember, you may bake your cake up to 3 months ahead of decorating day and freeze in heavy-duty foil. Always thaw cake completely before icing. Your cake will still be fresh and easy to ice because it will be firm. NOTE: If you're using one of the Wilton shaped pans, follow the specific instructions included with the pan. For 3-dimensional, stand-up cakes, use batters that bake a firm-textured cake (see specific pan's instructions).

Now Let's Begin

1. Preheat oven to temperature specified in recipe or on packaged mix.

2. Generously grease the inside of the cake pan, or pans, with solid vegetable shortening. Use a pastry brush to spread the shortening evenly. Make sure that all inside surfaces (sides, corners and any indentations) are well covered. (Fast and easy method: Use the latest grease/flour pan spray available at supermarkets. You just lightly spray the inside of pan evenly.) HINT: Simple

geometric shaped pans such as round, hexagon, square, etc. (not character or novelty shapes) pan bottoms may be lined with waxed paper after greasing. There's no need to flour pans. This will ensure easy unmolding, but more crumbs.

3. Sprinkle flour inside of pan and shake the pan back and forth so the flour covers all the greased surfaces. Tap out excess flour, and if any shiny spots remain, touch up with more shortening and flour. This important step will help prevent the cake from sticking to the pan.

4. Bake the cake according to temperature and time specifications in recipe or on package instructions. Remove cake from oven and let cool 10 minutes in pan on a cake rack. Larger cakes over 12-in. diameter may need to cool 15 minutes.

5. To remove cake from pan, place cake rack against top of cake and turn both cake pan and rack over. Lift off pan carefully. If cake will not release from pan, return it to a warm oven (250°) for a few minutes, and repeat procedure. Cool cake completely, at least 1 hour. Then brush loose crumbs off cake and it's ready to ice.

 GREASE
 FLOUR
 SHAKE
 PLACE RACK
 REMOVE

HOW TO COVER A CAKE BOARD

Many of your shaped cakes will look best on a full-covered cake board that follows the contours of the pan. **To make:**

1. Trace the shaped pan onto a Wilton cake board. Make with a pencil one-half to one inch larger than pan.

2. Cut out board with an artist's knife.

3. Trace board shape onto foil wrap, making outlines three to four inches larger than board. Cut out foil cover. Cut deep slits at several points around foil, leaving a half-inch uncut so it folds neatly around board.

4. Cover board with foil and tape securely to underside. If the cake is heavy, use two or more boards for added serving support. Stock up on strong Wilton cake boards, including circles and rectangles, and Fanci-Foil Wrap on pages 162-163.

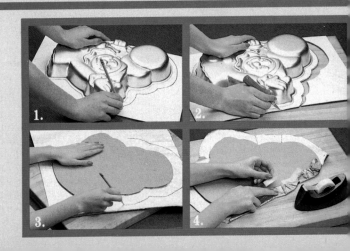

Icing Hints

Proper consistency is the key to making decorator icing that will shape the petals of a flower, show the details of a border or cover the surface of a cake. Therefore, it's important that you use the recommended icing and consistency for any technique. As a general rule, flowers require a stiff icing consistency, borders a medium-stiff consistency and writing or leaves a slightly thinned consistency. Icing that can peak to an inch or more is stiff, less than that is medium consistency. Icing that flows easily from a tip without running is a thin consistency. Every Wilton icing recipe is tested for taste and other important qualities. This chart will tell you each recipe's qualities, so you can determine which is the right one for your cake.

Have you tried Wilton Icing Mix (p. 125)?
It offers you everything the best homemade buttercream does! Creamy TASTE, luscious TEXTURE and the CONVENIENCE of a mix. Ideal for both frosting and decorating. So easy to make—just add butter and milk, the shortening's already in the mix. The 14 oz. size makes 2 cups of buttercream icing. Complete instructions on bag. It's available in creamy white (easy to tint) or chocolate flavor. The Snow-White and Deluxe recipes that follow are delicious variations to try with Wilton Buttercream Mix. Remember, having the right icing consistency is a must for good decorating.

Icing	Recommended Uses	Tinting	Flavor & Consistency	Icing Storage	Special Features
Buttercream (Wilton Mix or Homemade)	• Borders, writing • Roses, drop flowers & sweet peas • Icing cakes smooth	• Deep colors • Most colors deepen upon setting	• Sweet, buttery flavor • Medium-to-stiff consistency	• Refrigerate icing in an airtight container for 2 weeks	• Iced cake can be stored at room temperature for 2-3 days • Flowers remain soft enough to be cut with a knife
Snow-White Buttercream	• Borders, writing • Roses, drop flowers & sweet peas • Icing cakes smooth	• Deep colors • Most colors deepen upon setting • Gives true colors	• Sweet, almond flavor • Medium-to-stiff consistency	• Refrigerate icing in an airtight container for 2 weeks	• Iced cake may be stored for 2-3 days • Air-dried flowers have translucent look • Flowers remain soft to be cut with a knife • Good for wedding cakes • Tints true colors due to pure white color
Deluxe Buttercream	• Borders, writing • Drop flowers & sweet peas • Icing cakes smooth	• Deep colors	• Rich, creamy flavor • Medium-to-soft consistency	• Refrigerate icing in an airtight container for 2 weeks	• Texture remains soft on decorated cake • Iced cake may be stored at room temperature
Cream Cheese	• Basic borders, writing, stars, shells, drop flowers • Icing cake smooth	• Pastels	• Cream cheese • Medium-to-thin consistency	• Refrigerate icing in an airtight container for 1 week	• Iced cake must be refrigerated • Cream cheese flavor is especially good with spice cakes, carrot cakes, etc.
Stabilized Whipped Cream	• Borders, writing • Icing cake smooth	• Pastels can be achieved • Paste colors are best to use	• Creamy, delicate sweetness • Light, medium-to-thin consistency	• Use immediately	• Iced cake must be refrigerated • Texture remains soft on decorated cake • Especially good on cakes decorated with fruits
French Buttercream	• Basic borders • Writing • Icing cake smooth	• Pastels can be achieved	• Tastes similar to vanilla ice cream • Consistency similar to whipped cream	• Use immediately	• Store iced cake in refrigerator • Texture remains soft on decorated cake • Cooked icing gives a special flavor, similar to vanilla ice cream
Quick Pour Icing (Recipe on Candy Wafer & Fondant Mix, p. 106.)	• For icing cakes or cookies only	• Pastels	• Very sweet flavor • Pourable consistency	• Use immediately; excess fondant drippings can be reheated & poured again	• Dries to a shiny, smooth surface to coat petit fours and cookies • Seals in freshness
Royal	• Flower-making, figure piping, making flowers on wires • Decorating cookies & gingerbread houses	• Deep colors • Colors may fade upon setting	• Very sweet • Stiff consistency	• Store in airtight grease-free container at room temperature for 2 weeks	• Dries candy-hard for lasting decorations • Bowl & utensils must be grease-free • Cover icing with damp cloth to prevent crusting

Wilton ICING MIX RECIPES

BUTTERCREAM ICING

1 pkg. Wilton Icing Mix (p. 125)
Creamy White or Chocolate
6 Tbsps. butter or margarine
2-3 Tbsps. milk or water

Complete mixing instructions on packages.
YIELDS 2 cups.

SNOW-WHITE BUTTERCREAM

3 Tbsps. water
2 Tbsps. Wilton Meringue Powder (p. 125)
1 pkg. Wilton Icing Mix (p. 125)
1/4 cup solid vegetable shortening

Combine water and meringue powder; whip at high speed until peaks form. Add approximately half of the package of icing mix, beat well at medium-low speed. Add shortening; mix well. Add remaining icing mix; beat at medium-low speed until well blended. **YIELDS 1-3/4 cups.**

DELUXE BUTTERCREAM

1 pkg. Wilton Icing Mix (p. 125)
6 Tablespoons butter or margarine
1/4 cup whipping cream

Cream butter or margarine and icing mix together, beating at medium speed. Add whipping cream and beat at medium speed until light and fluffy.
YIELDS 2 cups.

Cake Icing Recipes

SPECIALTY ICING RECIPES

Be sure to refer to icing chart (p. 81) for the advantages of each.

BUTTERCREAM ICING

1/2 cup solid vegetable shortening
1/2 cup butter or margarine*
1 tsp. Clear Vanilla Extract (p. 125)
4 cups sifted confectioners sugar (approx. 1 lb.)
2 Tbsps. milk**

Cream butter and shortening with electric mixer. Add vanilla. Gradually add sugar, one cup at a time, beating well on medium speed. Scrape sides and bottom of bowl often. When all sugar has been mixed in, icing will appear dry. Add milk and beat at medium speed until light and fluffy. Keep icing covered with a damp cloth until ready to use. For best results, keep icing bowl in refrigerator when not in use. Refrigerated in an airtight container, this icing can be stored 2 weeks. Rewhip before using.
YIELD: 3 cups

*Substitute all-vegetable shortening and ½ teaspoon Wilton Butter Extract (p. 125) for pure white icing and stiffer consistency.

**Add 2 additional Tbsps. milk per recipe to thin for icing cake or use 3-4 Tbsps. light corn syrup per recipe.

CHOCOLATE BUTTERCREAM

Add 3/4 cup cocoa or 3-1 oz. unsweetened chocolate squares, melted, and an additional 1 to 2 Tbsps. milk to recipe. Mix until well blended.

For a unique change of pace, add Wilton Candy Flavors (p. 106) in Rum, Orange or Cherry, in place of vanilla extract.

FRENCH BUTTERCREAM ICING RECIPE

2/3 cup sugar
1/4 cup flour
1/4 tsp. salt
3/4 cup milk
1 cup cold butter, cut in several pieces
1 tsp. Clear Vanilla Extract (p. 125)

Place sugar, flour and salt in saucepan and mix thoroughly, stir in milk. Cook over medium heat and stir constantly until very thick. Remove from heat and pour into a medium mixing bowl. Cool at room temperature. Add 1/2 cup butter at a time (cut into several pieces) and beat at medium-high speed until smooth. Add vanilla and beat well. Chill icing for a few minutes before decorating. Iced cake must be refrigerated until serving time.

YIELD: 2 cups

STABILIZED WHIPPED CREAM RECIPE

1 tsp. unflavored gelatin
4 tsps. cold water
1 cup heavy whipping cream (at least 24 hours old and very cold)
1/4 cup confectioners sugar
1/2 tsp. Clear Vanilla Extract (p. 125)

Combine gelatin and cold water in small saucepan. Let stand until thick. Place over low heat, stirring constantly until gelatin dissolves (about 3 minutes). Remove from heat and cool slightly. Whip cream, sugar, and vanilla until slightly thickened. While beating slowly, gradually add gelatin to whipped cream mixture. Whip at high speed until stiff. YIELD: 2 cups. Cakes iced with whipped cream must be stored in the refrigerator.

CREAM CHEESE ICING

3-8 oz. packages slightly softened cream cheese
3 cups sifted confectioners sugar

Beat cream cheese until smooth. Add confectioners sugar and mix thoroughly. Beat at high speed until light and fluffy.

YIELD: 3-1/2 cups

SNOW-WHITE BUTTERCREAM RECIPE

2/3 cup water
4 Tbsps. Wilton Meringue Powder Mix (p. 125)
12 cups sifted confectioners sugar (approximately 3 lbs.)
1-1/4 cups solid shortening
3/4 tsp. salt
1/2 tsp. almond extract
1/2 tsp. Clear Vanilla Extract (p. 125)
1/4 tsp. Butter Extract (p. 125)

Combine water and meringue powder; whip at high speed until peaks form. Add 4 cups of sugar, one cup at a time, beating after each addition at low speed. Alternately add shortening and remainder of sugar. Add salt and flavorings; beat at low speed until smooth.

YIELD: 7 cups.

Note: Recipe may be doubled or cut in half. If cut in half, yield is 2-2/3 cups.

DECORATING WITH PREPARED ICINGS & CREAMS

CANNED ICING

For best results, refrigerate icing before using. If icing becomes too soft, place decorating bag in refrigerator until icing is firm enough for decorating. Each can yields about 1-1/2 cups icing.

FROZEN NON-DAIRY WHIPPED TOPPING

Non-dairy whipped topping must be thawed in the refrigerator before coloring or using for decorating. Can be used for decorating techniques similar to stabilized whipped cream. Do not allow to set at room temperature, as it becomes too soft for decorating. After decorating, store cake in refrigerator.

PACKAGE TOPPING MIX

Whipped topping mix can be used for decorating similar to stabilized whipped cream. However, use immediately after preparing. Do not allow to set at room temperature as topping becomes too soft for well-defined decorations.

ROYAL AND COLOR FLOW ICING RECIPES

ROYAL ICING

This smooth, hard-drying icing makes decorations that last. Ideal for making flowers, piping figures, overpiping and decorating cookies. Flowers and decorations made from royal icing will last for months, if stored properly, without softening. Royal icing decorations should be air dried. Allow several hours drying time for large decorations. Make sure bowl and utensils are grease free, since any trace of grease will cause royal icing to break down.

Royal Icing dries quickly, so keep icing bowl covered with a damp cloth at all times. Store in air tight container. Rebeat at low speed before using.

Note: Royal Icing is edible. Since it dries candy-hard, it is not recommended for icing your cakes. Use only for special effects you want to last.

To "paint" plastic cake trims with royal icing: Thin 1/2 cup icing with 1 Tablespoon water and add 1 teaspoon of Piping Gel (p.125) or light corn syrup for shine; to 1/4 cup icing, add 1/4 teaspoon piping gel when decorating confectionery coating candies.

ROYAL MERINGUE RECIPE

3 level Tbsps. Wilton Meringue Powder Mix (p.125)
4 cups sifted confectioners sugar (approx. 1 lb.)
6 Tbsps. water*

Beat all ingredients at low speed for 7 to 10 minutes (10 to 12 minutes at high speed for portable mixer) until icing forms peaks.
YIELD: 3 cups

*When using large counter top mixer or for stiffer icing, use 1 Tbsp. less water.

ROYAL EGG WHITE RECIPE

3 egg whites (room temperature)
4 cups confectioners sugar (approx. 1 lb.)
1/2 tsp. cream of tartar

Beat all ingredients at high speed for 7 to 10 minutes. Use immediately. Rebeating will not restore texture.
YIELD: 2-1/2 cups

COLOR FLOW ICING

To create candy-hard decorations using an outline and filling in method of decorating, use this success tested Color Flow recipe. You can trace emblems, insignias, original designs and patterns from Wilton Pattern Books (pp. 98-103) with this icing and the results will last.

1/4 cup + 1 teaspoon water
1 lb. sifted confectioners sugar (4 cups)
2 Tbsps. Wilton Color Flow Icing Mix (p.122)

In an electric mixer, blend all ingredients on low speed for 5 minutes. If using hand mixer use high speed. Color Flow icing "crusts" quickly, so keep it covered with a damp cloth while using it. Stir in desired Paste Icing Colors. Use full strength for outlining. To fill in outlines, soften full-strength Color Flow icing by adding 1/2 teaspoon of water at a time, (just a few drops as you near proper consistency) per 1/4 cup icing, until it becomes the right texture. Use grease-free spoon or spatula to stir slowly. Color Flow is ready for filling in outlines when a small amount dropped into the mixture takes a full count of ten to disappear. Let outlines dry thoroughly (1-2 hours) before filling in. Let Color Flow decorations dry for at least 24 hours. For complete directions and step-by-step information about Color Flow, see the **Wilton Way of Cake Decorating Volume I,** Chapter XIV, (sold on page 130).

Icing Your Cake

A beautifully decorated cake begins with a smooth, even coating of icing. This becomes the base to show off your pretty flowers and borders. Icing a cake properly is easy if you follow these basic steps. Most Yearbook cakes require 4-6 cups of icing to ice and decorate. See recipes on pages 81-83.

1. LEVEL CAKE

If you've followed the baking instructions on page 80, or the ones included with your Wilton pan, your layers should have a slight crown. However, if it is too high, or one side of the cake is raised more than the other, trim off the excess. Remove cake from pan, use a sharp, serrated knife, and move it sideways back and forth across the top of the cake in a saw-like fashion. A cake that's partially frozen is easier to trim.

2. FILL LAYERS

Place one cake layer on a cake board atop a cake stand, top side up. Fit bag with coupler and fill with icing. Make a dam by squeezing out a circle of icing about 3/4-in. high on cake top. Using a spatula, spread icing, jam, pudding or other filling on cake top. Next, position top layer, bottom side up.

3. ICE TOP

Thin your buttercream icing with milk or light corn syrup for easy spreading. The consistency is correct when the spatula glides over the icing. Put 3-in. wide waxed paper strips under the edges of the bottom layer to keep the cake stand free of icing drips. With large spatula place mound of icing on center of cake and spread across cake top pushing excess icing down onto cake sides. Always keep spatula on the iced surface, because once it touches the cake surface, crumbs will mix in with the icing.

4. ICE SIDES

Cover the sides of the cake with excess icing from the top, adding more icing if necessary. Work from top down, forcing any loose crumbs to the cake base. Again, make sure the spatula touches only the icing. Using an angled spatula (p. 124), can make icing the cake sides easier. For curved sides, hold the spatula upright against the side of the cake and, pressing lightly, turn cake stand slowly around with your free hand without lifting the spatula from the cake side surface. Return excess icing to bowl and repeat procedure until sides are smooth. For angled sides such as on a cross cake, do each straight side individually; hold spatula firmly to smooth.

5. SMOOTH TOP

Place spatula flat on one edge of cake top and sweep it across to center of cake. Lift off, remove excess icing and repeat, starting from a new point on edge of cake top. Repeat procedure until entire top surface of cake is smooth. To smooth center of cake, apply an even pressure to spatula as you turn cake stand around in a full circle. Lift off spatula and any excess icing. HINT: For smoother cakes, thin buttercream icing with milk or light corn syrup. This makes consistency best for easy spreading. Running a spatula under hot water, then smoothing icing, is not recommended.

SHEET AND OTHER FLAT SURFACED CAKES

Use the same icing procedure as shown here for sheet cakes, heart, oval, square and other shaped cakes with flat surfaces.

SHAPED CAKES

Most Wilton character and 3-dimensional cakes do not require icing before they're decorated. The decorating instructions with your pan show what to do.

HINT: Certain shaped cakes (especially 3-dimensional cakes) do require an iced surface. Ice smooth, then, after a slight crust has formed (about 15 min.), press plastic wrap against icing and smooth out spatula marks.

NOTE: Some cake designs require that you ice only small areas of the cake top smooth with a spatula. Make sure you ice slightly past area, so that edges will be covered with stars, etc.

CAKE ICER TIP

A fast and unique way to ice cakes, the Wilton Cake Icer Tip 789 (p. 119) fits into large Wilton Featherweight Decorating Bags, and allows you to cover flat-surfaced cakes with wide bands of icing. Hold tip flat against cake surface, serrated side up, and squeeze out a ribbed band of icing. Hold tip smooth side up, and squeeze out a smooth band of icing. For cake side, turn cake stand clockwise as you squeeze out a band of icing, wrapping it around the cake.

When the cake is completely iced, use a fork to blend ribbings and to join ribbed icing band seams together; use a spatula to blend smooth icing bands.

Color Techniques

Color brings cake decorations to life, therefore it's essential that you learn how to tint icings to achieve different decorating effects. Wilton Paste Icing Color is concentrated color in a creamy, rich base. It gives icing vivid or deep, rich color without changing icing consistency. See page 125 for a complete selection of quality Wilton Paste Icing Colors. Paste Icing Color kits are also available.

HOW TO TINT ICING

1. Start with white icing and add the color a little at a time until you achieve the shade you desire. Use a toothpick to add paste color; (use more depending on amount of icing). HINT: Tint a small amount of icing first, then mix in with remainder of white icing. Colors intensify or darken 1 to 2 hours after mixing, so keep this in mind when you're tinting buttercream icing. You can always add extra color to deepen the icing color, but it's difficult to lighten the color once it's tinted. Use White-White Icing Color to make your buttercream icing the purest snow-white!

2. To mix deep or dark, colored icing (such as red for roses), you may need a larger amount of Wilton Paste Icing Color. The color should still be added gradually, but use a clean small spatula each time to add the color. NEW! Wilton Red Paste Color has no after-taste! It's ideal for decorating large areas. Red-Red or Christmas Red Paste Color still is better to use in royal icing and for accent color, as each offers more color intensity. If you plan to use flavorings, make icing stiff consistency, then use enough flavoring to improve taste.

3. Always mix enough of any one color icing. If you're going to decorate a cake with pink flowers and borders, color enough icing for both. It's difficult to duplicate an exact shade of any color. As you gain decorating experience, you will learn just how much of any one color icing you will need.

IMPORTANT HINTS

1. Royal icing requires more base color than buttercream to achieve the same intensity.

2. Use milk, not water, in buttercream icing recipe when using Violet Icing Color, otherwise the icing may turn blue.

3. Substitute chocolate icing for dark brown colors. Use just 6 Tablespoons unsweetened cocoa powder, or 2 one-ounce squares of melted unsweetened baking chocolate, 1 Tablespoon milk, and add to 1½ cups white icing.

4. Add color to piping gel, color flow, gum paste, cookie dough, marzipan, cream cheese, sugar molds and even cake batter for striking decorating effects!

5. To restore the consistency of Wilton Paste Icing Colors that have dried out, add a few drops of Wilton Glycerin. Mix until proper consistency is reached. See page 125 for Glycerin.

6. Use a clean toothpick or spatula to add Wilton Paste Icing Colors each time, until you reach desired shade.

SPECIAL EFFECTS

Apply one or more stripes of full strength icing color to the inside of a parchment paper bag. (Paste icing color stains the plastic-coated bags.) Fill bag with white or pastel-colored icing and squeeze out multicolored borders, flowers, even figure piped clowns. HINT: For deep color effects (red roses), brush the entire inside of the parchment paper decorating bag with any paste color. Fill the bag with icing in a medium shade of the same color, and squeeze out deep dramatic decorations.

BRUSH STRIPING

Striping is a method used to give multiple or deep color effects to icing. To do this, one or more colors are applied to the inside of the parchment paper bag with a brush. Then the bag is filled with white or pastel-colored icing and, as the icing is squeezed past the color, out comes the striped decorations! See pictures below.

SPATULA STRIPING

Use a spatula to stripe the inside of a decorating bag with pastel colored icing. Then fill the bag with white icing, or another shade of the same color as the striping, and squeeze out decorations with pastel contrasts. Use the above color techniques when figure piping for exciting results. It's fun to experiment with color! Try to achieve natural-looking flower colors by using the spatula striping method. (Roses look especially beautiful with this effect.) Discover color—the key to decorating drama!

SPECIAL EFFECTS

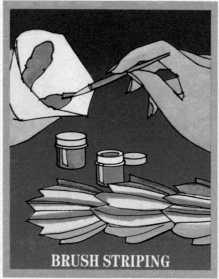

BRUSH STRIPING

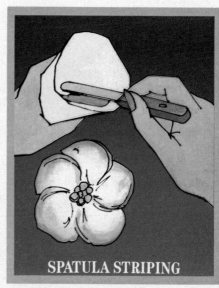

SPATULA STRIPING

Tiered Cake Assembly

A tiered cake is a work of art and architecture, whether it's two tiers or a towering multi-tiered masterpiece. The tiers refer to the number of different size cake layers, each usually separated by a set of separator plates and pillars. It's these separator plates and pillars (p. 160-161), combined with a network of wooden dowel rods (p. 160), that give the tiered cake a foundation and framework on which to build. The classic tiered cake assembly shown here can be adapted for any multi-tiered cake. Each tier is two cake layers deep, with the base tier deeper if there are more than three tiers above it. For more about tiered cakes, see our new *Dramatic Tier Cakes* book, see p. 135.

How To Assemble a Tiered Cake

1. Ice all tiers first. Place bottom tier on a sturdy base plate, or Tuk-N-Ruffle (p. 162) trimmed cake boards (2 or 3) cut 4-in. larger than tier diameter. On center top of this tier, press a cake board circle (p. 162) 2-in. smaller in diameter than the tier to be placed above it to imprint outline. Remove cake circle and push a dowel rod into lowest portion of cake within circular outline, until rod touches base plate. Lift up rod and use sharp pruning shears to cut off end at icing mark. Use this rod as a guide to cut six more dowel rods the same length. Push all seven rods into tier cake base so they're equally spaced within the circular outline and even with the cake top. NOTE: If you plan to position a small cake atop a novelty cake, ice the small cake on a cake board cut to fit. A dowel rod may be necessary to support the small cake. Ice all cakes on boards cut to fit when making any tiered cake.

2. With dowel rods in place, position next tier setting on cardboard base. Use cardboard circle 2-in. smaller in diameter to imprint an outline on second tier and repeat step 1 using five dowel rods. Now sharpen the end of another dowel rod with a kitchen knife or pencil sharpener and push through both layers of cake to cardboard circle base. Hit end of rod sharply with a tack hammer to drive rod through cardboard to bottom cake tier. Clip rod even with top of second tier using pruning shears. This serves to secure tiers, keeping them in place for transporting.

3. Insert pegs in base of separator plate, pillars on top; and push separator plate pegs into tier top.

4. Set top cake tier on corresponding size separator plate and position atop pillars for a three-tiered cake. Remove this top tier, and any tiers separated by plates, when transporting a cake. When cutting a tiered cake, always start with the top tier. Remove the tier, slice and serve.

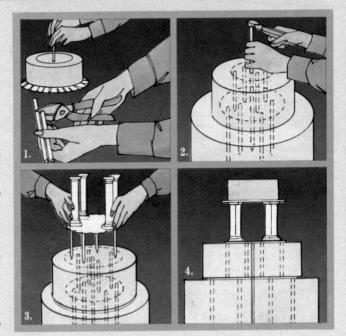

Helpful Hints

FOR FASTER DECORATING:

1. Buy several of the bags and tips you use most. It'll save changing bags so you'll save time.

2. Tips from the same basic group that are close in size may be substituted for one another, such as tips 15 and 16, 18 and 19, 101 and 102, 66 and 67, etc. The effect is a slightly smaller or larger decoration.

3. Use tip 20 or 21 or the super fast Triple-Star Tip (p. 121), when you want to cover a cake quickly with stars. You can also use zigzags for filling in large areas.

4. When using parchment bags, you may place a tip with a smaller opening over the tip you're using and tape it in place. This saves time changing bags and tips when you're using the same color icing.

FOR BETTER CAKE BAKING:

1. Packaged, two-layer cake mixes usually yield 4 to 6 cups of batter, but formulas change, so always measure.

2. If you're in doubt as to how many cups of batter you need to fill a pan, measure the cups of water it will hold first and use this number as a guide. Then, if you want a cake with high sides, fill the pan 2/3 full of batter. For slightly thinner cake layers, fill 1/2 full. Never fill cake pans more than 2/3 full. Even if the batter doesn't overflow, the cake will have a heavy texture.

3. For pans 3-in. deep or more, we recommend pound or pudding-added cake batters. For best baking results, fill pan half full only. Use pound cake batter when baking 3-D, stand-up cakes.

4. For easy unmolding, line bottom of basic geometric pan shapes with waxed or parchment paper after greasing. The cake will be slightly lighter and have tender crusts, but may have more crumbs than cakes baked in greased and floured pans.

FOR EASIER ICING

1. Thin buttercream icing with milk or light corn syrup for easy spreading.

2. To smooth the icing surface on 3-dimensional cakes such as the ball, egg, lamb or bunny cakes, let buttercream icing crust slightly. Then place plastic wrap over the icing and smooth over the surface gently with your hands. Carefully remove wrap. For a textured surface, follow the same procedure with a cloth or paper towel. See page 84 for icing techniques.

3. Canned icing works well for most decorating techniques, and will withstand humidity better than buttercream. It must always be refrigerated before using, to stiffen consistency. However, canned icing is not for flowers that require a stiffer consistency like the rose, mum and lily.

4. To make clean-up easier and quicker when decorating with buttercream icing, use a degreaser cleaner to dissolve icing from tools. It is especially important to have grease-free utensils when using royal or color flow icings.

DECORATING BAGS

After preparing the proper icing for your decorating, the next step is to prepare the decorating bag.

There are three types of decorating bags you may choose to use. Wilton Featherweight bags are coated polyester cones and Parchment Triangles are grease-resistant, disposable paper shapes you roll into bags. Clear, plastic Wilton Disposable Decorating bags are convenient and easy to handle. Each serves as an excellent container for your decorating tip and icing.

HAND POSITION

The angle at which you hold your decorating bag and tip must be correct in order to produce a desired decoration. To hold the decorating bag correctly, grip the bag near the top with the twisted or folded end locked between your thumb and fingers.

Generally, there are two basic positions for the decorating bag: The 90° angle and the 45° angle. In 90° angle, the decorating bag is held perpendicular to the decorating surface (see picture A). In the 45° angle position, the

FOR LEFT-HANDERS ONLY

If you are left-handed, hold the decorating bag in your left hand and guide the decorating tip with the fingers of your right hand. (see picture C). If the instructions say to hold the decorating bag over to the right, you should hold your decorating bag over to the left. A right-handed person will always decorate from left to right. A left-handed person should always decorate from right to left. The only exception to this rule is when you are writing or printing. When decorating a cake on a turntable, rotate the stand counterclockwise. For flower-making on a flower nail, turn nail clockwise in right hand as you pipe petals using left hand. Whether you're right or left handed, the amount of pressure and the steadiness with which it's applied to the decorating bag will determine

Easy-to-follow instructions are included with all Wilton Decorating Bags.

See page 117 for a complete selection of Wilton quality Decorating Bags and Couplers. The coupler allows you to change decorating tips on the same bag. It's a real timesaver when you want to use several different tips and the same color icing. Use couplers with Featherweight and Disposable Decorating Bags. Complete how to use coupler instructions are included with Wilton Decorating Bags.

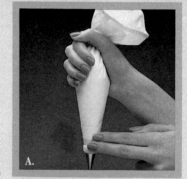

decorating bag is held at a slant to the decorating surface (see picture B).

Since most decorating tips are symmetrical, their positioning corresponds to that of the decorating bag. However, some tips are wider or serrated on one side; such as basketweave decorating tips on page 119, and have a correct position of their own. You will become acquainted with these positions as you learn to decorate. Guide the bag with your free hand.

the size and uniformity of any icing design. Some decorations require an even pressure, others a varying application of light, medium or heavy pressure. The more controlled the pressure, the more exact your decorations will be. Only practice can teach you the proper pressure application for each technique. Practice decorating on a Wilton Practice Board (p. 123) or the back of a cookie sheet using buttercream icing. Scrape practice decorations back into bowl and rewhip for use again. Be sure to rewhip frequently and keep the icing bowl covered with a damp cloth to prevent icing from crusting. If icing becomes too soft, place in refrigerator. Now you're ready to try your hand at cake decorating!

Decorating Tips & Techniques

The size and shape of the opening on a decorating tip identifies the basic group to which the tip belongs and determines the type of decorations the tip will produce.

PLAIN OR ROUND TIPS

Use for outline details, filling or piping in areas, printing and writing messages, figure piping, stringwork, beads, dots, balls, stems, vines, flower centers, lattice, cornelli lace. These tips are smooth and round—small plain tips include numbers 1, 2, 3, 4; medium, 5, 6, 7, 8, 9, 10, 11, 12; large, 1A, 2A. For fine stringwork, use 1S, 1L, 2L, 0L, 00L and 000; and oval tips for Philippine method flower making are 55 and 57. For fine, flat lines, use new Writing Tip 301. See p. 118.

PRINTING AND WRITING

Use thin consistency icing. Letters are combinations of straight and slanted lines, circles, half-circles and curves. It's important to practice these motions individually before combining them to form words.

To Print: Hold bag at a 45° angle to surface with back of bag to the right for horizontal lines, toward you for vertical. Raise the tip slightly and squeeze out lines. To end outline, stop squeezing, touch tip to surface and pull away.

To Write: Hold bag at a 45° angle with back of bag to the right. Use your arm, not just fingers, to form every line, letter or word. The tip should lightly touch the cake as you write.

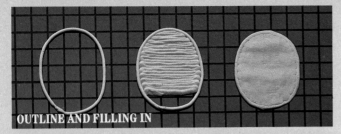

OUTLINE AND FILLING IN

To outline contours and details of shaped cake or for covering the marks transferred on your cake from a pattern...hold bag at a 45° angle and touch tip to surface. Now raise the tip slightly and continue to squeeze. The icing will flow out of the tip while you direct it along the surface. To end an outline, stop squeezing, touch tip to surface and pull away.

For Fill In: With thinned icing, squeeze out tip 2 or 3 side-by-side icing strings to fill area. For larger areas, use tip 4 or 5. Immediately smooth over strings with a dampened Decorator's Brush, spatula or finger dipped in cornstarch.

For Pipe In: Follow same procedure as Fill In, but do not thin icing. Squeeze with heavier pressure allowing icing to build up slightly. When necessary, shape with finger dipped in cornstarch.

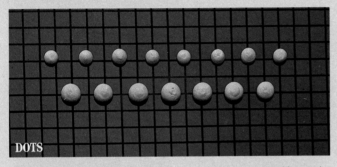

DOTS

Hold bag at a 90° angle with tip slightly above surface. Squeeze and keep point of the tip in icing until dot is the size you want. Stop pressure, pull away; use tip to clean point away or smooth with finger dipped in cornstarch. To make large dots or balls, lift tip as you squeeze to allow greater icing build-up.

BEADS, BEAD HEARTS AND SHAMROCKS

Hold bag at 45° angle with tip slightly above surface and end of bag pointing to the right. Squeeze and lift tip slightly so icing fans out into base. Relax pressure as you draw tip down and bring bead to point. Ideal for borders or piped in side-by-side rows to cover large areas.

For Hearts: Pipe two beads side by side and join points.

For Shamrocks: Pipe 3 bead hearts so points meet. Add tip 3 outline stem.

CORNELLI LACE

Use a 90° angle with tip slightly above surface. Pipe a continuous string of icing, curve it up, down and around until area is covered. Stop pressure; pull tip away. Make sure strings never touch or cross.

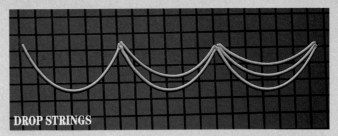

DROP STRINGS

With icing dots, mark 1½-in. horizontal intervals on your surface. Hold bag at 45° angle to the surface so that end of bag points slightly to the right. Touch tip to first mark and squeeze, holding bag in place momentarily so that icing sticks to surface.

Then pull tip straight out away from surface, allowing icing to drop into an arc. Stop pressure as you touch tip to second mark to end string.

Repeat procedure, attaching string to third mark and so on, forming row of drop strings. It's very important to let the string, not your hand, drop to form an arc. Try to keep your drop strings uniform in length and width.

For Double Drop Strings: Start at first mark again, squeeze bag. Let icing drop into a slightly shorter arc than arc in first row. Join end of string to end of corresponding string in first row and repeat procedure.

Always pipe longest drop strings first and add shorter ones. This technique is ideal for cake sides. Practice is important in making drop strings uniform.

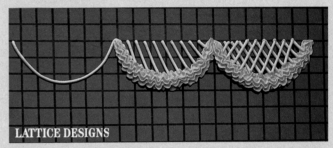

LATTICE DESIGNS

1. Starting at center of the shape to be covered with lattice, pipe tip 3 diagonal strings from top to bottom edge. Return to center and fill in rest of outline with diagonal strings, keeping them evenly spaced.

2. Starting at center of area again, pipe diagonal strings in the opposite direction. Repeat to fill in rest of outline. Cover edges of lattice with zigzag or star tip border.

STAR TIPS

The star-shaped openings create the most popular decorations...stars, zigzags, shells, rosettes and more. The most often used star tips are numbers 13 through 22. Star tips range in size from small to extra large. For deep ribbed decorations, try tips 23-31, 132, 133, and 195. Large star tips include numbers 32, 96, 4B, 6B, and 8B. Fine cut star tips are numbers 362, 363, 364, 172 and 199.

STARS

Hold bag at 90° angle with tip slightly above surface. Squeeze bag to form a star, then stop pressure, and pull tip away. Increase or decrease pressure to change star size. An entire cake or just one area can be covered with stars made very close together so that no cake shows between stars. Use the triple-star tip (p. 121) or use larger star tip to cover areas of cake in less time.

For Pull-Out Stars: Hold bag at 45° angle to surface. As you squeeze out icing, pull tip up and away from cake. When strand is long enough, stop pressure and pull tip away. Work from bottom to top of area to be covered with pull-out stars.

For Star Flowers: Squeeze and keep tip in icing until star petals are formed. Stop pressure and pull tip away. Add tip 2 or 3 dot center.

ROSETTES

Hold bag at a 90° angle with tip slightly above surface. Squeeze and move hand to the left, up and around in a circular motion to starting point. Stop pressure and pull tip away. For a fancy effect, trim center with a star.

For Spirals: Following rosettes technique, starting at outer edge, move tip in a clockwise direction in a continuous circular motion decreasing size of circles until center is reached. Stop pressure and pull tip away.

SHELLS

Hold bag at 45° angle with tip slightly above surface and end of bag pointing to the right. Squeeze with heavy pressure and slightly lift tip as icing builds and fans out into a full base. Relax pressure as you pull bag down towards you to make the tail. Stop pressure completely, pull tip away. When you make the shells, always work toward yourself, starting each new shell slightly behind tail of previous shell.

For Elongated Shells: Extend tail while relaxing pressure, until desired length is achieved.

For Upright Shells: Hold bag at 90° angle to cake sides. Follow same procedure as elongated shells.

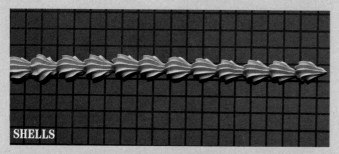

REVERSE SHELLS

Hold bag at 45° angle with tip slightly above surface. Squeeze to let icing fan out as if you were making a typical shell, then swing tip around to the left in a semi-circular motion as you relax pressure to form tail of a shell. Stop pressure, pull tip away. Repeat procedure, only this time, swing tip around to the right as you form tail of shell. Continue procedure, alternating directions for a series of reverse shells.

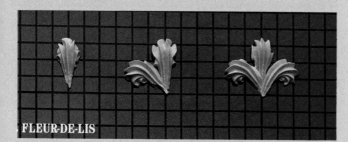

FLEUR-DE-LIS

Make a shell. Keep bag at 45° angle and starting at the left of this shell, squeeze bag to fan icing into shell base. Then as you relax pressure to form tail, move tip up slightly around to the right, relaxing pressure, forming tail similar to reverse shells. Join to tail of the first shell. Repeat procedure to right side of first shell.

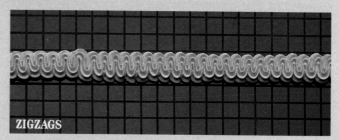

ZIGZAGS

Hold bag at 45° angle to surface, so that end of bag points out to the right, and fingertips gripping bag face you. Allow the tip to touch the surface lightly. Steadily squeeze out icing, moving hand in tight side-to-side motion for zigzag. To end, stop pressure and pull tip away. Use tip 16 to 21 for large areas to be covered with zigzags, tip 3 or 4 for small areas.

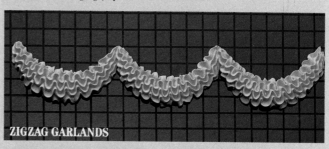

ZIGZAG GARLANDS

Hold bag as for basic zigzag procedure. Allow tip to touch the surface lightly and use light-to-heavy-to-light pressure to form curves of garland. To end, stop pressure, pull tip away. Practice for rhythmic pressure control so garlands are uniform.

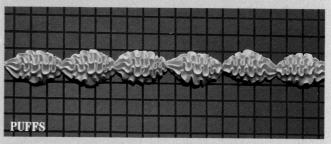

PUFFS

Hold bag at 45° angle to surface, fingertips on bag facing you. Touch tip to surface and use a light-to-heavy-to-light pressure and zigzag motion to form puff. Repeat procedure again and again as you move tip in a straight line to form row of puffs. To end row, stop pressure, pull tip away.

SCROLLS

Hold bag at 45° angle to surface so that end of bag points to the right. Use tip 3 to draw an inverted "C" center and use circular motion to cover inverted "C". You may overpipe with tip 13 or any small star tip. Use a heavy pressure to feather the scroll, relaxing pressure as you taper end. Add side petals like reverse shells.

REVERSE SCROLLS

With tip 3 squeeze out an inverted "C" scroll. Then, starting at the top of this "C," squeeze and move tip down, up and around for a backward "C". Cover outlines with tip 16. Add reverse shell side petals and you have a pair of reverse scrolls.

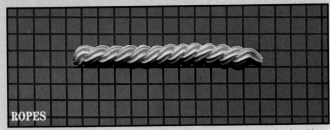

ROPES

Hold bag at 45° angle to surface with end of bag pointing over right shoulder. Touch tip to surface and squeezing bag, move tip down and up and around to the right forming a slight "s" curve. Stop pressure, pull tip away. Tuck tip under bottom arch of first "s" and repeat procedure. Continue joining "s" curves to form rope.

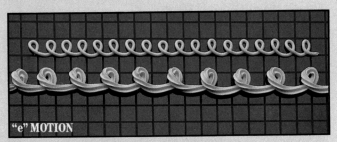

"e" MOTION

Hold bag at 45° angle to surface, fingertips on bag facing you. As you squeeze out icing, move tip down, up to the right and around as if writing the letter "e." Use a steady, even pressure as you repeat procedure. To end, stop pressure, pull tip away.

DROP FLOWER TIPS

These are the easiest flowers for a beginning decorator to execute. The number of openings on the end of the tip determines the number of petals the flower will have. Each drop flower tip can produce two different flower varieties— plain or swirled. Swirled drop flowers cannot be made directly on cake. Small tips include numbers 107, 129, 217, 220, 224, 225 (each form center holes), 135, 108, and 195. For large flowers, tips 1B, 1C, 1E, 1G, 2C, 2E and 2F. Use tip 190 or 225 and slightly stiffer consistency icing. Hold bag at a 90° angle with tip touching surface and pipe as you would a star. For swirled flowers: Curve wrist around to the left and, as you squeeze out icing, bring hand back to the right. Stop pressure, pull tip away. Add tip 2 or 3 dot centers. **For Stand-up Flower Stems:** On waxed paper, pipe tip 4 royal icing outlines (2-in. long). Add tip 352 leaves. Let dry. Attach flowers with icing. When dry, push into cake.

LEAF TIPS

The v-shaped openings of these tips give leaves pointed ends. With any leaf tip you can make plain, ruffled or stand-up leaves. Make leaves with center veins from small 65s, 65-70, to large, 112-115 and 355. Other popular numbers are 71-76, 326, 349, 352.

BASIC LEAF

Hold bag at 45° angle to surface, back of bag facing you. Squeeze and hold tip in place to let icing fan out into base, then relax and stop pressure as you pull tip towards you and draw leaf to a point.

STAND UP LEAF

Hold bag at a 90° angle to surface. Touch tip lightly and squeeze, holding tip in place as icing fans out to form base. Relax and stop pressure as you pull tip straight up and away, creating stand-up leaf effect.

PETAL TIPS

These tips have an opening that is wide at one end, narrow at the other. This teardrop-like shaped opening yields a variety of petals that form flowers like the rose, carnation, daisy, pansy and more (see pages 91-93). Petal tips can also make ribbons, drapes and swags; bows and streamers. Plain rose tips include numbers 101s, 101, 102, 103, 104, 124, 125, 126, 127 and giant roses, tip 127D. Swirled rose tips that make instant-curled petals are 97, 116, 118 and 119. Others include 59s, 59, 60, 61, 121, 122, 123, 62, 63, 64 and 150.

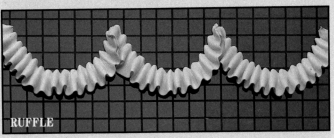

RIBBON DRAPE

Hold bag at a 45° angle to surface, fingertips on bag facing you. Touch wide end of tip to surface, angle narrow end out about ¼-in. away from surface. As you squeeze, swing tip down and up to the right forming ribbon drape.

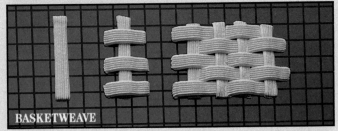

RUFFLE

Use same procedure as for ribbon drape. And, as you swing tip down and up to form a curve, move hand up and down slightly to ruffle the icing.

RIBBON TIPS

These are decorating tips with a smooth side for making smooth, wide icing stripes and/or one serrated side for making ribbed, wide icing stripes. When short ribbed horizontal stripes are interwoven in vertical rows the effect is that of a basketweave. Tips are 46 and 47. For smooth stripes, 44 and 45. For ribbed stripes, 48 and 327. Large ribbon tips include 1D, 2B and 789.

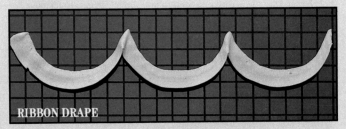

BASKETWEAVE

Use star or basketweave tip and medium consistency icing. You may use a small round tip as a vertical guide line if preferred.

1. Hold bag at 45° angle to cake with serrated side of tip facing up (or use round tip). Touch tip lightly to surface and squeeze out a vertical line of icing.

2. Next, hold bag at a 45° angle to surface, fingertips gripping bag facing you. Touch tip, serrated side facing up, to top left side of vertical line and squeeze out 3″ horizontal bar. Add two more horizontal bars, each about a tip width apart, to cover vertical line.

3. With bag and tip at 45° angle, make another vertical line of icing to right of first one, overlapping ends of horizontal bars. Use same procedure as step two to cover this line with horizontal bars, working them in spaces of bars in first row.

4. Repeat entire procedure, alternating vertical lines and horizontal bars, to create a basketweave effect. Other tips may be used for basketweave, but serrated tips 46-48 give icing a ribbed basket effect.

Making a Rose

THE FLOWER NAIL

The flower nail is a decorating tool used to make the most popular flower of all, the rose. It is also used to make pretty flowers like the violet, apple blossom and the daisy (see p. 93).

The key to making any flower on the nail is to coordinate the turning of the nail with the formation of a petal. The stem of the nail is held between your left thumb and forefinger, so you can turn the flat nailhead surface at the same time you're piping a flower with your right hand. Using the flower nail takes practice, but the beautiful results are well worth the effort!

NOTE: Left-handed decorators should use the nail opposite of above instructions.

Make all flowers on the nail with royal or stiffened buttercream icing (see p. 81 and 83), and the tips specified for each flower. Air dry flowers made in royal icing, and freeze buttercream flowers (buttercream roses can also be placed directly on iced cake) until firm at least 2 hours. Then, when you're ready to decorate, remove the frozen flowers, a few at a time, and position them on the cake. (Snow White Buttercream Icing flowers can be air dried).

For each flower you make, attach a 2-in. square of waxed paper to the nailhead with a dot of icing. Make a flower; remove waxed paper and flower together. For more about rose making, order the new *Wilton Celebrates The Rose*, p. 132.

MAKE THE ROSE BASE

1. Use tip 10 or 12. Hold the bag perpendicular at a 90° angle to nail with tip slightly above center of nailhead.

2. Squeeze with a heavy pressure, keeping bottom of tip in icing until you've made a full, round base.

3. Ease pressure as you raise tip up and away from nailhead, narrowing base to a dome head. The base is very important for successful rose-making. Be sure that it is secure to nail and can support all the petals. Practice until you feel comfortable with the technique.

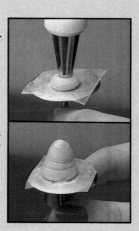

THE CENTER BUD

1. Use tip 104. Hold bag at a 45° angle to nail with wide end of tip just below top of dome, and narrow end pointed in slightly. Back of bag should be pointed over your shoulder.

2. Now you must do three things simultaneously...squeeze, pull tip up and out away from top of dome stretching icing into a ribbon band, as you turn the nail counterclockwise.

3. Relax pressure as you bring band of icing down around dome, overlapping the point at which you started.

1ST ROW OF 3 PETALS

1. Hold bag at 45° angle with end of bag pointed over your shoulder. Touch wide end of tip 104 to midpoint of bud base. Turn nail counterclockwise and move tip up and back down to midpoint of bud base forming first petal of rose.

2. Start slightly behind end of 1st petal and squeeze out 2nd petal same as first.

3. Start slightly behind end of 2nd petal and add a 3rd petal, ending this petal overlapping starting point of 1st petal. Now you have a full rosebud made on a nail to use just as you would a rosebud made on a flat surface (see p. 92).

2ND ROW OF 5 PETALS

1. Touch wide end of tip 104 slightly below center of a petal in 1st row, angle narrow end of tip out slightly more than you did for 1st row of petals. Squeeze and turn nail counterclockwise, moving tip up then down to form 1st petal in second row.

2. Start slightly behind this last petal and make a 2nd petal. Repeat this procedure for a total of 5 petals, ending last petal overlapping the 1st petal's starting point.

3RD ROW OF 7 PETALS

1. Touch wide end of tip 104 below center of petal in 2nd row, again angling narrow end of tip out a little more. Squeeze and turn nail counterclockwise and move tip up and down forming 1st petal. Repeat for a total of 7 petals.

2. Slip waxed paper and completed rose off nail. Attach another square of waxed paper and start again. Have several squares of waxed paper cut ahead of time so you can continue rose-making without stopping. HINT: An easy way to place a buttercream icing rose directly on your cake is to slide open scissors under base of rose and gently lift flower off waxed paper square and flower nail. Position flower on cake by slowly closing scissors and pushing base of flower with stem end of flower nail.

Practice is the key to perfect blooms!

Flowers

FLAT-SURFACE FLOWERS: ROSEBUDS, HALF ROSES AND SWEET PEAS

These are flowers you can make right on a cake, or any flat surface. To make all three, use tip 104 and royal, or stiffened buttercream icing (see pages 81, 83 for recipes). Attach a sheet of waxed paper to the back of a cookie sheet with dots of icing or use Wilton Practice Board, p. 123.

Make your practice flowers in horizontal rows and when you've filled the entire sheet, loosen the waxed paper with a spatula to remove it and start again.

When you're decorating a cake with lots of flat-surface flowers, make all the ones you need ahead of time using this same cookie sheet method. Let them dry, and they're ready when you're ready to decorate! Air dry flowers made with royal icing and freeze flowers made with buttercream until hard (at least 2 hours). Remove buttercream flowers with your spatula, a few at a time as you decorate, so they stay firm (Snow White Buttercream Icing flowers may be air-dried).

To attach a flower to the top or the sides of a cake, dot the cake with stiffened icing and set flower in position. Whether used individually as a border design, or arranged in clusters, sprays or bouquets, flowers add beauty to cakes, candy and cookies.

HALF ROSE

1. Make a rosebud without sepals and calyx. Hold bag at a 45° angle so that end of bag points to the right, fingertips gripping bag facing you. Touch wide end of tip 104 to bottom left side of bud. Squeeze, move it up, around to the right and down, relaxing pressure.

2. Make right petal. Hold bag in opposite position as far left petal. Touch wide end of tip to bottom right side of bud base. Squeeze, move up, around to the left and down to center of bud base. Stop pressure, pull tip away.

3. Make sepals and calyx with tip 3 and thinned icing. Follow same procedure as for step 3 of rosebud, starting at bottom center of half rose.

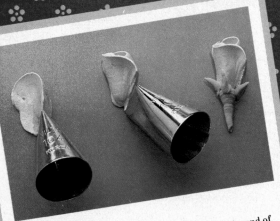

ROSEBUD

1. Make base petal. Hold bag at a 45° angle so that the end of bag points over your right shoulder, fingertips gripping bag facing you. Touch wide end of tip 104 to surface, point narrow end to the right. Squeeze, move forward ¼-in., hesitate so icing fans out, then move back as you stop pressure.

2. Make overlapping center petal. Hold bag in same position as step 1 with wide end of tip touching inside right edge of base petal, narrow end of tip pointing slightly up above base petal. Squeeze as icing catches inside edge of base petal and rolls into interlocking center bud. Stop pressure, touch large end back to surface and pull tip away.

3. Make sepals and calyx directly on cake with tip 3 and thinned icing. Hold bag at a 45° angle to base of bud with end of bag pointing towards you. Touch tip to bud. Squeeze and pull tip up and away from flower, relaxing pressure as you draw sepal to a point. Add three sepals and tip 3 calyx.

SWEET PEA

1. Make center petal. Hold bag at a 45° angle to surface so that back end of bag points toward you. Touch wide end of the tip to bottom of base petal, just inside cupped edge, point narrow end of tip straight up. Squeeze, raise tip slightly and let icing roll into center petal. Stop pressure, lower tip, pull away.

2. Make side petals. Touch wide end of tip to bottom left edge of center rolled petal, point narrow end up and out to the left. Squeeze, lift tip slightly, stop pressure, lower tip, pull away. Repeat procedure for right petal, starting at bottom edge of center petal.

3. Add calyx to flower base with tip 3 and thinned icing. Hold bag at 45° angle to surface so that end of bag points toward you. Insert tip into flower base and hold in place as you squeeze to build up pressure as you draw tip down, narrowing calyx to a point.

FLOWER NAIL FLOWERS

Use Royal or stiffened Buttercream Icing (see recipes p. 82-83) and the tips specified for each flower. We refer only to Buttercream Icing in the instructions that follow. If you use Snow-White Buttercream Icing for flowers, you may air dry them instead of freezing. When decorating with flowers or candy, always make extras to allow for breakage. Instructions usually call for more than you'll need.

Daisy

1. For best results, use Royal Icing (p. 83). Use tip 103 and dot center of nail with icing as guide for flower center. Hold bag at a 45° angle with tip almost parallel to nail surface, wide end of tip pointing to nail center, narrow end pointing out. Now, starting at any point near outer edge of nail, squeeze and move tip towards center icing dot. Stop pressure, pull tip away. Repeat procedure for a total of twelve or more petals.

2. Add tip 4 yellow flower center and press to flatten. For pollen-like effect dampen your finger, press in gold edible glitter, (see p. 122) and then flatten center.

Apple Blossom

1. Use tip 101 or 101s and hold bag at a 45° angle to flower nail with wide end of tip touching nail center, narrow end pointed out ⅛-in. away from nail surface.

2. Squeeze bag and turn nail as you move tip ⅛-in. out from nail center and back, relaxing pressure as you return to starting point.

3. Repeat procedure to make four more petals. Add five tip 1 dots for center.

Chrysanthemum

1. Hold bag at 90° angle to nail and pipe tip 6 mound of icing on nail center. Use tip 79 and very stiff royal icing for short petal effect. Hold bag at a 45° angle to outer base edge of mound, with half-moon opening of tip 79 pointing up. Squeeze row of ½-in. long cupped base petals using pull-out star technique.

2. Add second row of shorter petals atop and in between those in first row. Repeat procedure making each additional row of petals shorter than the previous row.

3. When entire mound is covered add a few stand-up petals to top and tip 1 center dots.

Daffodil and Jonquil

1. Use tip 104 for daffodil or tip 103 for jonquil. Hold bag at a 45° angle to nail, with large end of tip touching nail, narrow end pointed out and almost parallel to nail surface. Squeeze and as you turn nail, move tip out about ½-in. and back to center of nail to form petal. Repeat procedure for five more petals.

2. Dip your fingers in cornstarch and pinch ends of petals to form points.

3. Pipe row-upon-row of tip 2 string circles and top with tip 1 zigzag for center.

Narcissus

Use tip 102 and same procedure as for daffodil to make six ¾-in. long petals. Add tip 1 coil center and tip 1 zigzag.

Violet

1. Use tip 59s and same procedure as for apple blossom to make three ¼-in. long petals and two ⅛-in. base petals.

2. Add two tip 1 center dots.

Pansy

1. Fit two decorating bags with tip 104. Fill one with yellow icing, the other with violet. Hold bag with yellow icing at a 45° angle to nail center, squeeze and move tip out to edge of nail. Turn nail as you squeeze, relax pressure as you return to nail center. Repeat to form second yellow petal. Use same procedure to add two shorter yellow petals atop the first two.

2. Now with bag of violet icing, squeeze out a base petal that equals the width of the yellow petals, using a back and forth hand motion for a ruffled effect.

3. Use a decorator's brush to add veins of violet icing color after flower has air dried. Add tip 1 string loop center.

LILY NAIL FLOWERS

The Wilton Lily Nail Set (see p. 121) lets you make natural-looking flowers with bell-like shapes and cupped, turned-up petals. Different lily nail sizes relate to the size of flowers you can make. The larger the nail, the larger the flower. Always use royal icing for flowers made on the lily nail, (see p. 83 for recipe) since softer icing will not hold their deeply-cupped shapes. To make any flower on the lily nail, place an aluminum foil square in bottom half of nail. Press in top half to form a foil cup. Remove the top half. Lightly spray foil with vegetable oil spray. This makes it easier to remove from foil after icing has dried and reduces breakage. Pipe a flower on the foil cup and lift out flower and foil to dry. Repeat procedure.

Easter Lily

1. Probably the most popular lily nail flower of all. Use tip 68 and 1⅝-in. lily nail. Touch center well of nail with tip and squeeze, pulling petal up and over edge of foil cup. Decrease pressure as you reach tip of petal and hesitate before you stop pressure and pull tip away, drawing petal to a point.

2. Pipe 2 more petals as shown. then pipe 3 more petals in between the open spaces.

3. Add tip 14 star center and push in artificial stamens, (see p. 122).

Grapes

Grapes (p. 62)

Use tip 5 to pipe a tear drop-shaped base; then starting at the base and working up, pipe overlapping beads to cover base. Add tip 349 leaves and tip 1 "e"-motion tendrils. For more about Figure Piping, see The Wilton Way of Cake Decorating books (p. 130).

Wheat

Wheat (p. 62)

Use tip 5 to pipe outline stalks. Overlap for dimension. Add tip 4 pull-out bead grains. Pipe side, then center rows. Trim stalks with tip 103 ribbon bow. Ideal for Thanskgiving cakes, too.

Easy Candy Making

FOR BEST CANDY MAKING RESULTS, USE WILTON CANDY MELTS™* (p. 106.).

Candy Melts take the guesswork out of making candy at home. They melt easily, right to the ideal consistency for molding and dipping, and have a creamy, rich flavor. For a change of taste, they can be flavored with Wilton Candy Flavors (p. 106). See pages 100-107 for all the Wilton CandyMaker products. For more about candy making, order the *Candy Making for Beginners* book or the *Complete Wilton Book of Candy* (p. 106). Our Candy Making Home Study Course tells all (p. 128).

THINGS TO KNOW ABOUT CANDY MELTS.

For melting and molding directions, simply refer to the back of the Candy Melts package. Remember that constant stirring is very important to insure even heating, when using the double-boiler method. Here's a no-mess way of melting in microwave: Fill an uncut disposable decorating bag half-full of Candy Melts. Microwave 1 minute at half power; squeeze candy. Repeat at 30-second intervals until candy is completely melted. Then cut the tip and squeeze melted coating out into candy molds.

To Flavor: The creamy, rich taste can be enhanced by adding approximately ¼ teaspoon Wilton oil-based Candy Flavor (p. 106) to 1 lb. of melted Candy Melts. Never use alcohol based flavorings; they will cause coatings to harden.

To Color: Add Wilton Candy Colors (p. 106) to melted Candy Melts a little at a time. Mix thoroughly before adding more color. Colors tend to deepen as they're mixed. Pastel colored candies are most appetizing, so keep this in mind when tinting. Decorating with Candy Melts: To 1 cup of melted coating, add ¼ teaspoon light corn syrup. Mix well. More corn syrup may be added until coating is a piping consistency, smooth and slightly stiff. Mix well. Fill disposable decorating bag fitted with decorating tip and pipe decorations on candy. Work quickly. Allow coating to set until firm.

TO MOLD STAND-UP CANDY.

Use Wilton 2-pc. molds on p. 103. Cut mold in half along dotted line and snap together. Stand upright. Fill mold with melted coating and gently tap mold to release air bubbles. **To make hollow candy:** Place filled mold in refrigerator for about 5-10 minutes to harden the outside of the mold. Pour out excess. Return mold to refrigerator to harden completely. Unmold. To seal the bottom, cover cookie sheet with waxed paper. Pour a pool of melted Candy Melts that's larger than the opening. Position hollowed candy on top of pool. Let set. Trim excess coating away with a sharp knife. **For solid, stand-up candy:** Fill as for hollow method and refrigerate until firm (approx. 1½ hours). Unmold and trim excess. **To make a candy box:** Fill both halves of the Heart Box mold on p. 103 with melted coating and gently tap to release air bubbles. Place in refrigerator. After a few minutes, when outside is hardened, remove bottom half and pour out excess. Return to refrigerator to harden completely. Unmold. Decorate lid with melted Candy Melts or royal icing. Fill bottom with candy.

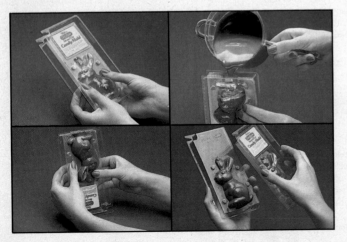

CANDY CUT-OUTS:
You'll love this new, easy method! You'll need melted Candy Melts™* and a 6 or 8-in. square pan (p. 167). Pour coating into center of pan. Tap gently on counter to break up bubbles and to spread coating evenly over bottom. Coating should be about ⅛-in. thick. Place pan in refrigerator for approximately 5-10 minutes (check occasionally, if coating becomes too hard it will be too brittle). Unmold onto hand or soft towels (tap pan gently, if neccessary). Place coating on work surface and with a sharp knife, score into desired shapes. Snap into pieces.

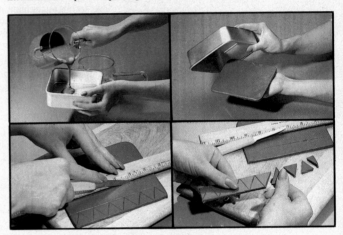

DIPPING CENTERS & MORE

Melt Candy Melts according to package directions. When completely melted, place a Candy Maker center (Center Mixes sold on p. 106), nuts, blotted fruit bits, mini-pretzels, cookies and more, one at a time, into coating. Roll around gently but quickly with Dipping Spoon or Fork (p. 106) until well-covered. Slip the dipper under the center. Scrape off excess coating against edge of bowl or pan. Drop right side up on waxed paper. As candy drops from dipper, twist the thread of coating clinging to dipper and make a swirl on top. Let set at room temperature for 15 minutes.

Hint: To reinforce set dipped candy bottoms and prevent leaks, spread melted coating on bottom and place on side until set.

TO CREATE MULTI-COLOR EFFECTS

"Painting" Method: Use a Decorator's Brush dipped in melted Candy Melts. Paint features or details desired. Let set. Fill mold. Refrigerate until set. Unmold. **"Layering" Method:** Pour melted coating into dry molds to desired height. Refrigerate until partially set. Pour contrasting color melted coating to desired height. Refrigerate until partially set. Repeat until desired numbers of layers are formed. Let candy harden in refrigerator. Unmold. Wilton Classic Candy Molds are available in a wonderful variety of unique and traditional shapes. Their generous depth makes painting and layering fun and easy. See pages 100-102 for our outstanding Classic Candy Molds selection.

HARD CANDY IS SO EASY TO MAKE WITH WILTON EASY MELTS™

Discover how quick 'n fun it is to create jewel-like, delicious hard candies. No thermometer is needed! Complete melt and mold directions right on package. When melting Easy Melts, be sure to use a heavy gauge aluminum saucepan to prevent burning. Mold luscious bite-size treats and lollipops in our quality Hard Candy Molds (p. 105). Be sure to wash molds and dry thoroughly before first use; oil molds before pouring candy syrup into them.

*brand confectionery coating.

Tempting Cake Recipes

PUMPKIN SPICE CAKE

½ cup butter or margarine
1⅓ cups sugar
2 eggs
1 cup canned pumpkin
⅔ cup buttermilk or sour milk
1 Tbsp. pumpkin pie spice
1¾ cups flour
2 tsp. baking powder
1 tsp. baking soda
1 tsp. salt

Cream butter and sugar until fluffy. Add eggs, one at a time, beating well after each addition. Combine pumpkin and buttermilk. Sift together flour, spice, powder, soda and salt; add to creamed mixture alternately with pumpkin mixture, mixing thoroughly after each addition. Bake in generously greased and floured Petite Fancy Ring Mold at 350° for 15 minutes or until cake tests done. Cool for 10 minutes; remove from pan. Cool completely before decorating. Yields enough batter to fill a one-cake-mix pan, two 8-in. layers, one 10-in. layer (baking time: 25-35 min.); or 12 Petite Fancy Ring Mold sections.

Decorate according to instructions on p. 44.

APPLESAUCE FRUITCAKES

See these giveable greats on page 51

1½ cups all-purpose flour
1 tsp. baking soda
½ tsp. baking powder
¼ tsp. each, ground cloves, nutmeg, cinnamon and salt
½ lb. candied cherries
¼ lb. mixed candied fruit
¼ lb. candied pineapple
6 dates
½ cup raisins
¾ cup pecans
¾ cup walnuts
¼ cup butter
½ cup sugar
1 egg
¼ cup water
¾ cup applesauce

Sift and mix flour, baking soda, baking powder, spices and salt; set aside. Cut up fruit* and coarsely chop nuts. Mix fruit and nuts. Cream butter and sugar. Add egg and beat well. Alternately add dry ingredients and water to creamed mixture, beating well after each addition. Mix in fruit, nuts and applesauce. Pour into paper-lined muffin cups. Bake 25 minutes at 350°. Yield: 24 cupcakes.

To decorate, see page 51.

*Hint: Fruit will remain evenly distributed, if you place in a plastic bag, add a small amount of flour and shake to coat evenly.

CHOCOLATE CHEESECAKE

This rich, elegant dessert serves 12. See it on page 64.
Ingredients for graham cracker crust for a 9-in. Springform Pan. 
5 oz. milk chocolate
3-8 oz. packages of cream cheese
¾ cup confectioners sugar
4 large eggs
⅓ cup coffee liqueur
¼ cup butter, melted
1 cup sour cream

Preheat oven to 350°F. Melt chocolate in a heavy saucepan over low heat. Beat cream cheese and sugar together in a large mixing bowl. Beat in eggs, one at a time; mix thoroughly after each addition. Mix in melted chocolate, liqueur, melted butter and sour cream. Blend well. Pour mixture in graham cracker crust-lined Springform Pan. Bake 45 minutes. Turn heat off and prop oven door open. Let cheesecake cool in oven until room temperature. Chill before decorating. (We recommend using unsweetened stabilized whipped cream.)

PUMPKIN ROLL

3 eggs, well beaten
1 cup sugar
⅔ cup pumpkin
1 Tbsp. lemon juice
¾ cup flour
1 tsp. baking powder
2 tsps. cinnamon
½ tsp. ginger
½ tsp. nutmeg
½ tsp. salt
1 cup chopped nuts

Grease and flour pan. Whip eggs until thick and foamy, about 5 minutes. Add sugar gradually to eggs. Fold in pumpkin and lemon juice. Sift together all dry ingredients and fold into egg mixture, beating just until batter is smooth. (You may use electric mixer on low speed.)

Pour into pan, spreading batter to corners. Sprinkle top with nuts. Bake 15 minutes at 375° or until cake springs back when touched lightly. Immediately loosen cake from edges of pan; invert on towel sprinkled with confectioners sugar. While hot, roll cake and towel from narrow end. Cool completely on wire rack.

CREAM CHEESE FILLING RECIPE

2-8 oz. packages cream cheese (softened)
½ cup butter (softened)
2 cups confectioners sugar
1 tsp. vanilla

Cream cheese and butter together, until blended. Add sugar and vanilla; mix well. Reserve 1 cup icing for decorating cake. Unroll cake; remove towel and spread remaing filling on inside. Roll up cake; wrap in waxed paper, then foil. Refrigerate until filling sets before decorating.

Decorate according to instructions on p. 44.

POUND CAKE

We recommend this recipe for all Wilton 3-D mold pans.* It's also ideal for cakes to be covered with fondant icing. Ingredient amounts in parentheses are for Snowman Pan. Yields 4 cups of batter. (2 recipes needed for 3-D cake.) Larger amounts yield 5 cups of batter. Enough to fill molds that snap together, the Bunny or Lamb Pan for example.

2 (1¼) cups all purpose flour
1¾ (1) cup sugar
2 (¼) tsp. mace
4 (2) eggs
½ (⅓) cup milk
1 (⅔) cup butter or margarine
1 (½) tsp. vanilla

Preheat oven to 350°. Grease and flour pan. Place all ingredients in a large bowl and beat at low speed until moistened. Beat at medium-high speed for 10 minutes. Pour into prepared pan. Bake 3-D pans for approximately 1 hour and 15 minutes; 50-60 minutes for Snowman Pan.

*Some 3-D pans will take more batter than this recipe yields. Refer to pan instructions for exact amount.

GINGERBREAD CAKE

Delight everyone with a Christmas Cottage. See it complete on page 52.

2 packages 2-layer spice cake mix
⅔ cup molasses
4 eggs

Preheat oven to 350°. Grease and flour House Pan. Prepare 1 cake mix as directed on package, except substitute ⅓ of molasses for ⅓ cup oil and use 2 eggs. Pour batter into prepared pan. Bake at 350° for 50-55 minutes or until toothpick inserted in center comes out clean. Cool 15 minutes; release from pan. Repeat for other half. Slice crowns so that cakes will fit together easily when iced. Bottom of house may have to be sliced so cakes will sit level.

To decorate, see p. 52.

DATE & FIG TART

Pastry:
1½ cups all-purpose flour
¼ tsp. salt
2 tsps. sugar
6 Tbsp. butter, chilled & cut
    in small pieces
1 Tbsp. shortening
1 egg, lightly beaten
½ tsp. lemon juice
1 Tbsp. ice water

Place flour, salt and sugar in mixer bowl. Add butter and shortening; mix only until mixture resembles coarse meal. Stir egg, lemon juice and ice water together; add gradually to flour-butter mixture, mix only until dough forms a ball. Wrap and chill dough for at least 1 hour. On a lightly floured surface, roll pastry ⅛-in. thick. Gently place dough in pan without stretching. Bake at 350° for 5 mins.

Filling:
⅓ cup butter, softened
⅔ cup sugar
3 eggs, separated
1 tsp. grated lemon peel
1 tsp. cinnamon
½ tsp. each, ground nutmeg &
    ground cloves
½ tsp. salt
¾ cup ground hazelnuts
½ cup flour
1 tsp. baking powder
⅔ cup chopped walnuts
½ cup each, finely chopped
    dried figs & dates

Preheat oven at 350°. Cream butter and sugar in large mixer bowl until light and fluffy. Stir in egg yolks, lemon peel, cinnamon, nutmeg, cloves, salt and hazelnuts. Beat egg whites until stiff. On low speed, blend egg whites into egg yolk mixture. Mix flour, baking powder, walnuts, figs and dates. Fold into egg mixture. Pour into pastry shell. Bake 40-45 mins. at 350° or until a wooden pick inserted in center comes out clean. Cool completely before decorating, see p. 76.

PENNSYLVANIA DUTCH CHOCOLATE CAKE

3 oz. unsweetened chocolate
½ cup water
1 cup sour cream
1¾ cups cake flour
1½ tsps. baking powder
1 tsp. baking soda
½ tsp. salt
¾ cup butter or margarine
1 cup sugar
¾ cup firmly packed
    brown sugar
3 large eggs
2 tsps. vanilla

Grease and flour two 8-in. round pans. Heat chocolate and water in heavy saucepan over low heat until chocolate is melted; stir constantly. Cool but do not allow chocolate to set up; add sour cream and blend well. Mix flour, powder, soda and salt together; set aside. Cream butter. Gradually add sugars; beat until light and fluffy. Add eggs, one at a time; mix well after each addition. Add dry ingredients alternately with chocolate mixture; mix well. Add vanilla. Pour into prepared pans. Bake at 350° for 30-35 minutes, or until wooden pick inserted in center comes out clean. Cool 10 minutes; release. Cool completely before decorating, see p. 79.

BLACK BOTTOM PIE

½ cup sugar
1 Tbsp. cornstarch
2 cups milk, scalded
4 beaten egg yolks
1 tsp. vanilla
1 cup semisweet chocolate chips
1 Tbsp. unflavored gelatin
¼ cup cold water
2 Tbsps. rum
4 egg whites
½ cup sugar

Pastry for double crust; divide into 2 balls. Roll-out dough; place one in pie pan. Use remainder to decorate (see p. 76).

Combine sugar and cornstarch in heavy 2-quart saucepan. Slowly add scalded milk to yolks. Add yolk mixture to sugar; blend well. Cook and stir over medium heat until mixture thickens and coats spoon. Remove from heat; add vanilla.

For black bottom: Add chocolate chips to 1 cup of custard; stir until melted. Pour into cooled 10-in. pastry shell; chill. Soften gelatin in cold water; add to remaining custard. Stir until gelatin is dissolved. Add rum and stir. Chill until slightly thickened. Beat egg whites until soft peaks form. Gradually add sugar and beat until stiff peaks form.

Fold in custard. Pour over chocolate layer; chill until set (approximately 2 hours).

See decorating instructions on page 76.

MARY TODD LINCOLN'S VANILLA ALMOND CAKE

1½ cups sugar
1 cup butter
1 tsp. vanilla
2¾ cups sifted cake flour
1 Tbsp. baking powder
1⅓ cups milk
1 cup finely chopped almonds
6 stiffly beaten egg whites

Preheat oven to 375°. Grease and flour two 8-in. round pans. Cream together sugar, butter and vanilla. Stir together cake flour and baking powder; add dry ingredients to creamed mixture alternately with milk. Stir in almonds. Gently fold in egg whites. Pour into prepared pans. Bake at 375° for 25-30 mins. Cool 10 mins.; release. Cool completely.

Fluffy Frosting:
1 cup sugar
⅓ cup water
¼ tsp. cream of tartar
dash of salt
2 egg whites, stiffly beaten
1 tsp. vanilla

In a heavy 1-qt. saucepan, combine sugar, water, cream of tartar and salt. Place over high heat; stir until sugar dissolves. Bring mixture to a boil. In mixer bowl, beat egg whites until stiff peaks form. While beating slowly, gradually pour hot syrup into egg whites until stiff peaks form, approx. 7 mins. Beat in vanilla. Fill, ice and decorate, see p. 78.

Dessert Recipes

BOSTON CREAM PIE

"Cake":

¼ cup butter
1 cup sugar
2 eggs, well beaten
1¾ cups flour

2 tsp. baking powder
¼ tsp. salt
½ cup milk
1 tsp. vanilla

Preheat oven to 350°. Generously butter 8-in. bevel and 8-in. round pans. Cream butter; add sugar gradually, beating well after each addition. Add eggs; beat well. Stir dry ingredients together; add to creamed mixture alternately with milk, beating after each addition. Add vanilla; blend well. Pour batter into prepared pans. Bake at 350° for approximately 30 mins. Let cool 10 mins. in pan; release. Cool completely.

Cream Filling:

5 Tbsps. flour
¾ cup sugar
¼ tsp. salt

2 cups milk, scalded
2 eggs
1 tsp. vanilla

Mix dry ingredients together in a double boiler and gradually add milk while stirring constantly. Cook mixture over boiling water until mixture thickens, approx. 3 min. Pour approx. ¼ cup of mixture into eggs and mix well; add to remaining milk mixture and cook 2 minutes. Remove from heat; add vanilla. Cool completely.

Glaze: ¼ cup whipping cream
¾ cup dark cocoa Candy Melts™* wafers, chopped

Heat whipping cream to a boil. Remove from heat. Stir in Candy Melts until smooth and completely melted. See page 77 for torting, filling, glazing and decorating instructions.

*brand confectionery coating

HAWAIIAN PINEAPPLE CAKE

1—2-layer white cake mix
1 package (4 serving size) toasted coconut instant pudding and pie filling
4 eggs

½ cup pineapple juice
⅓ cup light rum
¼ cup oil
2½ cups flaked coconut

Grease and flour Angel Food Pan. Blend all ingredients in large mixer bowl. Beat 4 minutes at medium speed. Pour into prepared pan. Bake at 350° for 40-50 minutes or until cake springs back when lightly pressed. Cool in pan 15 minutes; release. Cool completely before decorating. Ice with stabilized whipped cream (double recipe), p. 82; cover with 2½ cups flaked coconut. See p. 79.

NEW YORK STRAWBERRY CHEESECAKE

Crust:

1 cup all-purpose flour
¼ cup sugar
1 tsp. grated lemon rind
¼ tsp. vanilla extract

1 egg yolk
½ cup unsalted butter, chilled and cut into small pieces

Place all ingredients in large mixer bowl, combine together until dough forms a ball. Dust with flour; wrap in waxed paper. Refrigerate 1 hour. Preheat oven to 400°. Place chilled dough in 9-in. Springform Pan. Pat dough evenly over the bottom and sides (approx. 2-in. high). Bake for 10 min.; cool to room temperature.

Cheese Filling:

1¼ lbs. softened cream cheese
¾ cup sugar
1½ Tbsps. all-purpose flour
1 tsp. each grated lemon and orange rind

½ tsp. vanilla extract
3 eggs
¼ cup heavy cream

Preheat oven to 250°. Place cream cheese in a large mixer bowl; beat at high speed until smooth and creamy. Gradually beat in sugar until well blended. Add flour, grated rinds, vanilla, eggs and cream; beat well. Pour filling into cooled crust. Bake 1 hour; cool at room temperature. Chill before decorating, see page 77.

LADY BALTIMORE CAKE

1 cup butter
2 cups sugar
3½ cups sifted all-purpose flour
1¼ cups milk
1 Tbsp. baking powder

½ tsp. salt
1 tsp. each vanilla extract & almond extract
6 egg whites, stiffy beaten

Preheat oven to 350°. Grease and flour three 8-in. square pans. Cream butter and sugar until light and fluffy. Sift together flour, baking powder and salt; add to creamed mixture alternately with milk. Add flavorings; mix well. Fold in beaten egg whites. Divide batter equally in pans. Bake at 350° for 12-15 mins. or until cakes spring back when lightly touched. Let cool in pan for 10 mins.; release. Allow cakes to cool completely before decorating.

White Frosting:

2 cups sugar
⅔ cup water
½ tsp. cream of tartar
dash of salt
4 egg whites, stiffy beaten

2 tsp. vanilla
½ cup raisins, chopped
1¼ cups chopped walnuts
¼ cup chopped maraschino cherries

In a heavy 2-qt. saucepan, combine sugar, water, cream of tartar and salt. Place over high heat; stir until sugar is dissolved. Bring mixture to a boil. In mixing bowl, beat egg whites till stiff peaks form, approx. 7 mins. Beat in vanilla. Fold raisins, ¼ cup walnuts (reserve 1 cup for sides) and cherries into 3 cups icing for filling. Fill, stack layers, ice, decorate, see p. 78.

Cookie Recipes

GINGERBREAD COOKIES

See some friendly faces on page 50.

1/2 cup butter or margarine, softened	1 tsp. cinnamon
1/2 cup brown sugar	1 tsp. ginger
1/2 cup molasses	1/2 tsp. salt
3-1/2 cups all-purpose flour	1/4 tsp. cloves
1 tsp. baking soda	1/3 cup water

Preheat oven to 375°. Cream butter and sugar thoroughly with electric mixer. Beat in molasses. Blend all dry ingredients. Alternately add blended dry ingredients and water to the butter-sugar mixture. Dough will become stiff, so that last dry addition may need to be blended by hand. Work dough until it is a smooth consistency. If dough sticks to your hands, lightly dust them with flour. Careful though, too much flour makes dough dry and hard. When dough is easy to work, roll out and cut cookies. Bake on a lightly oiled cookie sheet at 375° for 8-10 min. When cool, decorate, see p. 50. Yields: Approximately 30 cookies.

COOKIE ICING RECIPE

Here's an icing that dries to a shiny, hard finish and tastes good, too. It works well for filling in cookie top designs that have been outlined with this special icing. Do outline and filling in with tip 2 or 3. When dry, cookies can easily be stacked.

1 cup sifted confectioners sugar
2 tsps. milk
2 tsps. light corn syrup

Place sugar and milk in bowl. Stir until mixed thoroughly. Add corn syrup and mix well. For filling in areas, use thinned icing (add small amounts of light corn syrup until desired consistency is reached).

EVEN EASIER! USE WILTON COOKIE MAKER COOKIE ICING MIX.
It's ideal for all cookie decorating. So versatile...can be flavored and made to different consistencies for icing, piping and filling. See p. 112 to order.

BROWN BUTTER COOKIES

Rich, chewy cookies with an almond flavor. As an alternate to cake, try this recipe for petit fours.

3/4 cup butter
1-2/3 cups confectioners sugar
1 cup powdered almonds
1/3 cup flour
5 egg whites

Preheat oven to 350°. Cook butter over medium heat just until light brown (watch closely, butter burns easily). Mix the sugar, powdered almonds and flour together. Gently stir in egg whites, then the hot butter. Baking: Generously butter Tartlet, Petit Fours and Pastry Molds or Mini Muffin Pan. Fill each mold halfway with the batter and place on a cookie sheet. Bake at 350° for 13-15 minutes. Remove immediately. Ice and decorate with melted Cookie Dips candy wafers. Yields approximately 2 dozen.

EASY FRUIT GLAZE

Add a slightly tangy flavor and glistening effect to cakes you plan to decorate simply with fruit and minimal icing trims.

Recipe
Heat fruit jelly or preserves (strain, if necessary). (Note: Use a currant jelly for dark fruits or apricot preserves for yellow cakes or light fruits.) Use the "juice" to glaze cake or fruit according to the following instructions.

For cakes: Fruit glaze may be used as a coating under fondant as well as a shiny glaze for cakes to be decorated with fruit. Prepare cake by brushing all loose crumbs from surface. Use a pastry brush to evenly coat completely cooled cake with warmed glaze.

For fruit: Drain canned, thawed or fresh fruit. Blot fruit dry with paper toweling, if necessary. Place fruit on rack over cookie pan. Spoon glaze over fruit to coat evenly. Let set until dry. Arrange on cake top.

ROLL-OUT COOKIES

Here's a success-tested, firm vanilla sugar cookie dough for cut-out cookies.

3/4 cup butter or margarine, softened	1 tsp. vanilla
3/4 cup sugar	2 tsps. baking powder
2 large eggs	2-3/4 cups flour

Preheat oven to 400°. In a large bowl, cream butter and sugar with an electric mixer. Beat in eggs and vanilla. Add baking powder and flour one cup at a time, mixing after each addition. The dough will be very stiff; blend last flour in by hand. Do not chill dough. Note: Dough can be tinted with Paste Icing Color. Add small amounts until desired color is reached. For chocolate cookies: Stir in 3-ozs. melted, unsweetened cocoa (if dough becomes too stiff, add water, a teaspoon at a time). Divide dough into 2 balls. On a floured surface, roll each ball in a circle approximately 12-inches in diameter and 1/8-in. thick. Dip cutters in flour before each use. Bake cookies on ungreased cookie sheet on top rack of oven for 6-7 minutes, or until cookies are lightly browned.

MOUTHWATERING BUTTER COOKIES

This cookie dough is ideal for molds or for piping. To use for cut-out cookies, just chill and roll out.

1 cup butter	3 cups flour
1 cup sugar	1 tsp. cinnamon or
2 large eggs	1 tsp. grated lemon rind

Preheat oven to 375°. (If using in cookie molds, bake at 325°.) Cream butter; add sugar gradually. Blend until very light and creamy; beat in eggs. Add flour and cinnamon (or lemon rind). Stir until blended. For molded cookie: Press dough into ungreased mold and pick 2 or 3 times with fork (to keep dough from puffing while baking). Dough should be slightly below the top of mold. Bake 10 minutes or until edges are just light brown. Remove from molds immediately. For pastry bag or cut-out cookies: Bake on an ungreased cookie sheet for 10-15 mins. Remove from sheet immediately. Recipe yields 5 dozen molded or 7 dozen piped cookies.

PRESENTING
THE WILTON COLLECTION OF
FINE PRODUCTS.

NOW,
BAKING
IS EASIER.
DECORATING
MORE FUN.
ENTERTAINING
MORE JUBILANT.
LIFE
MORE EXCITING!

CLASSIC CANDY MOLDS

Choose your favorites from these two pages! Each clear plastic sheet mold (7⁹/₁₆ x 8¼-in.) molds 5 to 16 candies. Use with Wilton Candy Melts (p. 106). Made in U.S.A.

Create a Party Mood Any Day With These Unique Shapes.

1. CORDIAL GLASSES.
6 molds, 1 design per sheet.
2114-P-1242. **$1.89 each**

2. ROSES. 10 molds, 2 designs per sheet.
2114-P-1511. **$1.89 each**

3. SEA LIFE. 10 molds, 5 designs per sheet.
2114-P-2702. **$1.89 each**

4. HEARTS & FLOWERS.
10 molds, 3 designs.
2114-P-4236. **$1.89 each**

5. PINEAPPLES & FLOWERS. 8 molds, 2 designs.
2114-P-513. **$1.89 each**

6. DIAMONDS II. 8 molds, 3 designs per sheet.
2114-P-531. **$1.89 each**

7. PEANUTS. 12 molds, 1 design per sheet.
2114-P-556. **$1.89 each**

8. LOCKETS. 12 molds, 3 designs per sheet.
2114-P-4208. **$1.89 each**

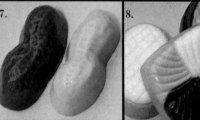

9. MINT DISCS. ¼-in. deep.
12 molds, 1 design per sheet.
2114-P-1226. **$1.89 each**

10. RIBBONS & SCROLLS.
10 molds, 2 designs per sheet.
2114-P-424. **$1.89 each**

11. FANCY CHOCOLATES I.
12 molds, 2 designs per sheet.
2114-P-1269. **$1.89 each**

12. FANCY CHOCOLATES II.
14 molds, 1 design per sheet.
2114-P-1285. **$1.89 each**

13. LEAVES. 10 molds, 2 designs per sheet.
2114-P-629. **$1.89 each**

14. SQUARES. 12 molds, 1 design per sheet.
2114-P-955. **$1.89 each**

15. CAMEOS. 10 molds, 2 designs per sheet.
2114-P-408. **$1.89 each**

16. ROUNDS. 8 molds, 2 designs per sheet.
2114-P-466. **$1.89 each**

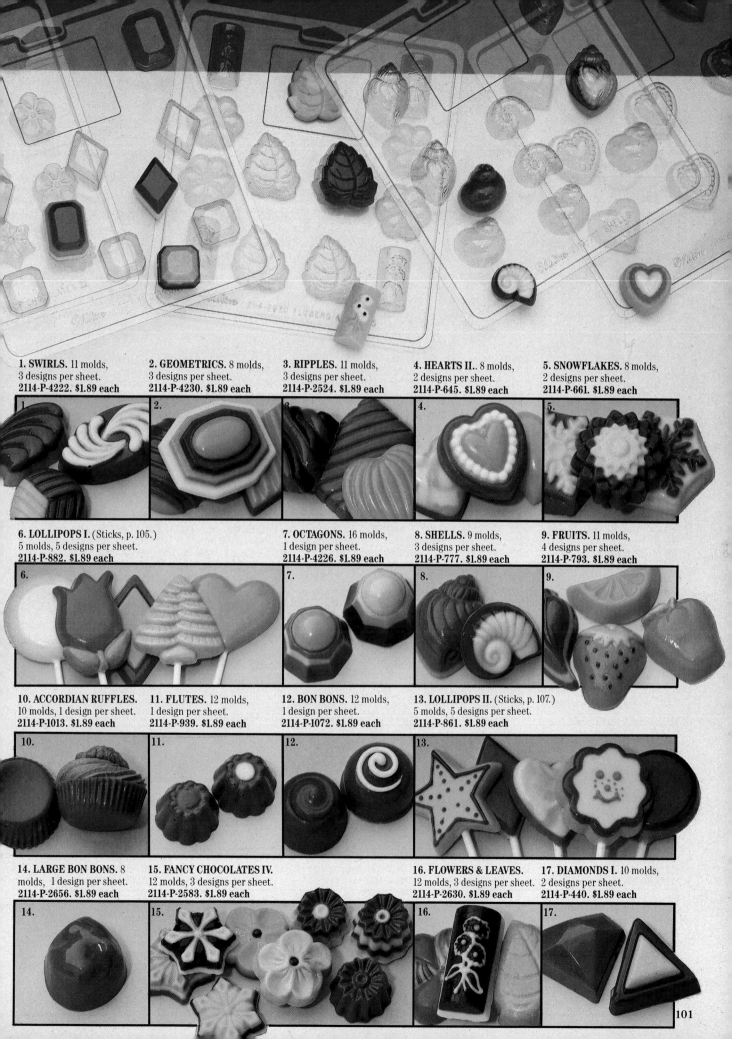

1. SWIRLS. 11 molds,
3 designs per sheet.
2114-P-4222. $1.89 each

2. GEOMETRICS. 8 molds,
3 designs per sheet.
2114-P-4230. $1.89 each

3. RIPPLES. 11 molds,
3 designs per sheet.
2114-P-2524. $1.89 each

4. HEARTS II.. 8 molds,
2 designs per sheet.
2114-P-645. $1.89 each

5. SNOWFLAKES. 8 molds,
2 designs per sheet.
2114-P-661. $1.89 each

6. LOLLIPOPS I. (Sticks, p. 105.)
5 molds, 5 designs per sheet.
2114-P-882. $1.89 each

7. OCTAGONS. 16 molds,
1 design per sheet.
2114-P-4226. $1.89 each

8. SHELLS. 9 molds,
3 designs per sheet.
2114-P-777. $1.89 each

9. FRUITS. 11 molds,
4 designs per sheet.
2114-P-793. $1.89 each

10. ACCORDIAN RUFFLES.
10 molds, 1 design per sheet.
2114-P-1013. $1.89 each

11. FLUTES. 12 molds,
1 design per sheet.
2114-P-939. $1.89 each

12. BON BONS. 12 molds,
1 design per sheet.
2114-P-1072. $1.89 each

13. LOLLIPOPS II. (Sticks, p. 107.)
5 molds, 5 designs per sheet.
2114-P-861. $1.89 each

14. LARGE BON BONS. 8
molds, 1 design per sheet.
2114-P-2656. $1.89 each

15. FANCY CHOCOLATES IV.
12 molds, 3 designs per sheet.
2114-P-2583. $1.89 each

16. FLOWERS & LEAVES.
12 molds, 3 designs per sheet.
2114-P-2630. $1.89 each

17. DIAMONDS I. 10 molds,
2 designs per sheet.
2114-P-440. $1.89 each

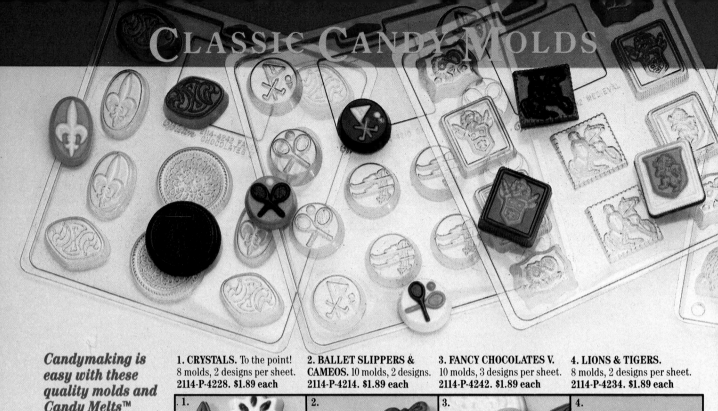

Candymaking is easy with these quality molds and Candy Melts™

Each clear plastic mold is 7⁹⁄₁₆ x 8¼-in.

1. CRYSTALS. To the point! 8 molds, 2 designs per sheet. 2114-P-4228. **$1.89 each**

2. BALLET SLIPPERS & CAMEOS. 10 molds, 2 designs. 2114-P-4214. **$1.89 each**

3. FANCY CHOCOLATES V. 10 molds, 3 designs per sheet. 2114-P-4242. **$1.89 each**

4. LIONS & TIGERS. 8 molds, 2 designs per sheet. 2114-P-4234. **$1.89 each**

5. TEDDY BEARS & GUM BALL MACHINES. Super sweet! 8 molds, 2 designs. 2114-P-4232. **$1.89 each**

6. PIANOS & TREBLE CLEF. 9 molds, 3 designs per sheet. 2114-P-4206. **$1.89 each**

7. SPORTS. Turn pro! 12 molds, 3 designs per sheet. 2114-P-4210. **$1.89 each**

8. MEDIEVAL. 10 molds, 4 designs per sheet. 2114-P-4212. **$1.89 each**

9. CLASSIC CARS. Vrrooom! 10 molds, 3 designs per sheet. 2114-P-4238. **$1.89 each**

10. CHINESE SYMBOLS. 12 molds, 4 designs per sheet. 2114-P-4220. **$1.89 each**

11. WATER FOWL. Best birds! 11 molds, 4 designs per sheet. 2114-P-4224. **$1.89 each**

12. LARGE EGGS. 2 x 1½ x ½-in. deep. 8 per sheet. 2114-P-1358. **$1.89 each**

13. EASTER BUNNIES. Critters in a row! 12 per sheet. 2114-P-1200. **$1.89 each**

14. EGGS. Measure about 1 x 1½-in. long. 14 per sheet. 2114-P-998. **$1.89 each**

15. HEARTS I. Love-ly. 12 molds, 3 designs per sheet. 2114-P-1030. **$1.89 each**

16. JACK-O-LANTERNS. 2½-in. wide. 3 per sheet. 2114-P-1056. **$1.89 each**

17. CHRISTMAS I. With 8 molds, 7 designs per sheet. 2114-P-4136. **$1.89 each**

18. CHRISTMAS II. With 10 molds, 9 designs per sheet. 2114-P-4152. **$1.89 each**

19. CHRISTMAS TREES. 12 molds, 1 design per sheet. 2114-P-1099. **$1.89 each**

3-D SPECIALTY MOLDS

Clear plastic molds made in U.S.A.
Use with Wilton Candy Melts™ (p. 106).

Plastic molds come in various sizes

1. NEW! BOTTLES. 2-pc. clear mold for solid or liquor-filled candies. About 2 in. high, 5 molds per sheet. **2114-P-2217, $2.49 each**

2. NEW! CONES. 2-pc. clear mold makes solid or hollow cones. Pipe in fillings! About 1¼ in. high, 5 molds per sheet. **2114-P-2215, $2.49 each**

3. EGG MOLD SET. Use these plastic 2-pc. molds for sugar, candy or ice cream treats. Includes one each: 5 x 4-in., 4½ x 3-in., 3 x 2-in. **1404-P-1040. $3.99 set**

4. PANDA MOLD. Clear plastic mold makes solid or hollow candy panda. Use with sugar or ice cream, too! About 3½-in. high. **2114-P-1463. $2.49 each**

5. PANDA STAND-UP MOLD. Aluminum 2-pc. mold/pan is perfect for candy, sugar, ice cream, even baking cakes! About 5-in. high. **518-P-489. $4.99 each**

1.

2.

3.

Plastic egg molds made in Hong Kong.

4.   5.

Aluminum Panda Mold made in Korea.

6. HEART BOX. Fill with candy! About 7-in. across. **1902-P-3218. $2.29 each**

7. VALENTINE HEART. With base, about 3½-in. high. **2114-P-3245. $2.49 each**

8. BASKET. Fill with drop flowers! About 3½-in. high. **2114-P-1404. $2.49 each**

9. LAMB. Easter treat is about 3¼-in. high. **2114-P-3229. $2.49 each**

10. BUNNY. Rare rabbit is about 4¼-in. high. **2114-P-1390. $2.49 each**

6.

7.

8.

9.

10.

11. PUMPKIN. Smiling friend is about 3-in. high. **2114-P-1447. $2.49 each**

12. TURKEY. Lil' Gobbler is about 3-in. high. **2114-P-1420. $2.49 each**

13. SNOWMAN. Winter buddy is about 4¼-in. high. **2114-P-3202. $2.49 each**

14. CHRISTMAS TREE. About 4¼-in. high. **2114-P-4012. $2.49 each**

15. SANTA. Molds a candy Santa about 4-in. high. **2114-P-1374. $2.49 each**

11.

12.

13.

14.

15.

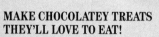

MAKE CHOCOLATEY TREATS THEY'LL LOVE TO EAT!

Each quality, clear plastic sheet mold is 7⁹/₁₆ x 8¼-in. Use with Wilton Candy Melts (p. 106). Made in U.S.A.

1. 3-D STRAWBERRY SHORTCAKE.™* Perky favorite stands 4-in. tall. **2114-P-1692. $2.49 each**

2. STRAWBERRY SHORTCAKE.™ 8 molds & 2 lollipops; 7 designs. **2114-P-1676. $2.29 each** *© 1983 American Greetings Corp.

3. MICKEY MOUSE® & FRIENDS. 6 molds & 2 lollipops; 6 designs. **2114-P-1781. $2.29 each** © 1984 Walt Disney Productions.

4. RAINBOW BRITE.™ So popular! 4 molds & 2 lollipops; 6 designs. **2114-P-2147. $2.29 each** © 1983 Hallmark Cards, Inc.

5. CLOWNS. Make 4 different oh-so-lickable lollipops! **2114-P-4110. $1.89 each**

6. BEARS. Fun-time mold makes 4 different lollipops. **2114-P-4055. $1.89 each**

7. CAT & MOUSE. The chase is on! Makes 4 different lollipop treats. **2114-P-4039. $1.89 each**

DESSERT MOLDS. Your favorite Sesame Street™ characters! Mold yogurt, jello, other tasty treats!

A. BIG BIRD™ STAND-UP MOLD. Lovable character stands about 4-in. high. **2114-P-2145. $2.49 each**

B. SESAME STREET™ I. Sheet mold has 4 molds & 2 lollipops; 6 designs. **2114-P-1765. $2.29 each**

C. SESAME STREET™ II. Add 6 different molds & 2 lollipops to your collection. **2114-P-1740. $2.29 each**

HARD CANDY MOLDS

SPARKLING HOMEMADE CANDIES EASY AS 1-2-3!

Special food-approved plastic is able to withstand the high temperature of hot candy syrup. Use with Easy Melts (p. 106), your favorite hard candy recipe, even Candy Melts! Sheet size: 7⁹/₁₆ x 8¼-in.

1. LOLLIPOP STICKS. Sturdy paper sticks are 4½-in. long. 50 sticks/pack.
1912-P-1006. $1.09 pack

2. LOLLIPOP BAGS. Plastic candy wraps. Fifty 3 x 4-in. bags/pack.
1912-P-2347. $1.99 pack

3. MICKEY MOUSE® & FRIENDS. 2 molds & 5 lollipops per sheet.
2115-P-316. $1.99 each
© 1984 Walt Disney Productions.

4. STRAWBERRY SHORTCAKE™ 2 molds & 5 lollipops per sheet.
2115-P-348. $1.99 each
© 1984 American Greetings Corp.

5. SMURFS.™ Cartoon fun! 7 lollipops per sheet.
2115-P-318. $1.99 each
© 1984 Peyo. Licensed by Wallace Berrie & Co., Van Nuys, CA

6. NEW! RAINBOW BRITE™ LOLLIPOPS. Cute! 6 lollipops, 3 designs per sheet.
2115-P-354. $1.99 each
© 1983 Hallmark Cards, Inc.

7. NEW! GARFIELD. Zany! 4 lollipops, 4 designs per sheet.
2115-P-360. $1.99 each
© 1984 United Features Syndicate, Inc.

    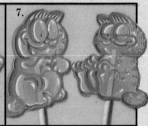

8. ROSE CAMEO. Dainty! 13 molds, 1 design per sheet.
2115-P-320. $1.99 each

9. NEW! RASPBERRIES. 16 molds per sheet.
2115-P-362. $1.99 each

10. ANIMALS. Man's best friends! 5 lollipops per sheet.
2115-P-350. $1.99 each

11. CLOWNS. Circus fun! 5 lollipops per sheet.
2115-P-344. $1.99 each

12. VARIETY LOLLIPOPS I. 5 lollipops per sheet.
2115-P-340. $1.99 each

13. STARS. Bright idea! 16 molds, 1 design per sheet.
2115-P-336. $1.99 each

14. SNOWFLAKES. 16 molds, 2 designs per sheet.
2115-P-332. $1.99 each

15. FAIRYTALE ANIMALS. 4 cute lollipops per sheet.
2115-P-342. $1.99 each

16. TREATS. Fun food! 5 lollipops per sheet.
2115-P-352. $1.99 each

17. VARIETY LOLLIPOPS II. 5 pretty lollipops per sheet.
2115-P-338. $1.99 each

    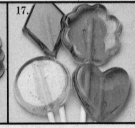

18. HEARTS. Little kisses! 15 molds, 1 design per sheet.
2115-P-322. $1.99 each

19. NEW! CLOVER. Lucky you! 16 molds per sheet.
2115-P-364. $1.99 each

20. CHICK IN EGG. For Easter! 12 molds per sheet.
2115-P-328. $1.99 each

21. RABBITS. Hop to it! 12 molds, 1 design per sheet.
2115-P-330. $1.99 each

22. NEW! EASTER LOLLIPOPS. 5 per sheet.
2115-P-356. $1.99 each

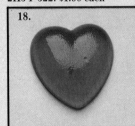  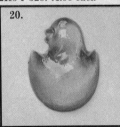  

23. HALLOWEEN. Spooky! 5 different lollipops/sheet.
2115-P-324. $1.99 each

24. PUMPKIN. Trick or Treat! 12 molds, 1 design per sheet.
2115-P-326. $1.99 each

25. BELLS. A sound idea! 16 molds, 1 design per sheet.
2115-P-314. $1.99 each

26. CHRISTMAS TREES. 13 molds per sheet.
2115-P-334. $1.99 each

27. NEW! HOLIDAY LOLLIPOPS. 5 designs.
2115-P-358. $1.99 each

   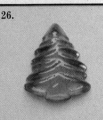 

Wilton CandyMaker

1. CANDY MELTS™ brand confectionery coating. 14 oz. bags. (Certified Kosher.) **$2.50 each**
LIGHT COCOA. (All-natural, cocoa flavor) 1911-P-544
DARK COCOA. (All-natural, cocoa flavor) 1911-P-358
ORANGE. (Available fall only.) 1911-P-584.
GREEN. 1911-P-404.   WHITE. 1911-P-498.
PINK. 1911-P-447.   PEANUT BUTTER.
YELLOW. 1911-P-463.   1911-P-562.

2. CANDY CRUNCHES. Add texture and flavor to your homemade candy. 8 oz. bags. **$1.99 each**
TOASTED COCONUT. 1913-P-994.
GOLDEN CRUNCH. 1913-P-996.

3. LIQUOR CREME MIX. Make liquor-flavored creme center candies. Just add fresh butter and liquor. 9 oz. **1911-P-1399. $2.39 each**

4. CANDY CENTER MIXES. For dipping, filling!
CREME CENTER MIX. 1911-P-1901…
CHOCOLATE FLAVORED. 1911-P-1903…
CHERRY. 1911-P-1905 . . . . **$2.39 each** (9 oz.)

ORANGE. 1911-P-2130…   MAPLE. 1911-P-2032…
RASPBERRY. 1911-P-2091…   LEMON. 1911-P-2059…
STRAWBERRY. 1911-P-2075 . . . . . **$3.99 each** (16 oz.)

5. CANDY WAFER & FONDANT MIX. Ice cakes smooth, make mints, more! 1 lb. can.
1911-P-1427. $3.99 each

6. MARSHMALLOW CENTER MIX. Perfect for filling 3-D candies (see molds, p. 103)! 1 lb. can.
1911-P-1443. $3.99 each

7. CANDY FILLINGS. Ready-to-use! **$3.99 each**
CARAMEL FILLING. 1911-P-1400. 16 oz.
COCONUT FILLING. 1911-P-1028. 16 oz.
NOUGAT FILLING. 1911-P-1488. 10 oz.

8. CANDY FLAVOR. Oil-based formula for flavoring Candy Melts.™ 1 oz. bottles. **$1.99 each**
PEPPERMINT.   RUM. 1913-P-705.
  1913-P-403.   ALMOND. 1913-P-802.
LEMON. 1913-P-431.   CREME DE MENTHE.
ORANGE. 1913-P-535.   1913-P-821.
CINNAMON. 1913-P-470.   MAPLE. 1913-P-720.
BUTTERSCOTCH.   CARAMEL. 1913-P-845.
  1913-P-497.   STRAWBERRY.
CHERRY. 1913-P-519.   1913-P-861.
PEPPERMINT HARD CANDY FLAVOR. 604-P-1176.

9. CANDY COLORS. ¾-oz. bottles. **$1.99 each**
RED. 1913-P-1124.   BLUE. 1913-P-1167.
YELLOW. 1913-P-1248.   ORANGE. 1913-P-1205.
GREEN. 1913-P-1183.   PINK. 1913-P-1140.
VIOLET. 1913-P-1221.

10. EASY MELTS.™ Easy-melting hard candy discs are pre-flavored and pre-colored. Use with Wilton Hard Candy Molds. 16 oz. bags. **$2.50 each**
CHERRY. 1911-P-1109.   RASPBERRY. 1911-P-1117.
GRAPE. 1911-P-1119.   ROOT BEER. 1911-P-1115.
LEMON. 1911-P-1107.   BLUE PEPPERMINT.
LIME. 1911-P-1103.   1911-P-1113.
ORANGE. 1911-P-1105.

11. THE COMPLETE WILTON BOOK OF CANDY.
902-P-1243. **$12.99 each**

12. CANDY MAKING FOR BEGINNERS—REVISED EDITION. 902-P-1361. **$1.99 each**

13. EASY-POUR FUNNEL. 5 x 4-in. wide; nylon.
1904-P-552. **$3.99 each**

14. CANDY THERMOMETER. Proper scale for hard candy, nougat, tempering chocolate, more!
1904-P-1168. **$12.99 each**

15-16. CANDY DIPPING TOOLS. White plastic, 7¾-in. long. **$1.99 each**
15. DIPPING FORK. 1904-P-749.
16. DIPPING SPOON. 1904-P-714.

17. 4-PC. DIPPING SET. Sturdy metal with wooden handles. 9-in. long. Spoon & 3 forks.
1904-P-838. **$12.99 set**

NOT SHOWN: 2-PC. DIPPING SET. Includes a 2-prong fork and spoon. (Shown in #17.)
1904-P-925. **$6.99 set**

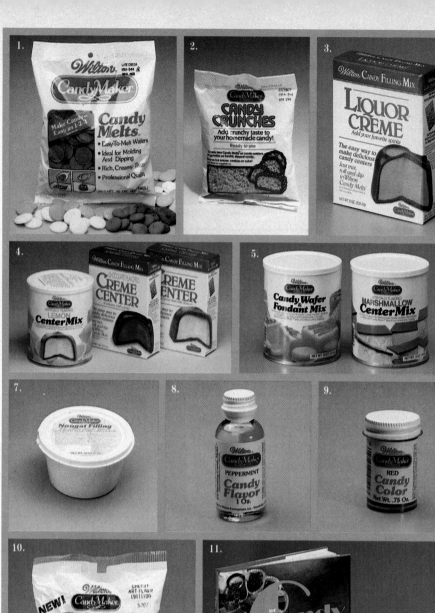

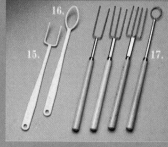

Wilton® CandyMaker™

1-2. NEW! SURPRISE KITS. Make candies in Mold/Tray (included) then reposition in Gift Box. Open special doors to reveal candy hidden inside!
1. Advent Calendar. 2114-P-2687. $3.99 kit
2. Easter Magic Door. 2114-P-2684. $3.99 kit

3. CANDY POPS KIT. Includes hard candy lollipop mold, sticks, bags and instructions. Use with Easy Melts™ (sold separately).
2114-P-2491. $4.99 kit

4. CANDYMAKING KITS. Includes 3 sheet molds, 1 stand-up mold, accessories and *Candymaking for Beginners* book. Use with Candy Melts™ (sold separately). **$6.99 kit**
CLASSIC. 2114-P-1978.
SWEETHEART. 2114-P-4322.
EASTER. 2114-P-3130.
HALLOWEEN. 2114-P-3350.
HOLIDAY. 2114-P-3296.

5. CANDY HOUSE KIT. Includes candy mold and instructions for 3 different candy houses.
2114-P-1992. $4.99 kit

6. GREAT EGGS!™ KIT. Make fantastic sugar or candy eggs! Includes 2 egg molds, tips, coupler, brush, 2 candy sheet molds, recipes, instructions.
2104-P-3616. $6.99 kit

7. LIQUOR CREMES KIT. 12 oz. liquor creme center mix, 12 oz. Dark Cocoa Candy Melts, candy cups, dipping spoon, two 1 lb. gift boxes, recipes & instructions. (You add liquor, butter.)
2114-P-1214. $9.99 kit

8. CLASSIC TRUFFLE KIT. Includes Truffle Mold, decorating bag, tips, dipping spoon, foil candy cups, recipes and instructions.
2114-P-2517. $4.99 kit

9. CANDY GIFT BOXES. Textured white boxes. Choose from three different sizes, each in sets of 3.
1/2-LB. SIZE BOX. 7⅜ x 4 x 1-in. deep.
  1912-P-2100. $1.99 set
1-LB. SIZE BOX. 9¾ x 5½ x 1-in. deep.
  1912-P-2240. $2.79 set

10. CANDY BOX LINERS. Waffle-padded paper sheets. Six 9¼ x 5½-in. sheets per pack.
1912-P-1543. 99¢ pack

11. FANCY CANDY WRAPPERS. Vibrant foil to protect your candy. Includes purple, blue, green, red and gold. 125 sheets, each 3 x 3-in.
1912-P-2290. $2.59 pack

12. CANDY GIFT BAGS. Present-perfect! 3 glassine-coated bags (3⅜ x 2½ x 7⅜-in. high) and 3 self-stick seals.
1912-P-1118. $1.99 pack

13. 1/2-LB. CANDY GIFT BOX. Attractive design. 3½ x 3½ x 3½-in. deep. Set of 3.
1912-P-1114. $2.29 set

14. CANDY CUPS. Packs of 100 (1-in. diam.). Choose gold foil or white glassine-coated paper.
GOLD FOIL. 1912-P-1227. $3.99 pack
WHITE. 1912-P-1243. 99¢ pack

15. CANDY BOX LABELS. Personalize your candy boxes or containers with these colorful stick-ons. 8 gummed labels, about 4-in. wide.
ALL-OCCASION CANDY LABELS.
  1912-P-2428. $1.59 pack
CHRISTMAS CANDY LABELS.
  1912-P-2479. $1.59 pack

Plastic dipping fork and spoon made in Hong Kong.
Dipping set and thermometer made in Japan.

PLEASE NOTE: All prices, certain products and services, reflect the U.S.A. domestic market and do not apply in Australia and Canada.

CLASSIC COOKIE MOLDS

Create unique cookies for gift-giving, entertaining and family treats.

Each mold includes an exclusive continental recipe specially developed by the Wilton kitchens. Two other recipes plus decorating ideas also included.

1. PRESS DOUGH INTO MOLD

2. BAKE

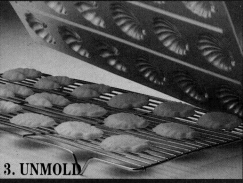

3. UNMOLD

BARCELONA CLASSIC COOKIE MOLD. Enter the world of strumming guitars, flamenco dancers and castanets. Serve Barcelona cookies. Make even the most intimate family dinner a colorful fiesta.
2306-P-106. $6.99 each

VENETIAN CLASSIC COOKIE MOLD. The perfect short-bread shapes. Serve plain or decorated. A delicious coffee break anywhere.
2306-P-105. $6.99 each

VIENNESE CLASSIC COOKIE MOLD. Violins humming a waltz. Glittering chandeliers. A midnight buffet and rich Viennese cookies. The cookie that makes every event romantic.
2306-P-102. $6.99 each

BAVARIAN CLASSIC COOKIE MOLD. Perfect to set a relaxing mood. White wine, flickering candles, rich dessert and Bavarian cookies!
2306-P-104. $6.99 each

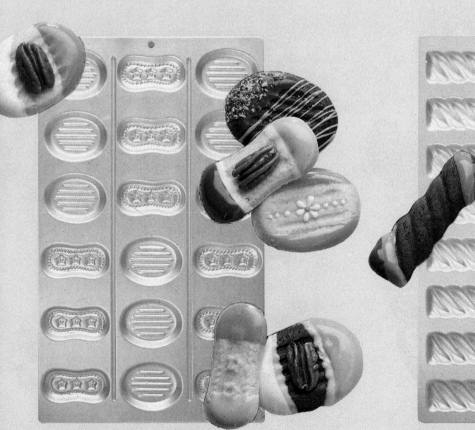

PARISIAN CLASSIC COOKIE MOLD. Mix simple and elegant decorating. Arrange Parisian cookies on a tray... Voila! A lovely delicious cookie centerpiece for every occasion.
2306-P-103. $6.99 each

MARSEILLES CLASSIC COOKIE MOLD. Great shapes for fancy, decorated dessert accompaniments or yummy cookie jar treats. A refreshing selection!
2306-P-101. $6.99 each

NEW! ENGLISH TEA CLASSIC COOKIE MOLD. The ideal shapes for English "biscuits." Simply delicious and elegant with tea, coffee, milk or just plain.
2306-P-107. $6.99 each

NEW! SALZBURG CLASSIC COOKIE MOLD. Two interesting shapes - one delicate, one fun. Crisp Cinnamon Snap cookie recipe included on mold for typically European flavor.
2306-P-108. $6.99 each

NEW! SWEDISH ALMOND TART CLASSIC COOKIE MOLD. The prettiest way to serve filled cookies. Equally delicious filled with jam, puddings, gelatins, more! Charming heart and apple shapes invite you to be creative. Continental Sandbakkel recipe included on label.
2306-P-109. $6.99 each

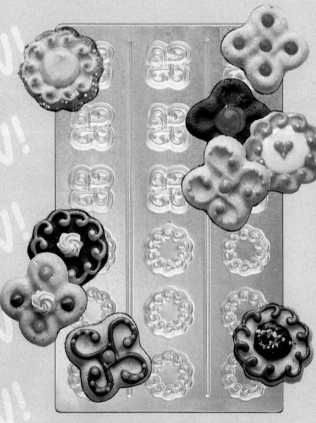

NEW! FLORENTINE CLASSIC COOKIE MOLD. Use the label recipe to create a delicate, classic touch of real lemon cookie. Fancy shapes are perfect for dipping and decorating.
2306-P-110. $6.99 each

HOLIDAY COOKIE MOLDS

A merry selection for holiday parties and treats. Perfect shapes for bread dough ornaments, too. For an extra-special hostess gift, include the mold with your tray of festive cookies. She'll be thrilled.

NEW! ANGEL/SOLDIER/HORSE COOKIE MOLD.
Children will love to munch these favorite shapes all season long. Bake up some for special package and tree trimmings.
2306-P-113. $6.99 each

NEW! WREATH/SNOWMAN/TREE COOKIE MOLD.
Perfect for ornaments or as a delicious treat for holiday visitors. They're all fun and easy to bake and decorate.
2306-P-112. $6.99 each

NEW! TEDDY BEARS COOKIE MOLD You'll have a tough time keeping your cookie jar filled with these playful characters. Follow label directions and perch Teddy on a lollipop stick for a special cookie pop treat!
2306-P-116. $6.99 each

Cookie Making Products

1.

Delight your family and friends with the wonderful flavor of homemade cookies. With these fine cookie making products, it's easier than ever to create delicious, beautiful cookies at home.

1. HOW TO MAKE GREAT TASTING FANCY COOKIES.
Soft-cover, 44-page book is filled with cookie making information, from the basics to the recipes, products and special decorating. Includes full-color photographs and easy-to-follow instructions. **902-P-3600. $1.99 each**

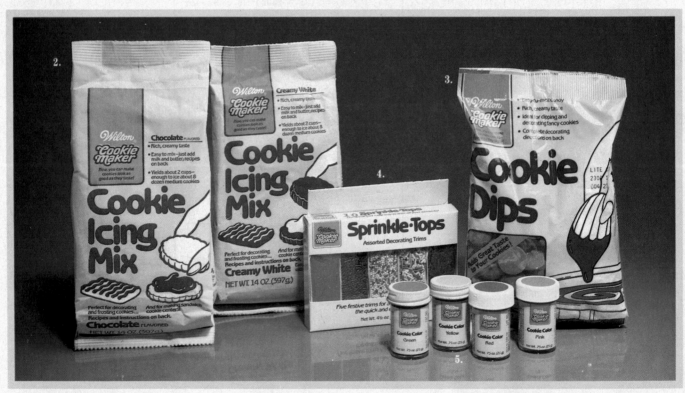

2. COOKIE ICING MIX.
Make creamy cookie icing or filling easily. Great for sandwich cookies! Just add butter and milk. Complete instructions on package. Creamy white and chocolate flavored. 14 oz. packages.
CREAMY WHITE. 2302-P-139. $1.99 each
CHOCOLATE FLAVORED. 2302-P-137. $1.99 each

3. COOKIE DIPS.*
Rich, creamy fast and easy-melting candy wafers perfect for dipping and drizzling cookies and pastries. White and light cocoa. 10 oz. packages.
*Certified Kosher.
WHITE. 2302-P-133. $1.99 each
LIGHT COCOA. 2302-P-131. $1.99 each

4. SPRINKLE TOPS—MULTI-COLORED DECORATING TRIMS.
Delightfully decorative cookie trims that easily add the festive look to any cookie. Chocolate Sprinkles. Rainbow Mix. Non-Pareils. Red Crystals, Green Crystals. **2302-P-120. $1.59 per package**

5. COOKIE COLOR.
Oil-based cookie color to tint white Wilton Icing Mix and Cookie Dips. ¾ oz. jars.
PINK. 2302-P-142. $1.99 each
RED. 2302-P-144. $1.99 each
YELLOW. 2302-P-146. $1.99 each
GREEN. 2302-P-148. $1.99 each

HOLIDAY COOKIE MAKING AND DECORATING KITS.
Each includes 2 cutters, 2 tips, 3 disposable decorating bags, 3 icing colors, 8-page instruction book with 6 designs.

1. FANCY COOKIE MAKING KIT. (Starter Set)
The ideal kit to introduce you to fancy cookie making. Five-pc. set includes 3 metal fancy cookie tips, one 12 in. pastry bag and an 8-page instruction book.
2301-P-135. $4.99 kit

2. FANCY COOKIE MAKING & PASTRY KIT.
Create luscious pastries, cookies, meringues. Kit includes one 16 in. pastry bag, cookie tips 1A, 1C, 1D, 6B, 230, one large coupler and 8-page recipe/instruction book.
2301-P-125. $9.99 kit

3. CHRISTMAS TREE & WREATH KIT.
2301-P-119. $3.99 kit

4. SANTA AND ANGEL KIT.
2301-P-117. $3.99 kit

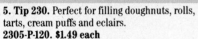

5. Tip 230. Perfect for filling doughnuts, rolls, tarts, cream puffs and eclairs.
2305-P-120. $1.49 each

6. Tip 1C. Ideal for cookie logs and jelly-filled shapes, meringue and whipped cream shells, too!
2305-P-114. $1.49 each

7. Tip 1A. Perfect for drop cookies, meringue mushrooms and for piping and filling cream puffs and eclairs.
2305-P-112. $1.49 each

8. Tip 6B. Great for meringue and whipped cream shells, cream puffs and more!
2305-P-118. $1.49 each

9. Tip 1D Pipes straight or zigzag bar cookies, smooth or striped tops. Just turn tip.
2305-P-116. $1.49 each

10. LARGE COUPLER. Make different cookies with the same pastry bag of dough. Change just the tips. Fits Wilton 14", 16", 18" bags.
2305-P-117. $1.49 each

11. COUPLER SET. Includes two standard couplers for use with standard decorating bags.
2104-P-4175. $1.29 set

12. ROUND DECORATING TIP SET. Includes three nickel-plated metal round decorating tips 2, 3, 4. Great for outlining, decorating and printing.
2104-P-4035. $1.79 set

13. STAR DECORATING TIP SET. Includes three nickel-plated metal star decorating tips 14, 16, 18.
2104-P-4094. $1.79 set

14. COOKIE PICKUP. Ideal for removing cookies from cookie sheet or pan. Quality stainless steel.
2305-P-134. $1.99 each

15. 16 IN. COOKIE MAKING & PASTRY BAG.
Heavy-duty, specially coated so grease won't go through. Easy to handle, flexible, soft and workable. Boilable, dishwasher safe, too!
404-P-1201. $5.99 each

16. 12 IN. VINYL COOKIE BAG. Flexible, easy-to-handle bag to use with cookie tips. Reusable and washable.
2305-P-136. $1.29 each

17. DISPOSABLE DECORATING BAGS. Heavy-duty, transparent plastic to use with icing or cookie dough. Fit standard tips and couplers.
2104-P-358. $2.99 pack of 12
2104-P-1358. $5.49 pack of 24

Plastic cutters made in Hong Kong

Now children can help make cookies or even make their own! Wilton plastic cutters are safe—no sharp edges to cut tiny fingers. Washable, dishwasher-safe, durable, non-rust, easy to clean, too! Perfect for children's modeling clay and dough.

CHILDREN'S ALPHABET A to Z SET. Adorable alphabet cutters with letters pressed into delightful figures. Perky birthday treats! Set of 26 washable, plastic cutters. 1-2½-in. wide; ⁵⁄₁₆-in. deep. **2304-P-104. $4.99 set**

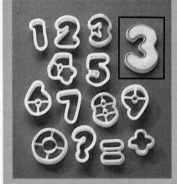

NUMBER SET. It's number one for birthdays, anniversaries, showers, school treats. Idea Tip: Teach youngsters easy addition, subtraction, multiplication! 13-pc. set includes 0 thru 9, =, +, and ? symbols. 2 x 1⅛ each. **2304-P-103. $4.99 set**

ALPHABET SET. The sweetest way to spell out a good cheer message or teach toddlers how to read easy words, including their names. Set of 26 washable cutters. 2 x 1⅛-in. each. **2304-P-102. $6.99 set**

HEART SET. Six different sizes for all sorts of lovely cookies. Perfect for Mother's Day. Valentine's Day, birthdays, anniversaries, more! Sizes range from 1¼ to 4⅛-in. Package of 6. **2304-P-115. $2.59 set**

STAR SET. Six super stars in graduated sizes. Great for all holiday and any day baking. You'll shine. 1⅝-in. to 4⅝-in. Washable plastic. **2304-P-111. $2.59 set**

ROUND SET. Favorite, versatile shape in six graduated sizes for cookies, hors d'oeuvres and more. From 1½-in. to 4-in. **2304-P-113. $2.59 set**

CRINKLE CUT SET. Fancy shapes are perfect for every occasion, including cookie gift-giving. Three sizes: 1½-in., 2½-in., 3-in. Washable plastic. **2304-P-125. $1.59 set**

PLAYING CARD SET. Four cutters in the playing card symbols. Perfect for hors d'oeuvres, breads, cookies, especially for bridge parties and other entertaining. 2½ x 2⅛-in. **2304-P-127. $1.59 set**

MINIATURE VARIETY SET. Tiny cutters for cookies, hors d'oeuvres, breads, more. Shapes for every occasion. Washable plastic 1-in. to 1⅝-in. high. Includes star, flower, heart, round and diamond. **2304-P-101. $1.59 set**

HOLIDAY SHAPES SET. All the festive shapes to make merry holiday eating and decorating. 5-pc. set includes Tree, Angel, Santa, Boy and Girl. Washable plastic. 3⅜-in. to 6-in. high. **2304-P-105. $2.59 set**

GINGERBREAD FAMILY SET. Bake and decorate yummy gingerbread family. Perfect with doll house cookies for a family surprise. 4-pc. set includes two 5½ x 4-in. and two 2½ x 1½-in. figures. **2304-P-121. $2.59 set**

ELEPHANT. Make a pretty pachyderm. He'll be the beauty of your cookie circus. Great party treats! 4⅜-in. high.
2304-P-132. 79¢ each

ICE CREAM CONE. A delicious favorite. Bake up a big batch, frost in favorite ice cream flavor frosting and let them choose. A real treat. 5⅛-in. high.
2304-P-135. 79¢ each

HORSE. Bake up a corral of these toy treats and the party crowd will giddyap to the kitchen for more. Decorate each cookie differently for individual party favors! 4¼ x 4¾-in.
2304-P-136. 79¢ each

TOY TRAIN. Make individual birthday expresses, bon voyage treats and more! They'll be "pulling out" of the cookie jar on an express schedule. 3¾ x 4¼-in.
2304-P-138. 79¢ each

CIRCUS CLOWN. No clowning around. He's fun to make and decorate. He'll shape up great with the giraffe, hobby horse and elephant for real circus fun. 5⅝ x 4½-in.
2304-P-137. 79¢ each

TEDDY BEAR. Decorate him cuddly and they'll want to hug him. Great for baby shower place cards. 5 x 4⅛-in.
2304-P-134. 79¢ each

GIRAFFE. The tallest member of the cookie animal menagerie. Fun to decorate...and eat! 5½-in. high.
2304-P-133. 79¢ each

DOLL HOUSE. Perfect for children's parties, or as a unique way to welcome new neighbors. Decorate to resemble home. 5⅝ x 3½-in.
2304-P-131. 79¢ each

Plastic cutters made in Hong Kong.

1. 10½-in. x 15½-in. COOKIE/JELLY ROLL PAN. 2105-P-1269. $7.50 each

2. MINI MUFFIN PAN. 2105-P-2125. **$5.99 each**

3. NEW! PETIT FOURS/PASTRY MOLD SET. Make cookies and pastries too! Set of 8. 2105-P-2093. **$7.99 set**

4. NEW! COOKIE COOLING GRID. Tight, interlocking design. Chrome-plated steel. (Taiwan) 2305-P-128. **$2.99 each**

5. TARTLET MOLD SET. Fabulous for filled cookies, mini pies, tarts and pastries. Set of 6. 2105-P-3794. **$3.99 set**

6. 16½ x 12½-in. COOKIE SHEET. Long grip for easier handling. 2105-P-2975. **$6.50 each**

7. 10-in. x 15-in. COOKIE SHEET. Roll and cut out cookies on sheet. 2105-P-1265. **$5.50 each**

8. 12-in. x 18-in. COOKIE PAN. Time-saving size bakes more cookies. 2105-P-4854. **$8.50 each**

COOKIE BAKEWARE AND ACCESSORIES

1. NEW! CARE BEARS™ EASTER EGG KIT.
This enchanting scene is so easy to create. Just tint eggs, punch out patterns and put them together. Kit contains 18 punch-outs, magic crayon, six packets of powdered egg tints and "The Care Bears Easter Egg Decorating Story."
2104-P-2389. $3.99 kit

2. NEW! CARE BEARS™ CHRISTMAS TREE KIT.
It's a trim-the-tree party centerpiece. The Care Bears gather to decorate your cookie tree. Includes punch-outs and star-shaped cookie cutters. A fun-to-make holiday treat!
2301-P-147. $3.99 kit

© MCMLXXXV American Greetings Corp.
*TM designates trademarks and character designs of American Greetings Corp.
Wilton Inc. Authorized user.

3. COOKIE HOLLY WREATH KIT.
Deck your table with boughs of holly! This festive sight is as much fun to make as it is to eat. Since wreaths are a symbol of love, it's an ideal treat year 'round. Alternate fall idea included. Kit contains 5 plastic cookie cutters, 1 plastic decorating tip, 4 packets of icing color, 3 decorating bags and illustrated instruction book.
2104-P-3664. $4.99 kit

4. CHRISTMAS COOKIE TREE KIT.
Reach for the stars and create this festive, impressive centerpiece cookie "tree"t. You get 10 plastic star cutters and illustrated instruction book.
2105-P-3424. $5.49 kit

Plastic parts made in Hong Kong.
Decorating bags made in Japan.

5. SANTA'S COOKIE SLEIGH KIT.
Loads of fun for everyone! Making an enchanting flight of fantasy is bound to become a holiday tradition. There are 3 different sleighs to try! Kit includes 4 durable plastic cutters, decorating tips, icing colors, disposable decorating bags and illustrated instruction book.
2105-P-2690. $5.49 kit

6. GINGERBREAD HOUSE KIT.
Build a dream come true. Sturdy punch-out pattern pieces make it easy to construct a gingerbread fantasy. Then comes the real fun…decorating. Illustrated instruction book tells you how.
2104-P-2946. $3.99 kit

7. EASTER BASKET COOKIE KIT.
Create this spring-fresh centerpiece treat…it's fun and easy. Kit comes with 3 embossed cookie cutters, punch-out basket pattern, decorating tips, bags and icing color.
2301-P-133. $4.99 kit

8. SWEETHEART COOKIE GREETING CARD KIT.
Here's the only way to win hearts. You'll really send that special someone with an edible message of love. Kit includes directions for 4 fast 'n easy designs, 4 greeting card boxes with liners, plastic heart cutter, icing color, decorating tip and bag.
2104-P-4310. $5.49 kit

COOKIE GIFT BOXES.
1912-P-2696. $1.99 pack of 4

1. FEATHERWEIGHT DECORATING BAGS

Lightweight, strong, flexible polyester bags contain your icing and are easy to handle, especially for beginners. Soft and workable, never stiff. Specially coated so grease won't go through. These bags may be boiled to thoroughly clean. Dishwasher-safe, too! Instructions included.

Size	Stock No.	Each
8-IN.	404-P-5087.	$1.89
10-IN.	404-P-5109.	2.99
12-IN.	404-P-5125.	3.99
14-IN.	404-P-5140.	4.99
16-IN.	404-P-5168.	5.99
18-IN.	404-P-5184.	6.99

QUICK-CHANGE PLASTIC COUPLERS.

Important decorating timesavers. They let you change tips without changing bags when using one color of icing. Instructions for using on Featherweight and Disposable Decorating Bags. Three sizes.

2. LARGE COUPLER.

Fits 14-in. to 18-in. Featherweight Bags. For use with large decorating tips. 1½ x 2½-in.
411-P-1006. $1.19 each

3. ANGLED COUPLER.

Reaches around tricky angles. Fits all bags and standard decorating tips. 1¼ x 1¾-in.
411-P-7365. 79¢ each

4. DISPOSABLE DECORATING BAGS

Popular 12-in. size bags of heavy duty, transparent plastic—flexible and easy to handle. Fit standard tips and couplers.
2104-P-358. $2.99 pack of 12.

24-COUNT VALUE PACK. Buy more & save!
2104-P-1358. $5.49 pack of 24.

5. STANDARD COUPLER.

Fits all decorating bags and standard tips.
411-P-1987. 59¢ each

6. HOLD-A-CONE.

Plastic organizer rack holds extra filled bags while you decorate. After washing bags, invert in holes to dry. White plastic. 5½ x 3⅜-in.
408-P-8769. $2.59 each

7. PARCHMENT TRIANGLES.

It's easy to make your own disposable decorating bags with our quality, grease-resistant vegetable parchment paper. Pre-cut in triangles for easy rolling. Complete instructions on package. Essential for color flow and color striping techniques.

12-IN.	2104-P-1206.	$3.99 pack of 100
15-IN.	2104-P-1508.	$4.99 pack of 100

8. TIP BRUSH.

Plastic bristle brush cleans tips thoroughly. 4-in.
414-P-1123. 99¢ each

9. TIP SAVER.

Reshapes bent tips and straightens prongs of metal. Directions included. Sturdy plastic.
414-P-909. $2.79 each

DECORATING TIPS

ROUND TIPS

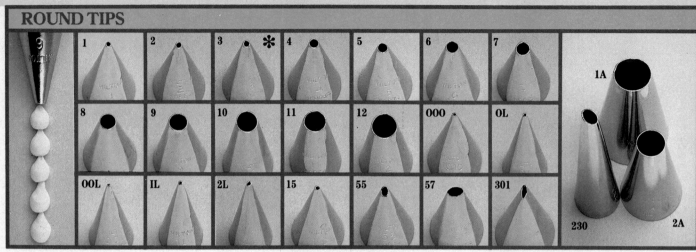

Smooth, circular openings. See pages 87-88 for how to use.

TIPS 1 THROUGH 12. Essential for outlining, writing, printing, dots, balls, beads...
Order 402-P-number. 59¢ each

TIP 000. For fine stringwork, lattice, beadwork.
402-P-1010. **99¢ each**

Stock up on these professional-quality, nickel-plated tips for all your decorating needs!

The "L" series for precision stringwork and beading.
TIP OL: 402-P-900. **$1.29 each**
TIP OOL: 402-P-903. **$1.29 each**
TIP IL: 402-P-901. **$1.29 each**
TIP 2L. 402-P-902. **$1.29 each**
*Use with parchment bags only.

TIP 1s. For delicate lattice, strings, beads.
402-P-1009. **99¢ each**

Oval openings for rounded lines, beads, Philippine-method flowers.
TIP 55. 402-P-55. **59¢ each**
TIP 57. 402-P-57. **59¢ each**

NEW! TIP 301. For "flat" lettering.
402-P-301. **59¢ each**

For figure piping and quick, showy borders...
TIP 1A. 402-P-1001. **$1.29 each**
TIP 2A. 402-P-2001. **$1.09 each**

TIP 230. Long and narrow for filling bismarcks, eclairs.
402-P-230. **$1.89 each**

MULTI-OPENING TIPS

The timesavers! Pipe intricate borders in a flash! Tips 41, 42, 43, 89 pipe rows of beads, dots, scallops, simultaneously.
TIP 41. 402-P-41. **59¢ each**
TIP 42. 402-P-42. **59¢ each**
TIP 43. 402-P-43. **59¢ each**
TIP 89. 402-P-89. **59¢ each**

TIP 134. Pipes a musical staff and even more lavish borders. 5 holes.
402-P-134. **$1.29 each**

Complete Decorating Tip Kits on Page 123.

Grass and hair tips...
TIP 233 (small). 402-P-233. **$1.09 each**
TIP 234 (large). 402-P-234. **$1.29 each**

NEW! TIP 235 Pipes a small star wreath.
402-P-235. **$1.09 each**

CLOSED STAR TIPS

Create deeply grooved shells, stars and fleurs-de-lis. Drop flowers have fine petals. See pages 88-90 for how to use.
TIPS 23 THROUGH 35, 132, 133.

Order 402-P-number. 59¢ each
Star-cut Cross Tips 49 through 54 pipe boldly carved decorations. A variety of unique effects can be created. The number of cuts in the tip opening determines how many petals or ridges your decorations will have.
Order 402-P-number. 59¢ each

Metal tips made in Korea.

✳ DENOTES POPULAR BEGINNER'S TIP. BE SURE TO ORDER!

OPEN STAR TIPS

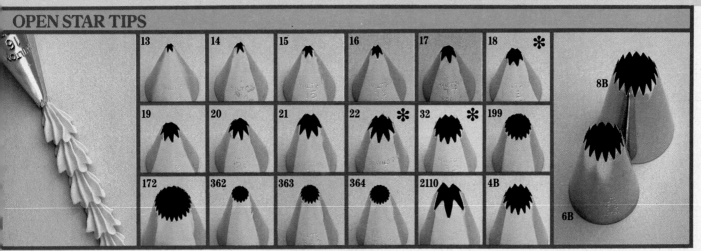

Pipe star techniques and some drop flowers.
See pages 88-90 for how to use.
**TIPS 13 THROUGH 22 & 32. Order
402-P-number. 59¢ each**
The finely-cut teeth of these tips pipe out
decorations with many ridges.

**TIPS 199, 172, 362, 363, 364.
Order 402-P-number. $1.09 each**
Giant open star tips create lavish icing
decorations. Ideal for piping pastry dough, too.

**TIP 2110. 402-P-2110. $1.09 each
TIP 4B. 402-P-4400. $1.09 each
TIP 6B. 402-P-6600. $1.09 each
TIP 8B. 402-P-8800. $1.29 each**

Deep-Cut Stellar Star Set (not shown).
Graduated sizes for tier shells, puffs and drop
flowers. Includes tips 501, 502, 504, 506, 508.
401-P-502. $3.59 set

PETAL TIPS

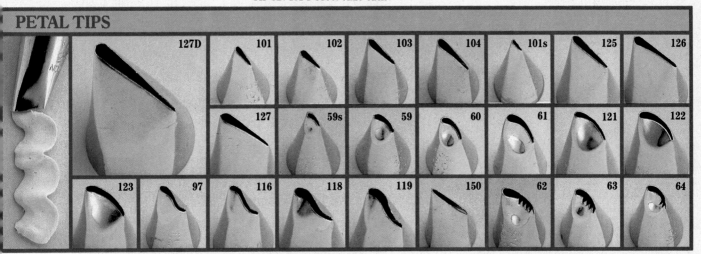

Create lovely icing blooms that rival nature—
roses, violets, daffodils, daisies and more. See
pages 91-93 for flower-making techniques. Use
petal tips to make ruffles, drapes and swags. See
pages 90-93 for how to use.

Standard Petal Tips (identical, except for size).
TIPS 101 THROUGH 104.

**Order 402-P-number. 59¢ each
TIP 101s. 402-P-1019. 99¢ each
TIPS 124 THROUGH 127.
Order 402-P-number. $1.09 each
TIP 127D (Giant Rose). 402-P-1274. $1.29 each
Curved Petal Tips:** For violets, pansies, ruffles…
**TIP 59s or 59°. 402-P-594. 59¢ each
TIPS 59, 60, 61. Order 402-P-number 59¢ each
TIPS 121, 122, 123.
Order 402-P-number. $1.09 each**

Swirled Petal Tips create lifelike curved petals.
**TIP 97. 402-P-97. 59¢ each
TIPS 116, 118, 119.
Order 402-P-number. $1.09 each
TIP 150.** For carnation petals.
402-P-150. $1.09 each

Cut Tips for zigzags, "e"-motion, ribbon bows.
TIPS 62, 63, 64. Order 402-P-number. 59¢ each

BASKETWEAVE TIPS

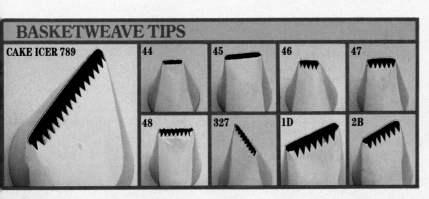

Pipe smooth and serrated stripes for
basketweave techniques, ribbons and bows.
Tips 44 and 45 pipe smooth stripes, while all
the rest make smooth and ribbed bars. Use
tips 1D, 2B and 789 for piping bar-shaped
cookies, too. See p. 90 for basketweave.
**TIPS 44 THROUGH 48.
Order 402-P-number. 59¢ each
TIP 327. 402-P-327. 99¢ each
TIP 1D. 402-P-1004. $1.29 each
TIP 2B. 402-P-2002. $1.09 each**

Cake Icer Tip. For icing cake top and sides
with extra-wide smooth or ribbed stripes.
Use 16-in. or larger decorating bag with
this 2 x 2½-in. tip. **409-P-789. $2.09 each**

119

DECORATING TIPS

DROP FLOWER TIPS

Have a variety of sizes on hand for making pretty, easy flowers in royal or buttercream icing. See how to on page 90.

Small Drop Flower Tips: For little plain or swirl flowers.
TIPS 106, 107, 108, 129, 217, 220, 224, 225.
Order 402-P-number. $1.09 each

Medium: For larger plain and swirl flowers.
TIPS 131, 177, 191, 193, 195. Order 402-P-number. $1.09 each
TIPS 109, 135, 140, 190, 194. Order 402-P-number. $1.29 each

Large: Use 14-in. decorating bag and large coupler (page 117). Ideal for giant blooms in icing or cookie dough.

TIP 2C. 402-P-2003. $1.09 each
TIP 2D. 402-P-2004. $1.09 each
TIP 2E. 402-P-2005. $1.09 each
TIP 2F. 402-P-2006. $1.09 each
TIP 1B. 402-P-1002. $1.29 each
TIP 1C. 402-P-1003. $1.29 each
TIP 1E. 402-P-1005. $1.29 each
TIP 1F. 402-P-1006. $1.29 each
TIP 1G. 402-P-1007. $1.29 each

SPECIALTY TIPS

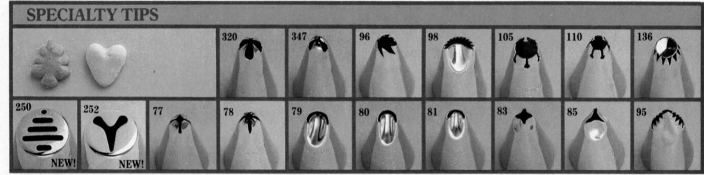

Pipe shells, ropes basketweaves with interesting, exciting effects. Discover each tip's possibilities in **The Wilton Way of Cake Decorating, Volume Three** (The uses of tips). To order, see page 131.

For shells, ropes, basketweave and more...
TIPS 320 & 347. Order 402-P-number. $1.09 each
TIPS 96, 98, 105, 110. Order 402-P-number. 59¢ each

TIP 136 makes icing ring candle holders.
402-P-136. $1.29 each

NEW! Tip 250. Pipes a Christmas tree, approx. ¾-in. high.
402-P-250. $1.29 each

NEW! Tip 252. Pipes out a heart in one squeeze.
402-P-252. $1.29 each

For the following, order 402-P-number. 59¢ each
TIPS 77, 78, 79, 80, 81 for flowers, zigzags, "e"-motion.

TIPS 83 (square) & 85 (triangle) for sculptured, 3-D printing, outlines, beads, zigzags.

TIP 95. French leaf for deeply-grooved borders.

RUFFLE TIPS

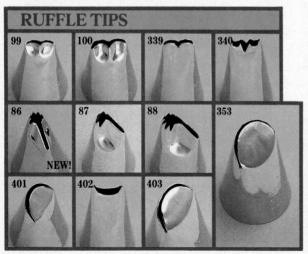

For garland, ribbon and ripple-type borders. See p. 90 for attractive ruffle-tip techniques.

Double Ribbon: For double fluted ruffles.
TIPS 99, 100. Order 402-P-number. 59¢ each
TIPS 339, 340. Order 402-P-number. 99¢ each

Star-cut: For shell and flute border in one step.
NEW! TIP 86 (Right-hander's).
402-P-86. 59¢ each
TIPS 87, 88 (Left-hander's).
402-P-number. 59¢ each

Ripple Ribbon: For wide zigzag borders, ears, tongues, feathers...
TIP 401. 402-P-401. 79¢ each
TIP 353. 402-P-353. 99¢ each
TIP 402. 402-P-402. $1.09 each
TIP 403. 402-P-403. $1.29 each

TIP SAVER BOXES. Keep decorating tips clean and organized in these sturdy plastic boxes.
A. 26-TIP CAPACITY 405-P-8773. $4.59 each
B. 52-TIP CAPACITY 405-P-7777. $6.59 each

✱POPULAR DECORATOR'S TIP...ORDER SEVERAL!

LEAF TIPS

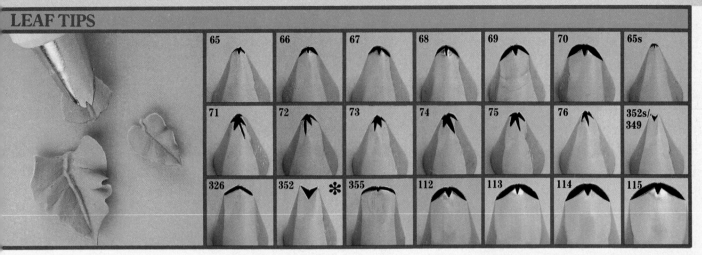

65	66	67	68	69	70	65s
71	72	73	74	75	76	352s/ 349
326	352 ✳	355	112	113	114	115

Collect several to make a variety of lush icing leaves...traditional, stand-up or ruffled variations. See page 90 for how to use.

Plain Cut: For natural-looking leaf with center vein.

SMALL: TIP 65 THROUGH 70. Order 402-P-number. 59¢ each
TIP 65s. 402-P-659. 99¢ each

Special Cut: For lilies, poinsettias, ferns, stand-up leaves; also shell borders and garlands.
TIPS 71 THROUGH 76. Order 402-P-number. 59¢ each

V-Cut: For never-fail pointed leaves, ferns.
TIP 352s/349 (small). 402-P-349. 99¢ each
TIPS 326 & 352 (large). 402-P-number. 99¢ each
Extra-large Plain Cut: Ideal for large cakes and lavish borders.
TIP 355. 402-P-355. 99¢ each
TIPS 112, 113, 114, 115. Order 402-P-number. $1.09 each

LILY NAIL SET

Place foil square in one lily nail. Press in top half to form a foil cup.

Essential for making cup flowers, such as lilies (see page 93). Here's how to use 2-pc. nails. Place aluminum foil in bottom half of nail and press in top half to form cup. Pipe flower petals. Set includes ½, 1¼, 1⅝, and 2½ inch diam. cups. Sturdy white plastic.
403-P-9444. $1.99 8-pc. set

AUSTRALIAN NET NAILS

Just rub a little vegetable oil on these curved nails and pipe latticework designs in royal icing. Let dry. Then lift off intricate, dimensional decorations.
A. AUSTRALIAN ARCH NAIL.
402-P-822. $1.79 each
B. AUSTRALIAN LARGE BORDER NAIL.
402-P-863. $1.99 each
C. AUSTRALIAN BASKET NAIL.
402-P-803. $1.79 each
D. AUSTRALIAN CRESCENT NAIL.
402-P-805. $1.79 each

METAL FLOWER NAILS

Turntables for piping glorious icing flowers, such as the rose!
E. FLOWER NAIL NO. 9. 1¼-in. diameter.
402-P-3009. 59¢ each
F. FLOWER NAIL NO. 7. 1½-in. diameter.
402-P-3007. 59¢ each
G. 2-IN. FLOWER NAIL. Use with curved and swirled petal tips, 116-123, to make large blooms.
402-P-3002. 99¢ each
H. 3-IN. FLOWER NAIL. Has extra large piping surface, ideal for use with large petal tips.
402-P-3003. $1.09 each
I. 1-PC. LILY NAIL. 1⅝-in. diameter.
402-P-3012. 79¢ each

TRIPLE-STAR TIP

This timesaving tip pipes three stars (size of tip 17 decorations) at once. Use with any size bag and cut to fit or use with large coupler and bag.
402-P-2010. $2.09 each

*For more about flower making, be sure to order the New **Wilton Celebrates! The Rose** book, see page 132.*

Plastic lily nail set and Tip Saver Boxes made in Hong Kong.

Metal tips and nails made in Korea.

PLEASE NOTE: All prices, certain products and services reflect the U.S.A. domestic market and do not apply in Australia and Canada.

GUM PASTE & SPECIALTY SUPPLIES

1. GUM PASTE FLOWERS KIT. Make beautiful, breathtaking gum paste flowers that look almost real! Create bouquets or single blooms for cakes, centerpieces, favors and more. Full-color how-to book gives you step-by-step instructions and wonderful ideas. Kit includes 24 plastic cutters, 1 leaf mold, 3 wooden modeling tools and 2 squares of foam for modeling. 30-pc. kit.
1907-P-117. $14.99 kit

2. GUM PASTE MIX. Easy-to-use…just add water and knead! Soon you'll have a workable, pliable dough-like mixture to mold into beautiful gum paste flowers and figures. 1 lb. can.
707-P-124. $4.99 each

3. GUM PASTE ACCESSORY KIT. Includes: 90' green florist tape, 30' fine florist wire, 20 pieces medium florist wire (18-in. lg.), 12-pc. chalk set and 144 yellow stamens.
1907-P-227. $9.99 kit

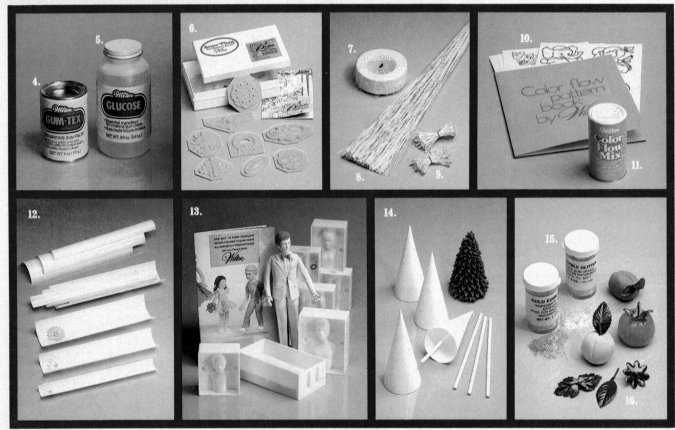

4. GUM-TEX™ KARAYA. Gives gum paste a pliable, elastic, easy-to-shape quality. 6 oz. can.
707-P-117. $5.49 each

5. GLUCOSE. Essential ingredient in making gum paste. 24 oz. pastic jar. **707-P-109. $4.29 each**

6. BAROQUE GUM PASTE MOLDS. Includes 12 classic molds, full-color instruction/idea booklet in a plastic storage box.
1906-P-1299. $10.99 set

7. FLORIST TAPE. Two 90-ft. rolls per package. White, ½-in. wide. **409-P-614. $2.29 pack**

8. FLORIST WIRE. Medium weight for a multitude of projects. 175 white wires (18-in. long) per pack. **409-P-622. $6.99 pack**

9. STAMENS. For realistic flowers. 144 per pack.
YELLOW. 1005-P-7875. $1.49 pack
PEARL WHITE. 1005-P-102. $1.49 pack

10. COLOR FLOW PATTERN BOOK.
Over 70 unique designs for dozens of occasions. Just outline and fill in. **408-P-350. $5.99 each**

11. COLOR FLOW MIX. Add water and confectioners sugar to this mix to make a smooth icing for outlining and filling in designs. 4 oz. can yields about ten 1½ cup batches.
701-P-47. $6.99 each

12. FLOWER FORMERS. Plastic stands allow icing leaves and flowers to dry convexed or concaved. Set of nine (11-in. long) in 3 widths: 1½, 2, 2½-in.
417-P-9500. $5.99 set

13. WILTON PEOPLE MOLDS. Create a whole family out of gum paste. Includes 3-part molds (man, woman, two children) and instruction book.
1906-P-5154. $15.99 set

14. TREE FORMERS. Make icing pine trees. Great for drying royal icing or gum paste decorations. Set of 4, 6½-in. high. **417-P-1150. $1.99 set**

15. EDIBLE GLITTER. ½-oz. plastic jar.
WHITE. 703-P-1204. $2.29 each
GOLD. 703-P-1212. $2.29 each

16. MARZIPAN LEAVES. 100 pieces per pack (4 designs). **1005-P-1000. $5.99 pack**

Stamens made in Korea. Plastic flower formers, tree formers, cutters, storage box, people molds made in Hong Kong. Gum paste book printed in U.S.A.

1. 60-PC. MASTER TIP KIT. Includes 52 nickel-plated metal tips that let you create practically every decorating technique. Tips for writing, figure piping, leaf and flower making, basketweave and many special effects. Also includes: standard and angled couplers, two #9 Flower Nails, 10-in. and 12-in. washable Featherweight decorating bags, *Beginners Guide To Cake Decorating* book and plastic tipsaver box. Individually $46.39.
401-P-7779. **$38.99 kit**

MASTER TIP SET. 52 decorating tips and tip-saver box only.
2104-P-7778. **$30.99 set**

2. 33-PC. DELUXE TIP KIT. Includes 26 nickel-plated metal tips for writing, borders, leaves, flowers and more. Plus: two #9 Flower Nails, standard coupler for easy tip changes, 10-in. and 12-in. washable Featherweight decorating bags, *Beginners Guide To Cake Decorating* book and plastic tipsaver box. Individually $27.86.
401-P-6667. **$22.99 kit**

DELUXE TIP SET. Includes 26 decorating tips and tipsaver box only.
2104-P-6666. **$17.99 set**

PLEASE NOTE: All prices and services reflect the U.S.A. domestic market and do not apply in Australia and Canada.

3. 15-PC. TIP KIT. Excellent choice for a new decorator or to add extras of most-used tips. Includes 10 nickel-plated metal tips, two 12-in. vinyl decorating bags, standard coupler, #7 Flower Nail, *Beginners Guide To Cake Decorating* book and plastic storage box. Individually $17.16.
401-P-4443. **$12.99 kit**

COLLECT ESSENTIAL CAKE DECORATING TOOLS AND TAKE ADVANTAGE OF THE SAVINGS ON COMPLETE SETS!

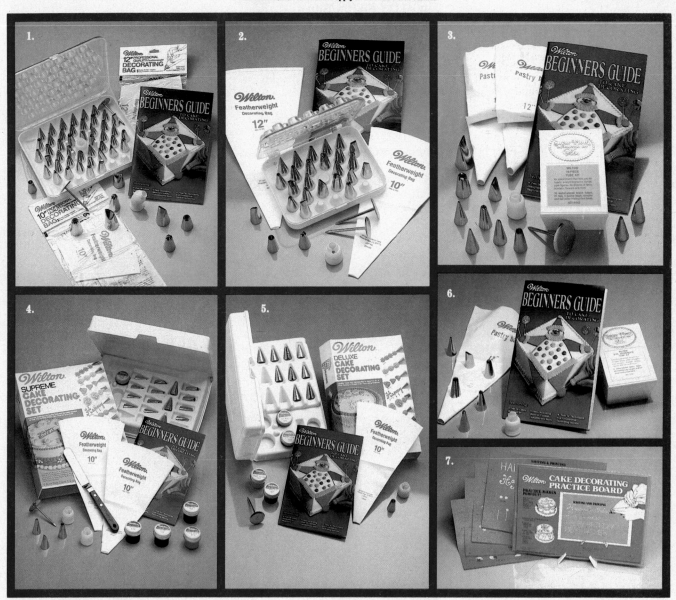

4. SUPREME CAKE DECORATING SET. Filled with 30 indispensable decorating tools, this set is an important investment for any level of cake decorator. You get 18 metal tips, two 10-in. Featherweight decorating bags, two couplers, five ½-oz. paste icing colors, #9 flower nail, 8-in. angled spatula, *Beginners Guide To Cake Decorating* book and plastic storage box. An excellent gift idea for your favorite decorator!
2104-P-3047. **$27.99 set**

5. DELUXE CAKE DECORATING SET. Designed to meet the needs of any decorator—beginner as well as expert. Contains 18 important pieces a talented decorator needs: 10 nickel-plated metal tips, 10-in. Featherweight decorating bag, coupler, #9 flower nail, four ½-oz. paste icing colors, *Beginners Guide To Cake Decorating* book and plastic storage box. Makes a thoughtful gift or a great treat for yourself!
2104-P-3063. **$17.99 set**

6. BASIC CAKE DECORATING SET. Starter set contains 6 metal tips, 12-in. vinyl bag, coupler and 40-page *Beginners Guide To Cake Decorating* book.
401-P-2221. **$7.99 set**

7. PRACTICE BOARD WITH PATTERNS. Learn or improve your decorating skills. Just slip pattern onto board under wipe-clean vinyl overlay and trace pattern in icing. Includes stand and patterns for flowers, leaves, borders, lettering (31 designs).
406-P-9464. **$6.99 each**

1.

2.

1. LEVELER/SPREADER. Ideal for leveling small cakes and ingredients. Handy for spreading filling. Rosewood handle with 9½-in. metal blade.
409-P-1014. $4.99 each

2. SERRATED LEVELER. Indispensable for leveling and splitting cake layers. Polished rosewood handle with 12-in. long stainless steel blade.
409-P-1016. $5.99 each

3. STAINLESS STEEL ICING BOWL. Store up to 3 cups of icing in this durable, handy container with snap-on plastic lid. 5¾-in. diameter.
415-P-250. $3.99 each

4. WEDDING KNIFE & SERVER SET. Gleaming stainless steel with serrated blades and handsome fluted shell patterned handles. Packaged in a gift box. 10½ and 12-in. long.
409-P-1211. $20.99 set

5. STAINLESS STEEL CAKE SERVER. Durable! Brown plastic handle with wide metal blade. Dishwasher-safe. 10¼-in. long.
409-P-2145. $4.99 each

QUALITY STAINLESS STEEL SPATULAS. Essential for spreading icing and filling. Flexible metal blades with rosewood handles.

6. 8-IN. TAPERED SPATULA. Angled blade for icing hard-to-reach corners, sides and small areas.
409-P-517. $2.59 each

7. 8-IN. SPATULA. Straight blade for putting icing on cake top and sides. Great for canapes, too!
409-P-6043. $2.59 each

8. 11.-IN. SPATULA. Makes short work of icing any tempting treat.
409-P-7694. $3.99 each

9. 8-IN. ANGLED SPATULA. Handy size, especially when smoothing icing around cake sides.
409-P-738. $2.59 each

10. 12-IN. ANGLED SPATULA. Essential when icing large areas on cake top.
409-P-134. $4.59 each

11. 14-IN. ANGLED SPATULA. Perfect for covering large cake areas with icing or filling.
409-P-274. $5.99 each

12. TOOL CADDY. Take your tools along or keep them organized at home. Room for 38 tips, 10 paste color jars, couplers, spatulas, practice board, books and more! Lightweight, stain-resistant molded polyethylene. A must for teachers! 16⅝ x 11¼ x 3½-in.
2104-P-2237. $17.99 each

Spatulas made in Japan. Plastic products made in Hong Kong.

QUALITY WILTON TOOLS MAKE DECORATING EASIER AND MORE FUN TO DO!
For better looking cakes, see our "Helpful Hints" on page 86. For decorating tips and flower nails, see pages 118-121.

3.

4.

5.

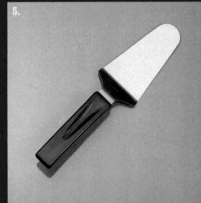

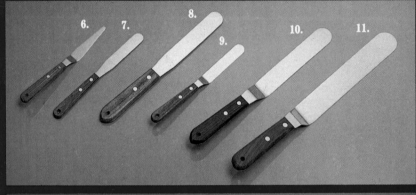

6. 7. 8. 9. 10. 11.

12.

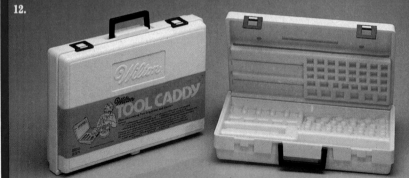

ICING MIX, COLORS & TOOLS

1. WILTON ICING MIX. It offers you everything the best homemade buttercream icing does: rich taste, luscious, smooth texture—PLUS it's convenient! All you do is add butter and milk...the shortening is already in the mix. It's ideal for frosting as well as decorating! So easy-to-use...complete instructions on package. 14-oz. size yields 2 cups of icing. In two delicious flavors—try them both!

CREAMY WHITE. 710-P-112. $1.99 each
CHOCOLATE FLAVORED. 710-P-114. $1.99 each

PLEASE NOTE: All prices, certain products and services reflect the U.S.A. domestic market and do not apply in Australia and Canada.

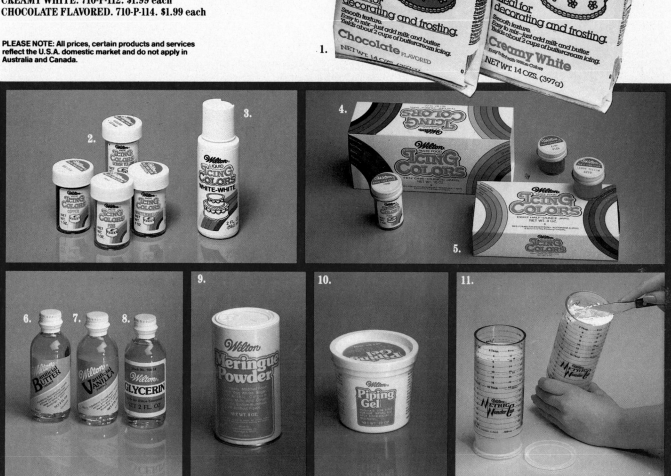

2. PASTE ICING COLORS. Concentrated colors in a creamy, rich base that's fast-mixing but won't thin your icing! 1-oz. plastic jars.

Each $1.29 (*except Red-Red and Burgundy, $1.89)

Lemon Yellow.	610-P-108.	Violet.	610-P-604.
Golden Yellow.	610-P-159.	Royal Blue.	610-P-655.
Orange.	610-P-205.	Burgundy.*	610-P-698.
Pink.	610-P-256.	Sky Blue.	610-P-700.
Christmas Red.	610-P-302.	Kelly Green.	610-P-752.
Watermelon.	610-P-353.	Leaf Green.	610-P-809.
Rose.	610-P-401.	Moss Green.	610-P-851.
Copper.	610-P-450.	Red-Red.*	610-P-906.
Brown.	610-P-507.	Black.	610-P-981.

NEW! WILTON RED (NO TASTE). Perfect for larger areas because it has no taste! 1-oz.
610-P-998. $1.89 each

3. WHITE-WHITE ICING COLOR. Add just a few drops to make your buttercream icing pure white! Great for wedding cakes. 2-oz. plastic bottle.
603-P-1236. $2.99 each

4. 10-ICING COLOR KIT. 1-oz. jars of paste colors: Violet, Leaf Green, Royal Blue, Brown, Black, Pink, Watermelon, Moss Green, Orange and Lemon Yellow. Convenient and money-saving!
601-P-5569. $11.99 kit

5. 8-ICING COLOR KIT. ½-oz. jars of paste colors: Christmas Red, Lemon Yellow, Leaf Green, Sky Blue, Brown, Orange, Pink and Violet.
601-P-5577. $7.99 kit

6. BUTTER EXTRACT. For a rich buttery taste. Use in icing, cakes and cookies, too! 2-oz.
604-P-2040. $1.39 each

7. CLEAR VANILLA EXTRACT. Perfect for decorating because it won't change your icing colors. Use for baking, too! 2-oz.
604-P-2237. $1.39 each

8. GLYCERIN. A few drops stirred into dried-out paste color restores consistency. 2-oz.
708-P-14. $1.99 each

9. MERINGUE POWDER MIX. For royal icing and meringue (see recipes on page 83).
4-OZ. CAN. 702-P-6007. $4.29 each
8-OZ. CAN. 702-P-6015. $6.99 each

10. PIPING GEL. Clear gel for glazing. Can be tinted with paste color for writing, color striping, stringwork, filling and more. 10-oz. container.
704-P-105. $3.29 each

11. METRIC WONDER CUP. 2 cup capacity measures cups, ounces and millimeters. Perfect for measuring shortening. With plastic shaker lid: 6 x 3-in.
415-P-105. $5.59 each

Tools and Pattern Presses

WILTON HAS THE TOOLS THAT SIMPLIFY DECORATING, GIVE MORE PRECISE, MORE PROFESSIONAL RESULTS!

1. 3-PC. CAKE TOP PATTERN PRESS SET. Sturdy plastic, 8-in. diameter patterns.
2104-P-3128. $5.99 set

2. DECORATING TRIANGLE. Pull across top or sides of iced cake. Each side creates a different effect. 5 x 5½-in.
409-P-990. 99¢ each

3. CAKE DIVIDING SET. Wheel chart marks 2-in. intervals on 6 to 18-in. diameter cakes. Triangle marker (6-in. high) marks precise spacing for stringwork, garland and more. Instructions included.
409-P-800. $8.99 set

4. DECORATOR'S BRUSHES. Essential for smoothing icing, glazing fruit, "painting" in special candymaking effects...and so much more! Set of 3.
2104-P-846. $1.49 set

5. DECORATING COMB. Add perfectly even ridges to a simple iced cake. White plastic, 12-in. long.
409-P-8259. $1.29 each

6. DIAL DIVIDER. Divide cake tops fast and accurately! For 6 to 16-in. diameter cakes. Sturdy plastic.
409-P-8607. $2.79 each

PATTERN PRESS SETS LET YOU CREATE FANCY DESIGNS QUICKLY AND EASILY... PERFECT FOR CAKE TOPS AND SIDES, MESSAGE AREAS, TOO!

Simply ice cake and press on patterns to transfer design to cake. Then cover marks with piped icing effects like outlines, stars, shells, dots. Combine patterns to create your own innovative designs!

7. 15-PC. DECORATOR PATTERN PRESS SET. A wide assortment of contemporary designs. Many patterns can be pressed on either side for easy symmetrical designs. Washable plastic.
2104-P-2172. $4.99 set

8. 9-PC. PATTERN PRESS SET. Traditional designs add artistic flair in a variety of patterns from 2½ to 5-inches high. Sturdy washable plastic.
2104-P-3101. $4.29 set

9. NEW! MESSAGE PATTERN PRESS SET. Six individual words let you combine patterns to create your own message. Includes: Happy, Birthday, Best, Wishes, Anniversary, Congratulations. Plastic, 2½ to 6¾ x ¾-in. high.
2104-P-2077. $2.99 set

Plastic products and brushes made in Hong Kong (except garland marker and wheel).

PLEASE NOTE: All prices, certain products and services, reflect the U.S.A. domestic market and do not apply in Australia and Canada.

WILTON SCHOOL

THE WILTON SCHOOL is accredited by the Illinois State Board of Education under the provisions of the Illinois Private Business and Vocational Schools Act. Skilled instructors offer personalized guidance and instruction. Wilton offers these six important courses.

MASTER COURSE. 2 weeks—70 hours. Cake decorating fundamentals that will turn you into a professional decorator. You'll go from basic stars to lavish wedding cakes.
Course fee $500.00

ADVANCED COURSE. 2 weeks—80 hours. Includes a detailed Gum Paste course, the Australian, Nirvana, South African methods and more. Previous decorating experience required.
Course fee $500.00

LAMBETH COURSE. 2 weeks—80 hours. You'll become an expert at the impressive English over-piped style of cake decorating. Previous decorating experience required.
Course fee $500.00

GUM PASTE COURSE. 15 hours. A mini-course that teaches the basics of the art of gum paste.
Course fee $125.00

PULLED SUGAR COURSE. 9 hours. Learn how to use pulled sugar to cover a cake, make flowers, candy dishes, ribbons, bows and more.
Course fee $125.00

CANDY MAKING CLASS. 1 week—30 hours. You will learn hollow molding, center making and hand dipping as well as how to make fondant, marzipan, truffles, candy cups and other fabulous confections. You will work with confectionery coatings and real chocolate.
Course fee $300.00

The Wilton School is located in Woodridge, Illinois (a suburb of Chicago). Course enrollment is limited, so don't delay. To enroll, or for more information, write to: School Secretary, Wilton School of Cake Decorating and Confectionary Art, 2240 W. 75th Street, Woodridge, IL 60517. Or call 312-963-7100 for free brochure and schedule.
You may charge your courses on VISA or MasterCard.

SPECIALTY HOME STUDY LESSONS

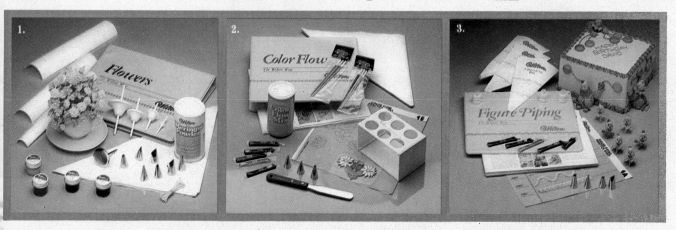

Now you can learn advanced decorating methods at home, at your convenience! Send for Flower Making, Figure Piping or Color Flow Lessons today. Basic skills are all you need to start. Includes all the specialty tools you'll need. You'll earn a certificate of completion from Wilton when you finish each course.
Each course is $19.99. Order any two for $36.98 (SAVE $3)…any three for $49.97. (SAVE $10). VISA and MasterCard accepted.

1. FLOWER MAKING. Learn to make 18 different icing flowers and glorious blossoms! You get 37 pages of illustrated instructions. Includes Artificial Flower Stamens, Flower Formers, Lily Nails, Meringue Powder Mix, and more! All products shown are included.
902-P-1094. $19.99*

2. COLOR FLOW. Learn how to outline and fill in with a special icing to create perfect designs. The essential ingredient is Wilton Color Flow Mix. You'll also get Wilton Hold-A-Cone, Decorator's Brushes, 8-in. spatula, 8½ x11-in. plastic-coated Practice Sheets and all products shown.
902-P-1078. $19.99*

3. FIGURE PIPING. Discover how to make fun figures atop your cakes. It's easy to do with step-by-step directions. Course provides six plastic clown heads, 8½ x 11-in. plastic-coated Practice Sheet, 3 vinyl Decorating Bags, 3 Couplers, and more! All products shown are included.
902-P-1086. $19.99*

127

CANDY MAKING HOME STUDY COURSE

LEARN HOW TO MAKE AND MOLD DOZENS OF DELICIOUS CANDIES IN JUST 5 EASY LESSONS! The Wilton Candy Maker™ Home Study Course is designed to teach even the most inexperienced student how to make and mold eye-catching, taste-tempting candies like these!

Step-by-step instructions, illustrations and photographs will take you from basic melting and molding techniques to advanced cooked candies. Special Candy Maker™ tools, supplies and ingredients are included.

TRY IT FREE FOR 15 DAYS—RETURN COUPON AT RIGHT AND WE'LL SEND LESSON 1 TO YOU ON APPROVAL!

LESSON 1
Melt and mold an assortment of candy treats in various shapes, flavors and colors. Make candy clusters and candies with nut centers. Combine creamy caramel, pecans and chocolatey coating to create chewy Caramel Turtles!

Lesson 1 includes:
Notebook Easel and Lesson Pages
3 lbs. Candy Melts™ brand confectionery coating
3 Plastic Sheet Molds
Disposable Decorating Bags
Lollipop Sticks
Pink Candy Color
Peppermint Candy Flavor
Caramel Filling (16 oz. container).

LESSON 2
Shape and dip creme center candies! Learn to use Wilton Creme Center Mix to make vanilla, peppermint and peanut butter creme centers. It's easy to mold and dip these candies! Covered cherries are another tasty treat you'll learn to make.

Lesson 2 includes:
Lesson Pages
4 lbs. Candy Melts™ brand confectionery coating
2 Plastic Sheet Molds
Panda 3-D Stand-Up Mold
Two Canisters Creme Center Mix
Disposable Decorating Bags
Plastic Dipping Spoon
Decorator's Brush
Candy Box, Liner, Label and Paper Candy Cups.

LESSON 3
Learn to turn plain candies into extraordinary tre by decorating with melted coating. Learn to make molded, layered and piped truffle candies—so ver creamy and rich! Try your hand at making ice crea candies to thrill a sweet tooth!

Lesson 3 includes:
Lesson Pages
5 lbs. Candy Melts™ brand confectionery coating
Heart Box 3-D Mold
Plastic Coupler and Decorating Tips
Disposable Decorating Bags
Green and Yellow Candy Colors
Lollipop Sticks
Lemon Candy Flavor
Foil Candy Cups.

LESSON 4
Mix and fix the most delicious candies! Mold candy cups to fill with liqueur or brandy. Learn how to make two cooked candies—light-as-air divinities and chewy nougats. Learn to shape an edible rose from special modeling candy recipe.

Lesson 4 includes:
Lesson Pages
3 lbs. Candy Melts™ brand confectionery coating
Cordial Cup Plastic Sheet Mold
Candy Box and Liner
Professional Quality Candy Thermometer.

LESSON 5
Make some super, sensational sweets! Learn how to make chewy jellied candies and shimmering hard candies in hard candy molds. Make delicate mints and petit fours with their smooth and creamy fondant-like icing.

Lesson 5 includes:
Lesson Pages
1 lb. Candy Melts™ brand
confectionery coating
2 Hard Candy Molds
Nylon Candy Funnel
Candy Wafer & Fondant Mix
Disposable Decorating Bags
Lollipop Sticks.

CAKE DECORATING HOME STUDY COURSE

LEARN CAKE DECORATING AT YOUR OWN PACE, AT YOUR CONVENIENCE! Even if you've never tried cake decorating before, the Wilton Home Study Course will show you how to decorate beautiful cakes for every occasion. Easy-to-follow 5-lesson course includes the specialty tools you need plus the step-by-step instructions, illustrations and photographs that make it easy! Products sent to complete your lessons would cost $89.50 if purchased separately.

TRY IT FREE FOR 15 DAYS—COMPLETE COUPON AT LEFT AND WE'LL SEND LESSON 1 TO YOU ON APPROVAL!

LESSON 1
Discover the easy way to pipe buttercream icing stars, zigzag borders and more! Learn how to prepare and color icing for your decorating bag, the correct angle to use, and how to control the pressure for expert results. Make a "Happy Birthday" cake!

Lesson 1 includes:
Notebook Easel and Lesson Pages
Decorating Tips 4, 16 and 18
Quick-Change Plastic Coupler
Two Jars of Paste Icing Color
Shaped "Happy Birthday" Cake Pan
12″ Featherweight Decorating Bag
Pattern Sheets and Practice Board
Cardboard Cake Circle.

LESSON 2
Make royal icing drop flowers, star flowers and leaves. Mold a sugar basket. Create a blooming basket cake. Learn how to achieve special effects with color and floral sprays plus how to print or write personalized messages!

Lesson 2 includes:
Lesson Pages
Flower Basket Sugar Mold
Stainless Steel Angled Spatula
Decorating Tips 3, 20, 67 and 131
Two Jars of Paste Icing Color
Meringue Powder (4 oz. canister)
Pack of 50 Parchment Paper Triangles
Cardboard Cake Circle
Six Pattern Sheets.

LESSON 3
Learn the proper techniques for making shells, rosebuds, sweet peas, ruffles, bows and more! Learn to make bouquets on a heart-shaped cake ideal for anniversaries, birthdays, Valentine's Day, weddings, showers.

Lesson 3 includes:
Lesson Pages
Four Pattern Sheets
Two 9″ Heart-Shaped Aluminum Pans
Decorating Tips 22, 103 and 104
12″ Featherweight Decorating Bag
Quick-Change Plastic Coupler
Cardboard Cake Circle
Jar of Paste Icing Color.

LESSON 4
Pipe daisies and chrysanthemums using a flower nail. Weave basketweave stripes. Create symmetrical cake designs, pipe rope borders and more. Use your new cake turntable to decorate a round cake.

Lesson 4 includes:
Lesson Pages
Trim 'N Turn Cake Stand
Decorating Tips 48 and 81
Cardboard Cake Circle
Flower Nails 7 and 9
Jar of Paste Icing Color
Six Pattern Sheets
Wilton Cake Marker.

LESSON 5
Shape a magnificent icing rose! Pipe stringwork and create a mini-tiered cake using the pans and separator set we'll send. After this lesson you'll qualify for your Wilton Certificate of Completion!

Lesson 5 includes:
Round Mini-Tier Kit (includes 3 cake pans, separator plates and columns)
Four Pattern Sheets
Decorating Tips 2, 12, 87 and 102
Cardboard Cake Circle
Lesson Pages.

THE WILTON METHOD OF CAKE DECORATING

Three Magnificent Volumes—All You Need to Master Every Method of Cake Decorating Popular Throughout the World!

THE WILTON WAY OF CAKE DECORATING, VOLUME ONE— THE BEAUTIFUL BASIC!

The one book you should own if you could own but one book on cake decorating! Provides the best groundwork on the basics, but adds a touch of magic even to simple techniques. It has helped many thousands of decorators achieve master status.

Starts right at the beginning and assumes no previous knowledge of cake decorating. It's a treasury of facts and ideas, a magnificent reference, a stimulating teaching tool covering all phases of Wilton-American decorating. Handsomely bound treasury will expand your basic knowledge of cake decorating to the fullest!

Over 600 full-color photos display the Wilton-American Method of Cake Decorating. This hard-cover book will take you from fast children's one-squeeze star cakes to gala tiered cakes, from icing borders and color techniques to lettering, flowers and color flow. Individual chapters cover sugar molding, 3-dimensional figure piping and working with marzipan. You'll discover ways to mold and decorate candy, ice cream and other foods for parties. Easy and delicious recipes, all tested by Wilton professionals, are included.

Hard-cover, 328 color pages. 8½ x11-in. Printed in Italy.
904-P-100. $29.99 each

Learn to pipe advanced trims like pretty Picot Lace!

Learn the techniques for making realistic Marzipan Treats!

Learn to make dozens of beautiful, lifelike Icing Flowers!

Learn to make artistic center-pieces and Sugar Mold Creations!

PATTERN BOOKS. Filled with all the easy-to-transfer patterns that you'll need to decorate the cakes shown in each Volume. Soft-cover, 9½ x 11-in.
VOLUME ONE PATTERN BOOK. 408-P-3007. $5.99 each
VOLUME TWO PATTERN BOOK. 408-P-1195. $5.99 each
VOLUME THREE PATTERN BOOK...NOW IN SPANISH, TOO!
ENGLISH VERSION. 408-P-1306. $5.99 each
NEW! SPANISH VERSION. 408-P-1348. $7.99 each

NEW!

THE WILTON WAY OF CAKE DECORATING, VOLUME TWO—ALL ADVANCED TECHNIQUES!

This 328-page encyclopedia contains the world's most breathtaking cake decorating techniques. It describes in great detail advanced Wilton-American methods, as well as all major foreign techniques: English (Nirvana and over-piped), Australian, Continental, Mexican, Philippine and South African. Over 670 color photos display every important detail close-up so you can master them all.

Volume Two is also a wonderful guide to piped and shaped flowers; it covers flowers from every state in the Union.

Learn to make gum paste flowers that look like live blooms! A new method makes it easy, fast and fun. Make realistic gum paste figures and more!

Explore shimmering pulled sugar techniques as taught by Norman Wilton. He shows you, step-by-step, how to make glistening masterpiece cakes—even a romantic pulled sugar swan!

Hard-cover, 328 color pages. 8½ x11-in.
Printed in U.S.A.
904-P-119. $29.99 each

PLEASE NOTE:
All prices, certain products and services reflect the U.S.A. domestic market and do not apply in Australia and Canada.

THE WILTON WAY OF CAKE DECORATING, VOLUME THREE—THE USES OF DECORATING TIPS.

There's never been a book like this—there's always been a need for one. Decorating tips are explained in depth! Knowing what each tip is capable of creating will make it possible for you to achieve your fullest decorating potential.

The 180 tips are divided into several families for easy learning.

Volume Three contains more than 400 color photos, covering over 40 beautiful borders, scores of flowers and many decorative motifs piped using various tips. A section on desserts, cookies and hors d'oeuvres offers beautiful party ideas. New ideas for figure piping and gum paste are explained and demonstrated.

Hard-cover, 328 color pages. 8½ x11-in.
Printed in U.S.A.
ENGLISH VERSION. 904-P-348. $29.99 each

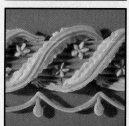

NEW! THE WILTON WAY OF CAKE DECORATING, VOLUME THREE—SPANISH VERSION.

Like no other book in the language, Volume Three in Spanish will bring decorating talents to the peak of perfection. This superb book, like the English version, is entirely devoted to the use of tips (tubes). In addition, it features a full chapter of beautiful quinceaños cakes. A "pictorial dictionary for the decorator" has been included so you can quickly learn the vocabulary of decorating as it is used in Volume Three. There is no other book in the Spanish language about cake decorating that so thoroughly and clearly explains the art of cake decorating.

Hard-cover, 328 color pages. 8½ x 11-in.
Printed in U.S.A.
904-P-1348. $29.99 each

NEW!
WILTON CELEBRATES
THE ROSE.

The most popular decorator's flower of all has been immortalized in this beautiful, full-color book. Easy-to-follow classic rose piping directions, plus a quick new method. How to create petal-perfect, delicious candy flowers. Modeling marzipan and gum paste into lovely roses. Stenciling pretty birthday and all-occasion cakes. A little treasury of rose-trimmed wedding cakes. There's even fresh rose-adorned cake designs. Tested recipes and patterns included. Soft-cover, 66 pages, 8½ x11-in.
916-P-1218. $6.99 each

2. CELEBRATE! WITH PARTY SPECTACULARS FROM A TO Z.
A star-studded collection of over 150 delightful cakes and treats. Combine shapes for lifelike stand-up animal cakes and learn how to construct a lighted gingerbread house! Hard-cover, 160 color pages: 8⅝ x 11¼-in.
916-P-936. $12.99 each

Celebrate! A to Z Pattern Book.
408-P-446. $5.99 each

3. CELEBRATE! III. Introduces the Sugar Plum Shop with exciting birth-day cakes plus Valentine's, Mother's and Father's Day cakes. Soft-cover, 160 color pages: 8½ x 10⅞-in.
916-P-308. $11.99 each

Celebrate! III Pattern Book.
408-P-229. $5.99 each

4. CELEBRATE! IV. Sugar Plum Shop offers 43 new birthday cakes. Elegant wedding cakes are included—one features a gum paste bridal couple. Discover the art of pulled sugar. 160 color pages: 8⅞ x 11¼-in.
916-P-456. $11.99 each

Celebrate! IV Pattern Book.
408-P-253. $5.99 each

5. CELEBRATE! V. Wilton Golden Anniversary edition features half a century of cake decorating know-how and helpful hints. Soft-cover, 160 color pages: 8½ x 10⅞-in.
916-P-553. $11.99 each

Celebrate! V Pattern Book.
408-P-2019. $5.99 each

6. CELEBRATE! VI. Weddings and showers, holidays and birthdays are presented. Even the Australian, Philippine and English overpipe styles. Soft cover, 160 color pages: 8⅞ x 11¼-in.
916-P-618. $11.99 each

1. CELEBRATE! WEDDING CAKES BY WILTON. You'll find large and small cakes, flowery and lacy cakes, simple cakes and ones to challenge you. Scores of exciting designs include some using foreign methods, many using staircases and fountains. Directions and patterns included. Hard-cover, 192 color pages: 8¾ x 11¼-in.
916-P-847. $12.99 each
Select one or several! These expert volumes are perfect for new ideas, reference and how-to's!

2. BEAUTIFUL BRIDAL CAKES THE WILTON WAY. A most impressive collection of wedding cake ideas! Select from an array of tiered wedding cakes designed using the Wilton method, plus continental, English, Australian and Philippine styles, too. You'll find cakes for intimate gatherings and gala affairs. Directions and patterns included for each cake. Hard-cover, 144 color pages: 8½ x 11¼-in.
908-P-117. $12.99 each

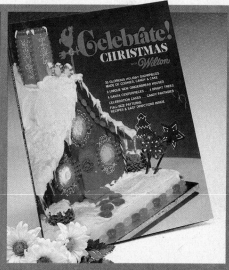

3. THE WILTON BOOK OF WEDDING CAKES. All about weddings, showers, rehearsal dinners, bachelor parties, anniversaries, more! Includes modern and traditional designs, towering tiers and simple creations. Information on planning, choosing flowers, selecting music and making arrangements included for bride-to-be. Hard-cover, 112 color pages: 8⅞ x 11¼-in.
908-P-109. $10.99 each

4. THE WILTON WAY TO DECORATE FOR CHRISTMAS. Make this your merriest Christmas ever! Includes delicious recipes and holiday decorating ideas: festive cakes, candy, cookies, fruit cake, cream puffs plus ornaments and ideas for table centerpieces. Includes patterns, instructions and close-up photographs to make these fun projects easy to do! Soft-cover, 96 color pages: 8½ x 11-in. Printed in Italy.
911-P-224. $6.99 each

5. CELEBRATE! CHRISTMAS. An idea book of Christmas magic! Gingerbread house designs cover many pages. We'll show you how to make candy trims and add icing decorations. We'll even show you how to light your dream house electrically. Includes centerpiece cookie and cake creations, delicious recipes and patterns. Soft-cover, 80 color pages: 8½ x 11-in.
916-P-774. $6.99 each

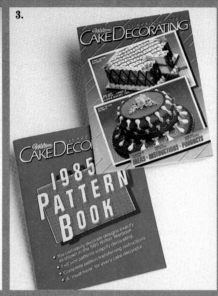

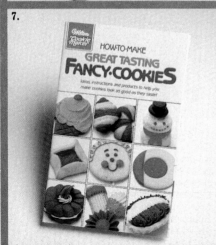

1-2. WILTON BEGINNERS GUIDE TO CAKE DECORATING. Clearly shows and tells Wilton cake decorating basics. You'll find ideas for beautifully decorated, hurry-up cakes and children's party treats—most take less than 1 hour to decorate. Soft-cover, 34 color pages, 5½ x 8½-in.
1. ENGLISH VERSION.
902-P-1183. $1.99 each
2. SPANISH VERSION.
902-P-1418. $1.99 each

3. 1985 WILTON YEARBOOK. Ideas, dessert and cookie recipes, candy making and so much more! Everything you need to add that special touch that means so much! Soft-cover, 192 color pages, 8¼ x 11-in.
1701-P-857. $3.99 each

1985 WILTON PATTERN BOOK. The patterns needed in the '85 Yearbook. Soft-cover, 8⅞ x 11-in.
408-P-8571. $3.99 each

4. 1984 WILTON YEARBOOK. Features a 16-pg. bonus pullout of Candymaking Ideas. Birthday and year 'round decorating ideas, too. Soft-cover, 8¼ x 11-in.
1701-P-847. $3.50 each

'84 YEARBOOK PATTERN BOOK. Soft-cover, 8⅞ x 11-in.
408-P-8408. $3.99 each

5. 1983 WILTON YEARBOOK. More great decorating and dessert ideas. Soft-cover, 8¼ x 11-in.
1701-P-836. $3.50 each

'83 YEARBOOK PATTERN BOOK. Soft-cover, 8⅞ x 11-in.
408-P-1829. $3.99 each

6. CANDY MAKING FOR BEGINNERS— REVISED EDITION. Filled with delicious candy recipes, ideas and products. Basic candy making techniques, like molding and dipping, are clearly explained. Learn how to make lollipops, dip fruit and create delightful treats with Wilton candy molds. Soft-cover, 44 color pages, 5½ x 8½-in.
902-P-1361. $1.99 each

7. HOW TO MAKE GREAT TASTING FANCY COOKIES. Now it's easy to make fancy, great tasting cookies. This little book is packed with kitchen-tested recipes, helpful hints, detailed instructions. Discover the delicious possibilities using jam, jelly, Cookie Dips,™ candy wafers, nuts, fruits and piped icing decorations. Soft-cover, 44 color pages, 5½ x 8½-in.
902-P-3600. $1.99 each

8. IT'S SO EASY BOOKS. Decorating ideas and instructions designed specifically for beginners. Timesaving designs that even busy, experienced decorators will appreciate. Collect the complete series for all of your happy occasions.
Soft cover, 5½ x 8½-in.
$.99 each.

BOY'S BIRTHDAYS. 902-P-3268.

GIRL'S BIRTHDAYS. 902-P-3241.

ADULT BIRTHDAYS. 902-P-3314.

TEEN BIRTHDAYS. 902-P-3225.

HAPPY EVENTS. 902-P-3284.

SPORTS EVENTS. 902-P-3209.

Our books are a wonderful gift idea for anyone who loves to bake, decorate and discover new talents. They're filled with impressive ideas and easy-to-follow instructions. Order several to give as gifts and treat yourself. We're sure you'll be pleased!

1. THE COMPLETE WILTON BOOK OF CANDY. Our candy specialists will show and tell you how to make luscious molded and dipped chocolates, dessert shells, fudges, truffles, confectionery coating candies, marzipan, hard candies and more. Recipes, with helpful hints, clearly explain how to make dozens of different confections you never would have thought possible to make in your own kitchen. Filled with numerous ideas, this beautiful book is a wise investment for beginning candy makers as well as those who have been making candy for years. Hard-cover, full-color, 176 pages, 7⅞ x 10⅛-in.
902-P-1243. $12.99 each

2. NEW! DRAMATIC TIER CAKES. The complete source of instruction on building tier cakes. Step-by-step picture lessons in the five ways to build a tier cake—starting with quickest and easiest. It shows how to achieve smooth level tiers, gives lots of quick shortcuts, the guaranteed way to safely carry a tier cake to the reception, tested recipes; use of stairways and fountains, decorating descriptions, a complete guide of products needed to execute cakes shown in the book. It's a must-have! Soft-cover, 80 color pages, 8½ x 11-in.
902-P-1725. $6.99 each

3. DISCOVER THE FUN OF CAKE DECORATING. Over 100 unique cake ideas, from fast and easy sheet cakes to glorious tiered wedding cakes, are shown with easy-to-follow, step-by-step instructions. A must for beginners, an indispensable reference for advanced decorators. Includes basic borders, flower making, figure piping, color flow and more. Complete with patterns and cake serving ideas. Hard-cover, 184 color pages, 8⅞ x 11-in.
904-P-206. $12.99 each

4. NEW! 1986 YEARBOOK. Order extras! Introduce others to the fun of cake decorating. Soft-cover, full-color, 8¼ x 11-in.
1701-P-867. $3.99 each

5. NEW! 1986 PATTERN BOOK. The easy-to-transfer patterns and instructions for duplicating delightful '86 Yearbook cakes. Soft-cover, 8⅞ x 11-in.
408-P-867. $3.99 each

6. THE WILTON METHOD ON FILM. The Wilton film, "The Art of Cake Decorating," is a great way to demonstrate the Wilton Method of Cake Decorating. Ideal to show to customers, at club meetings and in class. Full-color, 30-minute film features Norman Wilton expertly demonstrating beautiful icing decorations. Connie Riherd, professional instructor, creates lifelike gum paste flowers. Write for free information:
Wilton Enterprises, Film Productions, 2240 West 75th St., Woodridge, IL 60517

1.

4. NEW!
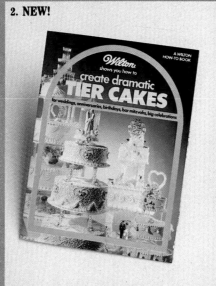

2. NEW!

5. NEW!
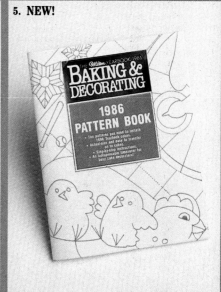

3.

6.

SEPARATOR SETS

1. CAROUSEL SEPARATOR SET.
Place this perky parade of ponies between two cakes to create an enchanting merry cake-go-round. Set contains 2 brown and 2 white snap-on 4-in. horse pillars, two 10-in. round plates—one clear acrylic, one plastic. Two 10-in. cardboard circles protect plates and add support.
2103-P-1139. $9.99 set

2. ABC BLOCK SEPARATOR SET.
It's easy as ABC to create enchanting tiered party cakes for showers, children's birthdays, and more! Complete set includes acrylic and white plastic two 10-in. round plates, four snap-on 4-in. high block pillars and two 10-in. cardboard circles for plate support. Use plates alone to serve single cakes or treats.
301-P-6016. $5.99 set

3. CAROUSEL CAKE TOP. Place our 10-in. high merry-go-round with dancing clowns and flying flags on a 10-in. or larger birthday or celebration cake. Awning big top, 6 each of poles, horses, flags and clowns included.
1305-P-9302. $4.99 set

4. CLOWN SEPARATOR SET. Tricky twosome balances a 6-in. round cake on top plate over any size base cake. You can stand them up on either their hands or feet to hold your cake. Set includes two 7-in. scallop-edged separator plates and two-snap-on clown supports. 4-in. high.
301-P-909. $6.99 set

YOUNG CHILDREN'S CAKE TOPS

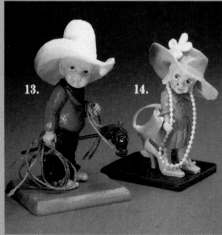

5. JUGGLER CLOWN. Turn your party cake into a 3-ring circus of fun. 4-in. high.
2113-P-2252. $2.09 each

6. POLKA DOT CLOWN. He'll make sure the party's great. Hand-painted. 4½-in. high.
2113-P-2848. $2.69 each

7. CIRCUS BALLOONS. 12 bright balloons in a bunch. 3-in. diam., 3 bunches per set.
2113-P-2366. $2.09 set

8. COUNTDOWN CLOWN. Turn his face to any age from 1 to 6. Hand-painted. 4½-in. high.
2113-P-2341. $1.39 each

9. COMICAL CLOWNS. Fun for all with a variety of faces. 2-in. to 2½-in. Set of 4.
2113-P-2635. $2.69 set

10. APPALOOSA ROCKING HORSES. Four painted ponies each 2½-in. high. Set of 4.
2113-P-2015. $3.09 set

11. NUMBER 1 KID. This super-fast cake trimmer lies flat on cake top or side. 3½-in. high.
2113-P-4565. $1.09 each

12. HONEY BEAR. You'll have a ball trimming your cake with this character. Hand-painted. 5-in. high.
2113-P-2031. $2.69 each

13. LI'L COWPOKE. Wee buckaroo will lasso cheers from the birthday kid. 5⅛-in. high.
2113-P-2406. $2.69 each

14. DOLLY DRESS-UP. They'll like her style. Necklace is detachable. 4½-in. high.
2113-P-1485. $2.69 each

15. SPACESHIP TOPPER SET. Silver-toned spacecraft with clear dome is 3¾-in. high; 4⅛-in. wide on 1¼-in. platform. One each 2¼-in. robot and 2⅛-in. spaceman hold standard candles.
2111-P-2008. $3.69 set

16. SPACEMEN & ROBOTS CANDLE HOLDERS. Silver-toned robots are 2¼-in. high; green spacemen are 2⅛-in. high (Candles not included.) 6-pc. set.
2111-P-2024. $3.09 set

FAMOUS CHARACTER CAKE TOPS

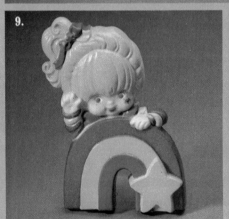

1. NEW! MASTERS OF THE UNIVERSE™ SET. Your decorating problems are ended when this mighty duo takes command of your cake top. 4⅛-in. high.
MASTERS OF THE UNIVERSE and associated characters are trademarks owned by and used under license from Mattel, Inc. © Mattel, Inc. 1983. All rights reserved.
2113-P-2393. $2.69 set

2. R2-D2™ & C-3PO™ SET. Friendly additions on cake top or sides. Hand-painted C-3PO, 4½-in. high and R2-D2, 2½-in. high.
2113-P-3607. $2.09 set

3. DARTH VADER™ & STORM TROOPER™ SET. Another powerful combination to put on the party cake. Darth Vader, 4½-in. high; Storm Trooper, 4¼-in. high. Handpainted.
2113-P-3641. $2.09 set
TM & © Lucasfilm Ltd. (LFL) 1983. All Rights Reserved. Wilton Enterprises Authorized User.

4. BIG BIRD WITH AGE†. What a surprise when everyone's favorite feathered friend announces the birthday child's age. 3⁹/₁₆-in. high.
2113-P-1430. $2.09 each

5. BIG BIRD PICK†. How easy it is to perk up the party cake or cupcakes with this mirthful bird. 3⅜-in. high.
2113-P-3815. $1.69 pkg. of 6

6. COOKIE MONSTER PICK†. No fooling around. He's a real friend when the decorating has to be fast. 3⅛-in. high.
2113-P-3813. $1.69 pkg. of 6

7. SESAME STREET CANDLE SET†. Let the lovable Sesame Street bunch burn brightly for the birthday boy or girl. 6-pc. set 2- to 2¾-in. high.
2811-P-1004. $2.99 set
†© 1984 Children's Television Workshop. BIG BIRD, COOKIE MONSTER, OSCAR THE GROUCH, BERT and ERNIE© 1984 Muppets, Inc. All rights reserved.

8. SESAME STREET SET††. BIG BIRD, OSCAR THE GROUCH, COOKIE MONSTER, BERT and ERNIE. 2-in. to 3¼-in. high.
2113-P-1728. $3.09 set
††© 1982 Children's Television Workshop BIG BIRD, COOKIE MONSTER, OSCAR THE GROUCH, BERT and ERNIE© 1982 Muppets, Inc. All rights reserved.

9. RAINBOW BRITE.™ She's the quickest, easiest way to add brightness and love to your celebration cakes. Lay flat on cake top or side. 3½-in. high.
2113-P-4798. $1.69 each
© 1983 Hallmark Cards, Inc.

10. BIRTHDAY BEAR CARE BEAR.™ This cuddly optimist brings his special rainbow of birthday wishes to the party cake. Rainbow is age indicator, 1 to 6. 3⅝-in. high.
2113-P-1475. $2.09 each

11. STRAWBERRY SHORTCAKE. Lay flat on cake top or sides. Hand-painted. 3½-in. long.
2113-P-4646. $1.39 each

12. "BERRY" NICE STRAWBERRY SHORTCAKE. She'll be a standout at any celebration. Hand-painted. 3-in. high.
2113-P-4522. $2.69 each

SPORTS CAKE TOPS

1. JAUNTY JOGGER. You're sure to win any cake decorating marathon without huffing and puffing with this little runner. Hand-painted. 4¼-in. high. 2113-P-2066. **$2.69 each**

2. IN-STEP JOGGER. It's no sweat to decorate with this! 3¾-in. high. 2113-P-4816. **$2.09 each**

3. TENNIS STAR. Set her on the winner's congratulations or birthday cake. You'll be loved for it. 4-in. high. 2113-P-2112. **$2.09 each**

4. GOLF PRO. Have this determined lady tee off on a celebration cake and you'll look like a decorating pro. 4-in. high. 2113-P-1975. **$2.09 each**

5. LITTLE LEAGUER. All set for the game; he'll be a big hit. 4½-in. high. 1306-P-7436. **$2.09 each**

6. FEMALE BASKETBALL TOPPER SET. These gals will be super scorers on your special-event cakes. 5¼ & 4⅛-in. high. 2113-P-4417. **$2.69 set**

7. BASKETBALL PLAYER. Dashing dribbler is bound to star on party cakes. Hand-painted. 3¾-in. high. 2113-P-9354. **$1.69 each**

8. HOCKEY PLAYERS SET. You'll skate through the decorating with these fast-moving champions. 2-pc. set. Each 3¼-in. high. 2113-P-2474. **$3.69 set**

9. FRUSTRATED FISHERMAN. He's all tied up trying to bring the big catch to the party. 4½-in. high. 2113-P-2384. **$2.99 each**

10. FISHY SITUATION. A little surprise sure to get smiles at the party table. Hand-painted. 5-in. high. 2113-P-2074. **$2.69 each**

11. END OF DOCK FISHER-MAN. Good for a laugh. Just ice cake; swirl with spatula to resemble water and set on top. 5-in. high. 2113-P-4832. **$2.69 each**

12. GONE FISHIN' SIGNBOARD. Gets your message across on any cake. Pipe on icing greeting. 4½-in. high. Pack of 2. 1008-P-726. **$1.39 pack**

13. PRIZE CATCH FISHER-MAN. With his sole catch he's perfect on Father's Day and birthday cakes. 7-in. high. 2113-P-2228. **$2.09 each**

14. BASEBALL SET. Your perfect cake can't miss with this winning team to top it. Includes batter, catcher, pitcher and 3 basemen. Hand-painted. Each 2 in. tall. 2113-P-2155. **$2.69 set**

15. SUPER SKATER GIRL. With this speed demon, the decorating is as fast as she is. Hand-painted. 4½-in. high. 2113-P-4204. **$1.69 each**

16. SUPER SKATER BOY. This daredevil will help you beat the clock with your decorating, too! Hand-painted. 4¾-in. long. 2113-P-4247. **$1.69 each**

17. BASEBALL TOPPER SET. You're safe if you put this trio on your athlete's cake. It's sure to steal the show. Ump 2¾-in.; catcher 2-in.; player, 4½-in. long. 2113-P-2473. **$2.69 3-pc. set**

1. SENSATIONAL SOCCER PLAYER. Everyone will get a big kick out of this super sport atop your celebration cake. 5-in. high.
2113-P-2627. **$2.69 each**

2. GOOD SPORT COACH. He looks sweet, but he's really a tiger. Have him highlight a winning team or coach's party cake. 4½-in. high.
2113-P-4140. **$2.69 each**

3. BUMBLING BOWLER. In spite of his defeat, his clumsy feat will turn your cake into a winner. 4½-in. high.
2113-P-2783. **$2.69 each**

4. GYMNAST. Lookin' good on birthday and celebration cakes. Hand-painted. 3½-in. high.
2113-P-4689. **$2.09 each**

5. TENNIS RACKETS. Court success and save decorating time with this whacking good pair. Place on cake top or sides. 2¾-in.
2113-P-3267. **$1.09 each**

6. COMICAL GOLFER. Down on all fours, trying his hardest, he'll be good for a laugh. 2-in. high. 4¼-in. wide, 5⅛-in. long.
2113-P-2554. **$2.09 each**

7. GOLF SET.* A stroke of genius in easy decorating. Includes 4½-in. high golfer plus 3 each. 2½-in. wide greens 4-in. high flags. 5-in. clubs and golf balls.
1306-P-7274. **$2.09 set**

8. ARMCHAIR QUARTER-BACK. Most of us know this guy. Change screen to suit his taste. Man in chair, 3⅜-in. high; TV, 2¼-in. high.
2113-P-1302. **$2.69 set**

9. SHARP SHOOTER. He'll fire up fun on birthdays or Father's Day. Hand-painted. 6-in. high.
2113-P-2422. **$2.99 each**

10. FEMALE BOWLER. She'll make your decorating roll right along. Perfect for birthday and banquet cakes. 5¼-in. high.
2113-P-2503. **$2.69 each**

11. MALE BOWLER. The number one choice for your bowler's bash. 6⅛-in. high.
2113-P-2538. **$2.69 each**

12. BOWLING PIN SET. Set on cake top to resemble bowling alley and bowl them over. Ten 1½-in. tall pins with four ½-in. balls. 14 pc. set.
1306-P-4909. **$1.69 set**

13. YOU'RE NUMBER 1! Just push this big 1 into any good news and winning day cakes to tell them they're tops. Pack of 6.
2113-P-4492. **$1.39 pack**

14. CAMPUS CHEERLEADER. She'll pep up any party. 5⅛-in. high.
2113-P-2708. **$1.69 each**

15. TELEPHONE TEENS. Party line for fun. 3 girls. 3 boys. 2 x 2¾-in. high.
1301-P-706. **$3.69 6 pc. set**

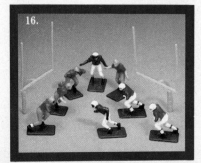

16. SUPER BOWL FOOTBALL SET. Decorate a super cake in a hurry and win lots of fans! Great for birthdays as well as Super Sunday. Eight 2-in. high players and two 4½-in. high goal posts included.
2113-P-2236. **$3.09 10 pc. set**

Plastic products made in Hong Kong.

*CAUTION: Contains small parts. Not intended for use by children 3 years or under.

HOLIDAY CAKE TOPS

1. PILGRIM PALS. Give thanks for a bountiful year with this symbolic Thanksgiving pair. Set includes 3½-in. boy and 3¼-in. girl. 2113-P-3119. **$1.69 set**

2. STARS 'N STRIPES. Display your patriotic pride atop or on the side of summer and holiday cakes. 3¼-in. high. 2113-P-4727. **$1.09 each**

3. BOPPIN' BUNNY. This happy hopper will bring glee to the Easter celebration. Fill detachable basket with candy. 5½-in. high. 2113-P-2465. **$2.69 each**

4. LITTLE TRICKERS. This trio is a treat on a Halloween cake. Pumpkin, 2⅞-in. high; Ghost, 2½-in. high; Monster, 3¼-in. high. 2113-P-3380. **$3.09 set**

5. EASTER BUNNY PICK. 2-in. on 1¾-in. pick. 2113-P-4476. **$1.39 pack of 6**

6. BUNNY FAMILY.* 2½-in. mom; three 1½-in. high babies. 1305-P-7547. **$1.69 set**
*CAUTION: Contains small parts. Not intended for use by children 3 years or under.

7. BLACK POT. Fun with Wacky Witch. Fill with candy. Cauldron is detachable. 4½-in. high. 1207-P-5222. **$1.09 each**

8. WACKY WITCH. She'll bewitch all with her charms on or besides the party cake. 5¼-in. high. 2113-P-6118. **$2.09 each**

9. JACK-O-LANTERNS. 2-in. spooky pumpkins will get screams of glee. 2113-P-3135. **$1.69 set of 4**

10. BLACK CAT PICK. 1¼-in. on 1¾-in. pick. 2113-P-4301. **$1.39 pack of 6**

11. JACK-O-LANTERN PICK. 1⅝-in. on 1¾-in. pick. 2113-P-4328. **$1.39 pack of 6**

12. HAPPY GHOST. Ghostly fun. 4⅜-in. high 2113-P-3356. **$1.09 each**

13. HOLLY WREATH. Boughs and berries. 3½-in. 2113-P-4784. **$1.09 each**

14. SNOWMAN PICK. Jolly fellow 1⅝-in. on 1¾-in. pick. 2113-P-4360. **$1.39 pack of 6**

15. CHRISTMAS TREE PICK. 1⅝-in. on 1¾-in. pick. 2113-P-4344. **$1.39 pack of 6**

16. SANTA CLAUS. Ho! Ho! Ho! He's a merry touch to add to a holiday confection. Hand-painted. 4½-in. high. 2113-P-4506. **$2.69 each**

17. SANTA 'N TREE. Santa 2⅝-in. tall; tree 3⅜-in. high. 2113-P-1647. **$1.69 2-pc set**

18. CHRISTMAS CAROLLERS. A harmonious trio. 2113-P-2813. **$2.69 each trio.**

With this sign of luck your decorating can't run amuck.

19. EMERALD SHAMROCK. 2113-P-3313. **$1.09 each**

20. LUCKY LEPRECHAUN. 4½-in. high. 2113-P-1957. **$2.69 each**

21. SHAMROCK PICK. 2113-P-4387. **$1.39 each**

22. LEPRECHAUN PICK. 1⅜-in. on 1¾-in.-pick. 2113-P-4441. **$1.39 pack of 6**

A show of love to place on special cakes!

23. HEART CHARM. 3¾-in. wide. 2113-P-3518. **$1.09 each**

24. VALENTINE PICKS. 1½-in. heart on 1½-in. pick. 1502-P-1011. **$1.39 pack of 12**

ADULT CAKE TOPS

1. BIG FORTY CAKE PICK. Too busy living it up to decorate? Do it fast and easy with this perfect pick. 1⅜-in. on 1½-in. pick. **2113-P-4482. $1.39 each**

2. FATHER TIME & BABY NEW YEAR. The perfect pair to welcome the new year. Use them separately for other events, too. Father Time, 3¾-in. high; Baby New Year, 2¼-in. high. **2113-P-3089. $2.69 set**

3. OL' SMOKY. This careless cooker will fire up lots of laughs for birthdays, Father's Day, picnics and more. Man, 5⅛-in. tall; Grill, 2⅜-in. high. **2113-P-2694. $2.09 set**

4. BACKYARD GARDENER. Plant this hoer atop birthday, Father's Day, special event cakes and more! He's got lots of get up and grow. 4¼-in. high. **2113-P-1973. $2.09 each**

5. ALL THUMBS. Our handyman special is a whimsical way to trim your favorite handyman's cake. 4⅞-in. high. **2113-P-2686. $2.09 each**

6. PARTY GUY. Your life-of-the-party will love this fellow sitting on his birthday, get well, bachelor's party cake and more! 3⅛-in. high. **2113-P-3739. $2.69 each**

7. BIG BOSS. He means business —funny business, that is. He'll take the work out of decorating your best boss's birthday, anniversary, retirement cake. **2113-P-3798. $2.69 each**

8. LAZY BONES. This snoozer is a super cake accent for Father's Day and more. 2½-in. high on 5½-in. base. **2113-P-2414. $2.69 each**

9. NUMBER 1 MOM. Show her who's first with you on Mother's Day, her birthday and more! She'll love your cake—you'll love the easy decorating. Pink/white 3½-in. high. **2113-P-3224. $1.09 each**

10. NUMBER 1 DAD. This says it all. The best for a Super Dad. Quick decorating, too. Blue/white 3½-in. high. **2113-P-3240. $1.09 each**

Plastic products made in Hong Kong.

All prices, certain products and services reflect the U.S.A. domestic market and do not apply in Australia and Canada.

1.

2.

3.

4.

5.

6.

7.

8.

9.

10.

HAPPY EVENTS CAKE TOPS

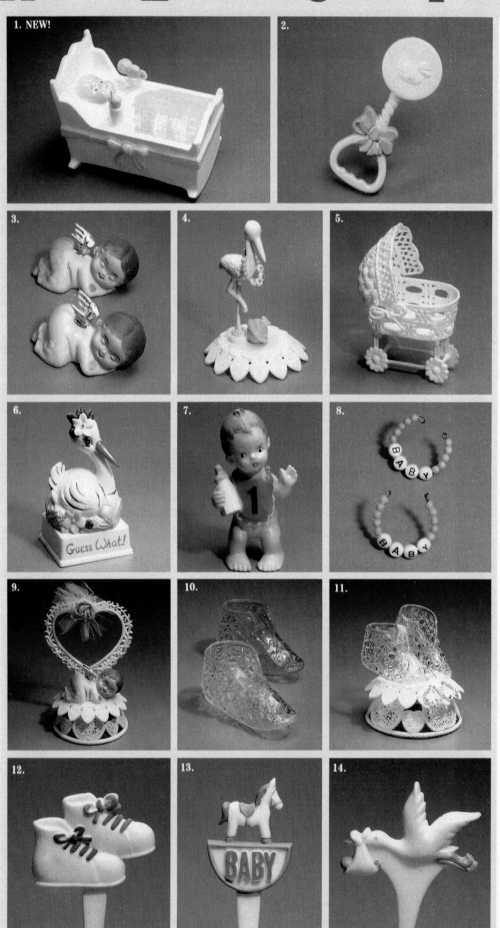

BABY SHOWERS & CHRISTENINGS

1. NEW! BABE IN CRADLE. All the lovable sweetness of a newborn baby shines in this porcelain figure. An ideal cake trim and baby shower memento for the new mother. 2112-P-2118. **$4.99 each**

2. BABY RATTLES. Don't be rattled about decorating your baby shower cake if you have these adorable add-ons in hand. Lay flat on cake top or sides. 2113-P-3283. **$1.09 pack of 2**

3. SLEEPING ANGELS. Sweet slumbering cherubs for a simply beautiful cake. Pink and blue gowned infants. 2¾ x 1½-in. 2113-P-2325. **$1.69 pack of 2**

4. MR. STORK. He's preparing for his very special delivery. Perfect shower cake surprise for the mom-to-be. 115-P-1502. **$4.99 each**

5. DAINTY BASSINETTE. Perfect for your cake, party favors or place cards. Fill with candy and attach name card with ribbons. 2111-P-9381. **$1.09 each**

6. MAMA STORK. Colorful, hand-painted nesting bird is full of mischief. 3⅞-in. high. 1305-P-6303. **$1.69 each**

7. TINY TODDLER. Perfect little imp for baby's first birthday. 5½-in. high. 1103-P-7429. Blue. **$1.69 each** 1103-P-7437. Pink. **$1.69 each**

8. BABY BRACELET. Familiar beads spell out the happy news. Ideal for quick, clever decorating. Pink and blue. 1-in. diameter. 2111-P-72. **$1.69 pack of 4**

9. LULLABY ORNAMENTS. Cherubic baby on filigree base is a sure charmer. 6-in. high. 115-P-921. Blue. **$4.99 each** 115-P-948. Pink. **$4.99 each**

10. CRYSTAL-CLEAR BOOTIES. Lace these dainty booties with pastel ribbon and fill with candy or flowers. 4¼-in. long. 1103-P-9332. **$1.69 pack of 2**

11. BOOTIE ORNAMENT. Crystal clear booties on filigree hearts. Add pink or blue trim. 111-P-2500. **$6.99 each**

12. BABY SHOES CAKE PICK. Scatter these tiny shoes around your shower cake to tell moms the patter of little feet is near. 2113-P-3811. **$1.39 pack of 6**

13. ROCKING HORSE CAKE PICK. Round up these rockin' ponies to trim your cake and you'll have time to rock at the party! 2113-P-3809. **$1.39 pack of 6**

14. STORK CAKE PICK. Land this fellow on your cake top and fly through the decorating. 2113-P-3805. **$1.39 pack of 6**

BRIDAL SHOWER, COMMUNION & GRADUATION CAKE TOPS

1. NEW! BRIDAL SHOWER DELIGHT. This delicate miniature umbrella on stand is perfect for all bridal shower cakes. Use it as an attractive individual table centerpiece, too. 6-in. high.
115-P-201. $6.99 each

2. PARTY PARASOLS. Perfect party favors, cake tops, gift ties. 4-in. parasols, 5-in. snap-on handles.
2110-P-9296. $1.69 pack of 4

3. RELUCTANT GROOM COUPLE. Add a humorous touch to the engagement or wedding shower cake. 5½-in. high.
1316-P-9520. $4.99 each couple

4-5. NEW! COMMUNION BOY and COMMUNION GIRL. Childhood innocence in all its glory is beautifully expressed in these kneeling earthenware figurines. A perfect addition to the Communion cake.
COMMUNION BOY.
  2112-P-2114. $2.99 each
COMMUNION GIRL.
  2112-P-2116. $2.99 each

6. COMMUNION ALTAR. Boy or girl at prayer will be a meaningful addition on the joyous event cake. Tulle veil on girl. Each 3 x 2½-in.
Boy. 1105-P-7886. $2.09 each
Girl. 1105-P-7878. $2.09 each

7. SHINING CROSS. Lay flat or push into cake. Embossed gold-tone finish with detachable pick. 3¾-in. high.
1105-P-7320. $1.09 each

8. SUCCESSFUL GRAD. He's got his future in his hands. Perfect tribute to the proud grad. 4½-in. high
2113-P-4549. $1.69 each

9. GLOWING GRAD. She's radiant with happiness and success. Place her on your grad's cake to share her joy. 4½-in. high.
2113-P-1833. $1.69 each

10. GLAD GRADUATE. Eager and ready for the world, he'll make your cake. 4¾-in. high.
2113-P-1817. $2.09 each

11. MORTARBOARD AND DIPLOMA CAKE PICK. Perk up your graduate's cake and you'll both be congratulated for a job well-done.
2113-P-3803. $1.39 pack of 6

12. RINGS AND RIBBON CAKE PICK. Transform a simple cake into a joyful celebration of love. Quick and easy trimming.
2113-P-3807. $1.39 pack of 6

13. GOOD LUCK KEY CAKE PICK. The key to success. It's also the key to fast decorating.
2113-P-3801. $1.39 pack of 6

1. NEW!

2.

3.

4. NEW!

5. NEW!

6.

7.

8.

9.

10.

11.

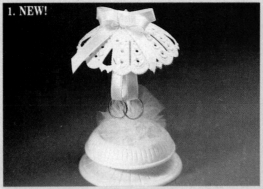

12.

13.

WEDDING CAKE PORCELAINS

Our collection of exquisite Wedding Cake Porcelains offers the discriminating bride the opportunity to express her very personal style.

Each features a stunning, stylized couple of fine porcelain in a traditional or contemporary setting. All are tastefully adorned with satin ribbons and handmade blooms. The crystal-look base of Promise and Rhapsody coordinates beautifully with our crystal-look plates, pillars and new Fountain Cascade.

Whichever elegant Wedding Cake Porcelain you choose, it's sure to become a treasured keepsake. Who knows, maybe it will be atop your child's wedding cake someday.

Be sure to see the Wedding Porcelains used on our wedding cakes, pages 70, 71 and 74.

1-2. NEW! DEVOTION. Symbolic and streamlined. The grace and sleekness of the lucite-look chapel window makes Devotion the perfect one for a sophisticated, traditional bride to select. 8⅜-in. high.
$24.99 each
1. PINK. 117-P-421
2. LILAC. 117-P-423
Also available:
WHITE. 117-P-425

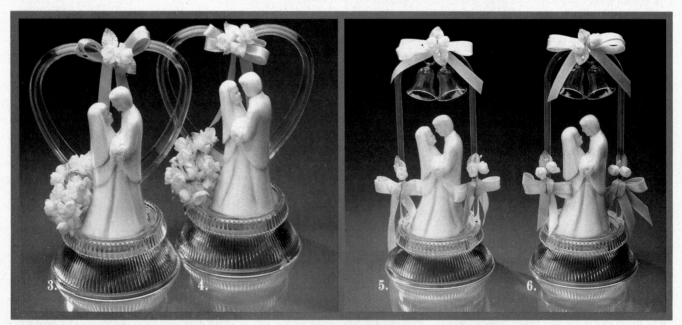

3-4. PROMISE. This lighthearted romantic is a lovely choice for the bride who likes classic styling with contemporary flair. Can't you just see it atop beautiful heart-shaped tiers? 9⅝-in. high.
$24.99 each
3. BLUE. 117-P-309   Also available:
4. PINK. 117-P-311   LILAC. 117-P-307

5-6. RHAPSODY. Modern, yet traditional. The winsome belled arch will look simply stunning atop elaborate wedding tiers. 9½-in. high.
$24.99 each
5. WHITE. 117-P-301
6. PINK. 117-P-305
Also available:
LILAC. 117-P-303

Porcelain Plates made in Japan.
Couple, brass nameplate and flowers made in Korea.
Plastic parts made in Hong Kong.
Assembled in U.S.A.

144

1. CHERISH. Are you a romantic? If so, then Cherish is the perfect choice for you. It's classic, charming and sentimental. Let the lovely motif of the porcelain wedding plate inspire your cake's decorations. Three delightful patterns are available. Ornament is 8¼-in. high; plate is 7⅛-in. diameter. Includes an engravable brass nameplate to attach to base. With special assembly instructions.
$34.99 each
1. LILAC. 117-P-173

Also available:
PINK. 117-P-157
YELLOW. 117-P-190

2. PORCELAIN WEDDING PLATES. What a delightful idea...the bride and groom can serve their pieces of wedding cake on matching plates. Thoughtful thank you gifts for the bridesmaids, too. Collectibles to treasure; packaged in attractive gift cartons.
$12.99 each
2A. FAITH. 201-P-1660. Rings and ribbons in lilac tones.
2B. JOY. 201-P-1724. Wild flowers in yellow tones.
2C. HOPE. 201-P-1635. Bells and flowers in pink tones.

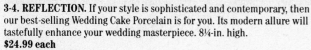

3-4. REFLECTION. If your style is sophisticated and contemporary, then our best-selling Wedding Cake Porcelain is for you. Its modern allure will tastefully enhance your wedding masterpiece. 8¼-in. high.
$24.99 each
3. PINK. 117-P-297
4. BLUE. 117-P-130
Also available:
LILAC. 117-P-270

5-6. CAPTIVATION. Radiant and engaging. Captivation will appeal both to the sophisticated or traditional bride. The pretty ribbon-covered canopy makes it perfect for spring and garden wedding cakes. 10-in. high.
$24.99 each
5. LILAC. 117-P-211
6. WHITE. 117-P-254
Also available:
PINK. 117-P-238

WEDDING ORNAMENTS

Choose from traditional, or contemporary charming hand-painted couples, enhanced with handmade fabric flowers, beautifully detailed plastic trims, satin ribbons, airy tulle and lacy ruffles.

1. SWEET CEREMONY.
Pretty bead heart, dotted with tulle and a bloom. An openwork chapel bell. Traditional couple. Delicate filigree heart base. 10-in. high.

$12.99 each

BLACK COAT. 101-P-22011.

WHITE COAT. 101-P-22028.

2. LOVE DUET.
Symbolic double rings. Lovebirds. Elegantly detailed openwork gate. Fabric flowers. Embossed base. 8-in. high.

103-P-43903. **$8.99 each**

3. SPELLBOUND.
Picturesque garden gazebo. Graceful doves. Kissing Couple. Delicate flower vines. 9-in. high.

$12.99 each

YELLOW FLOWERS. 110-P-406.

PINK FLOWERS. 110-P-422.

4. TENDERNESS.
Romantic Kissing Couple. Lavish sprays of white roses and lily of the valley. Burst of tulle, dotted with a satiny rose. Filigree heart base. 10½-in. high.

110-P-112. **$14.99 each**

5. HEART-TO-HEART.
Engaging Kissing Couple. Lace-trimmed filigree heart frame. Pretty fabric bloom. Airy openwork heart base. 9-in. high.

110-P-376. **$15.99 each**

6. LOVE TOKEN.
Lace-covered three-ring dome. Puff of tulle and filigree bell. Darling Kissing Couple. Floral scroll base. 11-in. high.

110-P-538. **$14.99 each**

Plastic parts made in Hong Kong.
Flowers made in Korea.
All ornaments are hand-assembled in the U.S.A.

1. SPRING SONG.
A pretty pair of songbirds. Yellow-centered and fantasy flower spray. A burst of tulle. Filigree heart base. 9½-in. high. Be sure to see the Petite version of this popular ornament on page 151.
111-P-2802. $14.99 each

2. NEW! HARMONY.
Elegant bisque porcelain couple. Tulle-trimmed openwork heart. Pairs of glittery openwork bells. Flowery touches. Sleek beveled pedestal base. 8½-in. high.
$19.99 each

BLACK COAT. 116-P-100.

WHITE COAT. 116-P-200.

3. TENDERHEART.
Bisque porcelain couple. Delicate filigree heart, outlined with lacy ruffles. Satin ribbons and fantasy flowers. Openwork heart base. **$19.99 each**

COAT	FLOWERS	NO.
BLACK.	WHITE.	112-P-100.
BLACK.	PINK.	112-P-200.
BLACK.	BLUE.	112-P-300.
WHITE.	BLUE.	112-P-400.
WHITE.	PINK.	112-P-500.
WHITE.	WHITE.	112-P-600.

4. MOONBEAM'S EMBRACE.
Double archway of delicate star flowers and white cascading blossoms. Lovely bisque porcelain couple on filigree heart base. 10½-in. high.
$19.99 each

WHITE COAT. 112-P-1000.

BLACK COAT. 112-P-2000.

5. ROSE CASCADE.
Beautifully detailed bisque porcelain couple. Enchanting archway of rose, lily of the valley, fantasy flowers and leaves. A pretty puff of tulle, dotted with a single bloom. On delicate heart base. 11½-in high.
$18.99 each

WHITE COAT. 112-P-9000.

BLACK COAT. 112-P-8000.

6. RELUCTANT GROOM.
Whimsical wedding couple. Dainty yellow-centered fabric and tulle flower arch accented with filigree bell. Lacy heart base. Ideal for bridal shower or groom's cakes, too. 10-in. high.
110-P-1003. $16.99 each

Glorify your beautiful tribute to love with our traditional hand-painted couples, pure white lovebirds, filigree or satin bells. Each flaunts pretty handmade florals, bursts of tulle, elegantly detailed plastic trims or tender touches of lace.

1. CIRCLES OF LACE. Lovely lace-covered triple-ring arch. Topped with airy tulle and delicate filigree bell. Handsome bride and groom. Floral scroll base. 12-in. high.
$13.99 each
BLACK COAT. 114-P-8014.
WHITE COAT. 114-P-8022.

2. ENCHANTMENT. Charming arched trellis and pretty picket fence. Elegant white orchids and dainty baby blooms. Traditional couple. Filigree heart base. 10-in. high.
$14.99 each
BLACK COAT. 114-P-9002.
WHITE COAT. 114-P-9023.

3. MANTILLA. Gleaming golden cross. Openwork cathedral window. Yellow-centered fabric and tulle flower sprays. Loving couple. Filigree heart base. 11-in. high.
$15.99 each
BLACK COAT. 114-P-45416.
WHITE COAT. 114-P-45424.

4. HEARTS TAKE WING. Graceful kissing love birds. Filigree heart adorned with tulle ruffles. Baroque scroll base. An eye-catching choice. 10½-in. high.
103-P-6218. **$10.99 each**

5. ROSEBUD BRILLIANCE. Lovebirds and rosebuds. Airy, filigree domed canopy. Bride's overskirt is made of tulle. 8½-in. high.
$10.99 each
BLACK COAT. 101-P-44315.
WHITE COAT. 101-P-44323.

6. MORNING ROSEBUD. Tulle-trimmed bride and handsome groom. Moveable openwork gate. Graceful doves and dainty fabric roses. Embossed base. 8-in. high.
$9.99 each
BLACK COAT. 101-P-44013.
WHITE COAT. 101-P-44020.

1. NEW! CHAPEL BELLS. Satiny bead-framed bells on openwork trellis. A heart of lace. A flounce of tulle. Sprays and clusters of tulle and fabric fantasy flowers. White beveled pedestal base. **$15.99 each**

IVORY.	103-P-2419.	WHITE.	103-P-2413.
LILAC.	103-P-2411.	PINK.	103-P-2415.
	BLUE.	103-P-2417.	

NEW! SWEETHEARTS & SPRING LOVE.

We're delighted to introduce this fresh, blushing bride and groom of hand-painted bisque porcelain. They'll enhance and romance your wedding tiers with their lighthearted sweetness and innocence.

2. SWEETHEARTS. Lavish and lovely. Billowy, cloud-soft tulle with a dash of lace. Glittering double bells. Sleek lucite-look heart. Ribbon bow and tulle puff. Delicately floral embossed base. 9-in. high.
107-P-200. $23.99 each

3. SPRING LOVE. Sunny and sentimental. Charming arched trellis and picket gate. A fluttering dove, rosebuds and bells. A misty gathering of tulle and lace. Beveled pedestal base. 7¾-in. high.
107-P-100. $23.99 each

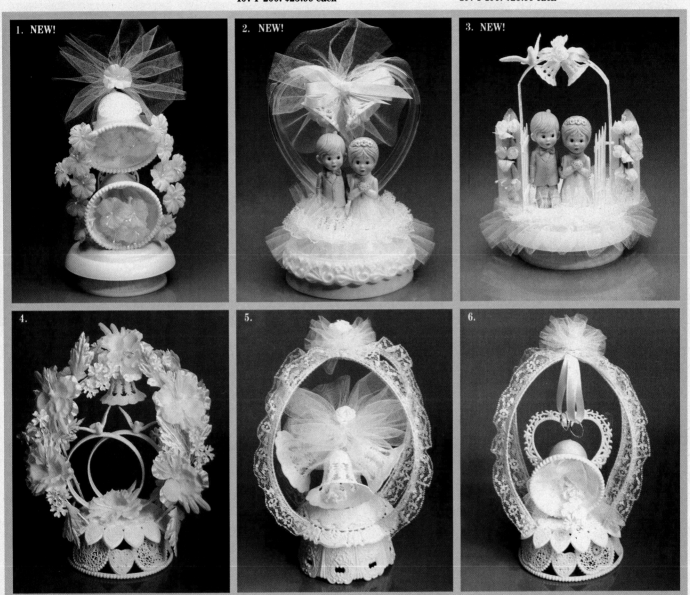

4. CIRCLES OF LOVE. Doves alight on symbolic double rings. Eye-catching sprays of giant and dainty fabric flowers. Filigree bell and airy heart base. 10-in. high.
103-P-9004. $14.99 each

5. WEDDING BELLS. Pretty lace-covered bands. A cluster of charming filigree bells. Touched with tulle puffs and dotted with roses. 10½-in. high.
103-P-1356. $14.99 each

6. EVERLASTING LOVE. Lace ruffled arches, trimmed with tulle. Wedding bands suspended from pretty satin ribbon. Satin-covered bell and openwork heart. A cascade of tulle and fabric flowers. 10-in. high.
103-P-236. $14.99 each

Plastic parts made in Hong Kong. Flowers made in Korea.
All ornaments are hand-assembled in U.S.A.

ANNIVERSARY ORNAMENTS

Traditional wreaths or hand-painted couples, adorned with fluffs of tulle, handmade floral sprays or festive bows. Lovely keepsakes after the party is over!

1. NEW! GOLDEN MOMENTS.
A fluff of tulle and airy fantasy flowers with gold leaves. Classic numeral wreath. Crystal-look base. 6¼-in. high.
102-P-305. $11.99 each

2. NEW! SILVER MOMENTS.
The same beautiful ornament in silver will add elegance to 25th wedding anniversary cakes.
102-P-303. $11.99 each

3. ANNIVERSARY WREATH.
Traditional numeral wreath. Matching ribbon bow. Peaceable doves. Filigree heart base. 9-in. high.
$7.99 each
25TH SILVER. 102-P-1513.
50TH GOLD. 102-P-1520.

4. ANNIVERSARY WALTZ.
Embossed 25th or 50th year emblem wreath. Lace-edged ribbon bow. Handsome couple. Gown matches color of wreath. Filigree heart base. 9-in. high.
$9.99 each
25TH SILVER. 102-P-5519.
50TH GOLD. 102-P-5527.

Beautiful Ways To Highlight The Years of Caring and Sharing

5. 50 OR 25 YEARS OF HAPPINESS.
Gleaming gold or silver finished anniversary wreath. Encircled with lush blooms and gold or silver leaves. A giant flower accents filigree heart base. 10-in. high.
$14.99 each
50 YEARS GOLD. 102-P-223.
25 YEARS SILVER. 102-P-207.

6. PETITE ANNIVERSARY.
Choose silver 25th or golden 50th numeral wreath. Graceful doves perch on the filigree heart base. 6¾-in. high.
$4.99 each
50TH. 105-P-4273.
25TH. 105-P-4265.

7. PETITE DOUBLE RING DEVOTION.
Ceremonial gold or silver double wedding bands. Lady's gown coordinates with rings. On filigree heart base. Ideal for smaller celebration cakes. 5½-in. high.
$6.99 each
25TH SILVER. 105-P-4613.
50TH GOLD. 105-P-4605.

8. PETITE ANNIVERSARY YEARS.
Embossed white wreath holds snap-on numbers—5, 10, 15, 20 and 40. Trim with tinted icing flowers or ribbons in coordinating cake colors. Also features pair of doves and filigree heart base. 5¾-in. high.
105-P-4257. $4.99 each

Plastic parts and trims made in Hong Kong. Flowers and Bisque Couple made in Korea. Assembled in U.S.A.

The perfect choice for smaller tiered cakes.
Engaging combinations of hand-painted couples, ornate plastic trim,
handmade fabric flowers, tulle puffs and delicate touches of lace.

1-3. NEW! PETITE ELEGANCE.
A pretty duo of satiny bells.
Cascading spray of fantasy flowers.
Filigree open heart backdrop. Triple-loop satin bow. Beveled pedestal base. 5½-in. high.
$8.99 each.

Select Petite Elegance in these lovely colors!
1. IVORY.   106-P-341.
2. PINK.   106-P-343.
3. BLUE.   106-P-347.

Petite Elegance is also available in . . .
WHITE.   106-P-345.
LILAC.   106-P-349.

4. PETITE SPRING SONG. Lovebirds coo on a branch just for two. Dainty blooms and fantasy flower arch. Airy puff of tulle. Filigree heart base. 7-in. high.
106-P-159. $8.99 each

1. NEW!

2. NEW!

3. NEW!

4.

To Have and To Hold, To Admire and Adore

5.

6.

7.

8.

5-6. HAPPY HEARTS. Engaging bisque porcelain couple. Contemporary cut-out heart. A fluff of tulle, trimmed with ribbon and a bloom. A graceful spray of delicate blossoms. Elegant pedestal base. 6-in. high. Choice of white or black coat.
$13.99 each.

	COAT	COLOR	NO.
5.	WHITE.	PINK.	108-P-219.
	WHITE.	BLUE.	108-P-211.
	WHITE.	LILAC.	108-P-215.
6.	BLACK.	LILAC.	108-P-213.
	BLACK.	BLUE.	108-P-209.
	BLACK.	PINK.	108-P-217.

7. PETITE DOUBLE RING COUPLE.
Elegant simplicity. Fluttering lovebirds. Impressive wedding bands. Traditional couple on filigree heart base. 5½-in. high.
$6.99 each
BLACK COAT. 104-P-42413.
WHITE COAT. 104-P-42420.

8. LOVERS IN LACE. Graceful arches, lavished with lace ruffles and dotted with a generous puff of tulle. The traditional couple looks so perfect. 7-in. high.
$8.99 each
BLACK COAT. 104-P-818.
WHITE COAT. 104-P-826.

1-3. NEW! PETITE TENDER HEART.

Winsome bisque porcelain couple. Lace ruffled filigree open heart. Pretty roses and ribbon bow. Beveled pedestal base. 5¾-in. high.
$13.99 each

COUPLE	COAT	BRIDE	NO.
WHITE	WHITE	BLONDE	108-P-522.
WHITE	BLACK	BLONDE	108-P-524.
WHITE	BLACK	BRUNETTE	108-P-626.
WHITE	WHITE	BRUNETTE	108-P-624.
BLACK	BLACK	BLACK	108-P-324.
BLACK	WHITE	BLACK	108-P-422.

4. PETITE WHITE BIRDS. A regal pair of songbirds perch on gracefully curving boughs. Lace-covered arched dome. Tulle pompon and filigree bell. Openwork heart base. 6-in. high.
111-P-133. $6.99 each

5. LA BELLE PETITE. Delicate, openwork chapel bell. Graceful spray of dainty blooms. Filigree open heart, lavished with tulle. Openwork heart base. 5½-in. high.
106-P-248. $6.99 each

6. PETITE BELLS OF JOY. A pretty cluster of filigree bells, dotted with a rose. Lovely, lacy bands. A tuft of tulle. Filigree heart base. 6½-in. high.
106-P-2658. $8.99 each

1. PETITE DOUBLE RING.
Fluttering doves and double bands
symbolize endless joy. Adorned with
tulle. Filigree heart base. 5½-in. high.
106-P-4316. $4.99 each

2. PETITE HEAVENLY BELLS.
Graceful doves and angelic cherub.
A pretty medley of filigree bells.
Embossed heart base. 7-in. high.
111-P-3000. $6.99 each

3. ADORATION. Charming dancing
cherubs. Elegant scroll-embossed
base. Add icing flowers and ribbons
in coordinating cake colors.
4½-in. high.
111-P-141. $5.99 each

4. PETITE TRIPLE BELLS. Elegant
filigree bell trio, dotted with tulle and
a sentimental rose. Airy, embossed
heart base. 5½-in. high.
106-P-4250. $6.99 each

5-8. NATURAL BEAUTY. Sweet
songbirds perched side-by-side.
Delicate rose sprays and satiny ribbon
bow. Filigree heart frame and base.
A wonderful selection of colors.
6-in. high
$7.99 each
5. PEACH. 106-P-1104.
6. LILAC. 106-P-1147.
7. PINK. 106-P-1120.
8. NEW! BLUE. 106-P-1184.
Also Available:
WHITE. 106-P-1163.

9-10. PETITE DAINTY CHARM.
Tulle-trimmed bride and handsome
groom. A fan of tulle and delicate
floral spray. Filigree heart base.
5½-in. high.
$8.99 each
Choose Petite Dainty Charm in:
9. WHITE. 104-P-32310.
10. LILAC. 104-P-1172.
Also Available:
PINK. 104-P-1156.

When planning a large wedding cake,
be sure to consider using a petite
ornament between your cakes. Most
of our petite ornaments coordinate
beautifully with larger ornaments.

1. NEW! STYLIZED PORCELAIN COUPLE. The same elegant bride and groom as seen on Promise, Rhapsody, Reflection and Captivation Wedding Cake Porcelains, pp. 144-145. 4⅝-in. high.
202-P-218. **$8.99 each**

2-3. NEW! BRIDESMAID & GROOMSMAN. Elegant bisque-porcelain figurines. See how lovely they look on p. 74. Gowns can be painted to coordinate.
BRIDESMAID (4¼-in. tall). 202-P-225. **$3.99 each**
GROOMSMAN (4¼-in. tall).
BLACK COAT. 202-P-223. **$3.99 each**
WHITE COAT. 202-P-221. **$3.99 each**

4. PETITE GARDEN HOUSE. 5 x 9-in. Easy to assemble.*
205-P-8298. **$4.19 each**

5. PICKET ARCHWAY. 5½ x 5¼-in. swinging gate and trellis.
205-P-343. **$2.79 each**

6. ARCH CANOPY TRELLIS. 3½ x 6¾-in.
205-P-6015. **$2.79 each**

7. WISHING WELL. Movable parts. 3 x 4¾-in.
205-P-327. **$3.79 each**

8. FILIGREE HEARTS. Openwork frame.
7-IN. 205-P-1500. **$2.28 pack of 3**
4-IN. 205-P-1528. **$2.40 pack of 6**

9. SEED PEARL HEART. Delicate 7 x 6½-in. frame.
205-P-1005. **$3.27 pack of 3**

10. KISSING COUPLE. Tender twosome. 4-in. high.
202-P-171. **$4.19 each**

11. BRIDAL COUPLE. Tulle-trimmed bride.
CLASSIC COUPLE 4½-IN. TALL.
BLACK COAT. 202-P-8110. **$4.19 each**
WHITE COAT. 202-P-8121. **$4.19 each**
PETITE COUPLE. 3½-IN. TALL
BLACK COAT. 2102-P-820. **$3.79 each**
WHITE COAT. 203-P-8220. **$3.79 each**

12. ANNIVERSARY COUPLE. Gold or silver gown. 4½-in. tall.
25TH SILVER. 203-P-2827. **$3.79 each**
50TH GOLD. 203-P-1820. **$3.79 each**

13. SWIRLS. Latticework. 1¼ x 2½-in.
1004-P-2100. **$2.49 each**

14. LACY HEARTS. Lovely! 3¾ x 3½-in.
1004-P-2305. **$2.40 pack of 12.**

15. SCROLLS. Graceful! 2¾ x 1¼-in.
1004-P-2800. **$1.92 pack of 24**

16. CURVED TRIANGLE. Fancy! 3 x 3¼-in.
1004-P-3001. **$2.49 pack of 12**

17. CONTOUR. Latticed. 3¾ x 2¾-in.
1004-P-2003. **$2.49 pack of 12**

18. CURVED GOTHIC WINDOW. 5 x 9-in. 2 pcs.*
205-P-3059. **$3.79 each**

19. HEART BASE. White openwork. 2-pcs.*
4¼ x 2-IN. 201-P-7331. **$2.79 each**
3¼ x 1½-IN. 201-P-7846. **$2.19 each**

20. GARDEN GAZEBO. Dome-top. 4-pcs.*
4¼ x 8½-in.
205-P-4100. **$4.19 each**

21. PETITE GOTHIC ARCH. 5 x 7¼-in. 2-pcs.*
205-P-2672. **$2.79 each**

22. FLORAL SCROLL BASE. 4½-x 2½-in. 2 pcs.*
201-P-303. **$2.79 each**

23. ITALIAN FILIGREE ARCHWAY. 2 pcs. Romantic arch with heart base. 4½-x 7-in.
205-P-8115. **$4.19 each**

24. GATETOP ARCH. Openwork gates and heart base. 2-pcs. 8-in. high.
205-P-3482. **$2.79 each**

1. CHERUB CARD HOLDER. Charming place markers (card not included). 1⅝ x 3⅜-in.
1001-P-9373. **$3.20 pack of 4**

2. ANGEL FOUNTAIN. Fill with icing flowers. 3¾-in. high.
1001-P-406. **$1.99 each**

3. ANGEL WITH HARP. 3½-in. high.
1001-P-7028. **$3.56 pack of 4**

4. MEDITERRANEAN CUPID. 4-in. high.
1001-P-601. **$2.09 each**

5. MUSICAL TRIO. A noteworthy band for cakes and centerpieces. Each 3½-in. high.
1001-P-368. **$2.29 pack of 3**

6. CLASSIQUE VASE. Fill with real icing or gum paste flowers. 8-in. high.
1008-P-7364. **$3.59 each**

7. FROLICKING CHERUB. Graceful addition. 5-in. high
1001-P-244. **$2.79 each**

8. WINGED ANGELS. A pair per package. 2½ x 2-in.
1001-P-457. **$2.52 for 3 packages**

9. KISSING LOVEBIRDS. Romantic adornment. 5½-in. high.
1002-P-206. **$3.99 each**

10. ANGELINOS. Captivating! 2 x 3-in.
1001-P-503. **$3.24 pack of 6**

11. KNEELING CHERUB FOUNTAIN. Accent with dainty icing flowers. 4-in. high.
1001-P-9380. **$1.99 each**

12. IRIDESCENT DOVES. 2 x 1½-in.
1002-P-508. **$2.64 pack of 6**

13. IRIDESCENT GRAPES. 3-in. long.
1099-P-200. **$3.79 pack of 4**

14. LARGE FLUTTER DOVES. 4 x 2¾-in.
1002-P-1806. **$2.49 pack of 2**

15. SMALL DOVES. 4 x 2¾-in.
1002-P-1709. **$1.44 pack of 12**

Not Shown:
GLITTERED SMALL DOVES. Non-edible glitter-coated.
1006-P-166. **$1.69 pack of 12**

16. FILIGREE BELLS.

STOCK NO.	IN. HIGH	PRICE
1001-P-9446	1-IN.	$1.68/12
1001-P-9421	2-IN.	$1.68/6
1001-P-9438	2¾-IN.	$2.28/6
1001-P-9403	3-IN.	$1.50/3
1001-P-9410	4¼-IN.	$1.89/3

17. IRIDESCENT BELLS.

STOCK NO.	IN. HIGH	PRICE/PACK
1001-P-8016.	1½-IN.	$3.59/12
1001-P-8024.	1¾-IN.	$2.40/6
1001-P-8032.	2-IN.	$2.64/6
1001-P-8040.	3-IN.	$3.39/3

18. GLITTERED BELLS.

STOCK NO.	IN. HIGH	PRICE/PACK
1007-P-9060.	1¼-IN.	$1.68/12
2110-P-9075.	1¾-IN.	$1.09/6
1007-P-9087.	2-IN.	$1.74/6
2110-P-9090.	3-IN.	$2.19/6
1007-P-9109.	5-IN.	$3.09/3

19. HEART BOWL VASE. Fill with icing or fresh blooms. 3¼-in. high.
1008-P-9685. **$2.29 each**

20. ARTIFICIAL LEAVES. 144 leaves per package. Green or white cloth; gold or silver foil.
Order 1005-P-number

	1⅞-IN.	1¼-IN.
GOLD.	6518. $2.29	6712. $1.99
SILVER.	6526. $2.29	6720. $1.99
GREEN.	4655. $2.29	4670. $1.99
WHITE.	6501. $2.29	

21. LARGE DOUBLE WEDDING RINGS. 3⅜-in. diam.
GOLD. 201-P-3007. **$1.79 each**
SILVER. 201-P-3147. **$1.79 each**
PEARL. 201-P-1007. **$1.49 each**

22. FLOWER SPIKES. Fill with water, insert and add flowers. 3-in. high.
1008-P-408. **$2.49 pack of 12**

23. PUSH-IN CANDLE HOLDERS. Pegs/holders.
1107-P-8131. **$1.69 pack of 12**

24. SMALL WEDDING RINGS. With slit for interlocking. ⅝-in. diam.
SILVER. 1002-P-1016. **$1.59 pack of 24**
GOLD. 1002-P-1008. **$1.59 pack of 24**

25. OLD-FASHIONED FENCE. 12 2½-in. posts, 1-in. pegs, 144 snap-together links.
1107-P-8326. **$2.49 set.**

26. STAIRSTEPS. 24 1-in. high snap-together stairs with 3-in. candleholders.
1107-P-8180. **$5.29 set**

1. CRYSTAL-CLEAR CAKE DIVIDER SET.*
White plastic separator plates are held by ½-in. diameter clear plastic twist legs which penetrate cake and rest right on plate (dowel rods not needed). Includes one each: 6 in., 8 in., 10 in., 12 in., 14 in. and 16 in. plates plus 24 clear plastic twist legs (7½ in. high). **Save 25% on set.**
301-P-9450. $45.99 set

PLATES	NUMBER	PRICE
6 IN.	302-P-9730	$ 2.99 each
8 IN.	302-P-9749	$ 3.99 each
10 IN.	302-P-9757	$ 4.99 each
12 IN.	302-P-9765	$ 6.99 each
14 IN.	302-P-9773	$ 8.99 each
16 IN.	302-P-9780	$10.99 each

7½ IN. TWIST LEGS.
303-P-9794. $3.99 pack of 4

9 IN. TWIST LEGS. Add extra height and space.
303-P-977. $3.99 pack of 4

2. TALL TIER STAND SET.* Holds up to six impressive tiers! Includes: five twist-apart columns 6½ in. high with 1 bottom and 1 top bolt; 18 in. footed base plate; 16 in., 14. in., 12 in., 10 in., and 8 in. separator plates (interchangeable, except footed base plate). White plastic.
Buy individually or save 25% on set.
304-P-7915. $45.99 set

*Assemble at reception hall.

PLATES FOR TALL TIER STAND.

SIZE	NUMBER	PRICE
8 IN.	302-P-7894	$ 3.99 each
10 IN.	302-P-7908	$ 4.99 each
12 IN.	302-P-7924	$ 5.99 each
14 IN.	302-P-7940	$ 8.99 each
16 IN.	302-P-7967	$11.99 each
18 IN.	302-P-7983	$14.99 each

COLUMNS.

6½ IN.	303-P-7910	$ 1.59 each
7¾ IN.	304-P-5009	$ 2.59 each
13½ IN.	303-P-703	$ 4.29 each

TOP COLUMN CAP NUT. 304-P-7923. 79¢ each
GLUE-ON PLATE LEGS. 304-P-7930. 59¢ each
BOTTOM COLUMN BOLT. 304-P-7941. 99¢ each

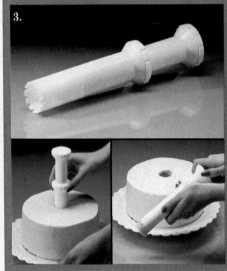

3. CAKE CORER TUBE. Prepare your tiers quickly and neatly for the Tall Tier Stand column. Serrated edge removes cake center with one push. Ice cake before using. Plastic 7 in. long solid center fits into 6½ in. long hollow corer to eject cake bits. Cleans easily in soapy water.
304-P-8172. $1.99 each

4. SUPER STRONG CAKE STAND. Molded embossed base holds up to 185 pounds of cake! High impact polystyrene material and underweb of ribbing make this stand super strong. 2¾ in. high with arched sides. Full 18 in. diameter accommodates larger cake bases.
307-P-1200. $12.99 each

5. 4-ARM BASE STAND. Replace Tall Tier Base Plate (shown in #2) with this support, then add separator plates (shown in #2) up to 12 in. diameter. For proper balance, add up to 3 graduated tiers to center column. Heavy-duty white plastic. Base bolt included.
304-P-8245. $11.99 each
BASE BOLT ONLY. 304-P-8253. 59¢ each

1. CRYSTAL-LOOK TIER SET. This dynamic plate and pillar combination features an elegant cut-glass look. Pillars have many faceted cuts that catch the light. The transparent round plates are edged with the same diamond-look cuts and have been strengthened to support the largest cake. Set includes two 17 in. plates and four 13¾ in. pillars. Combine with our crystal-look wedding ornaments and Kolor-Flo Fountain (p. 158) for a romantic look. Plastic. **Save $1.95 when you buy the set!**
301-P-1387. $39.99 set

17 IN. CRYSTAL-LOOK PLATE. 302-P-1810. $12.99 each
13¾ IN. CRYSTAL-LOOK PILLAR. 303-P-2242. $3.99 each

All plastic products made in Hong Kong.

2. FILIGREE PLATFORM AND STAIRWAY SET. Connect your decorated cakes with this impressive pair of stairs for an exciting formal presentation. Position ornament on the center of the graceful filigree platform. Includes two stairways (16¾ in. long) and one platform (4¾ in. x 5 in.). White plastic. **Save $3.98 when you buy the set!**
205-P-2109. $9.99 set

ONE STAIRWAY ONLY. 205-P-1218. $4.99 each
PLATFORM ONLY. 205-P-1234. $3.99 each

PLEASE NOTE: All prices, certain products and services, reflect the U.S.A. domestic market and do not apply in Australia and Canada.

3. FIVE-COLUMN TIER SET. Glorify your formal creation with five 13¾ in. Roman columns and two 18 in. round scallop-edged separator plates. A beautiful choice to use with Wilton wedding ornaments and the Kolor-Flo Fountain. White plastic.
301-P-1980. $29.99 set

13¾ IN. ROMAN PILLARS. 303-P-2129. $2.99 each
18 IN. ROUND SEPARATOR PLATE. 302-P-1225. $8.99 each

4. ARCHED TIER SET. Impressive way to support tiers over the Kolor-Flo Fountain (page 158). Set includes: six 13 inch arched columns, two 18 inch scroll-edged round separator plates and six angelic cherubs to attach to columns with royal icing or glue.
301-P-9752. $44.99 set

18 IN. PLATE. 302-P-504. $12.99 each
13 IN. PILLARS. 303-P-9719. $3.99 each
13 IN. PILLARS. Save $4.95 on pack of six. 301-P-9809. $18.99 pack

1. FLOWER HOLDER RING.
White plastic holder is perfect for fresh or silk flower arrangements. Position at base of the Kolor-Flo Fountain. 12¼ in. diameter, 2 in. high.
305-P-435. $4.99 each

2. FILIGREE FOUNTAIN FRAME.
The perfect finishing touch around the Kolor-Flo Fountain! Eight lacy, white plastic scallops snap together easily. 9 in. diameter, 3½ in. high.
205-P-1285. $2.99 each

3. ROUND SEPARATOR PLATES.
Dainty scalloped edge accents cakes beautifully, includes eight 4 in. plastic legs.
14 IN. ROUND PLATE. 302-P-148. $5.29 each
16 IN. ROUND PLATE. 302-P-946. $7.29 each

4. LACY-LOOK PILLAR.
Elegant white plastic pillar adds a pretty touch. Insert fabric to coordinate with bride's color scheme for an original accent. 12 in. high.
303-P-8976. $2.99 each

5. ROMAN COLUMN.
Handsome 10¼ in. classicly styled pillar may be used with Kolor-Flo Fountain (remove one fountain tier). Clean lines make white plastic pillars so elegant!
303-P-8135. $2.59 each

6. NEW! FOUNTAIN CASCADE SET.
Crystal-look plastic circles add new beauty to Kolor-Flo Fountain. Dome-shapes redirect water over their surface in undulating rivulets. Set includes 3 pieces: 2½, 4½, and 8 in. diameter. (Kolor-Flo Fountain sold separately.)
306-P-1172. $14.99 set

7. THE KOLOR-FLO FOUNTAIN.
The ultimate cake highlight. Cascading waterfall with sparkling lights is the perfect way to enhance elegant formal tiers. Add icing color to tint the water a delicate coordinating pastel shade. Add fresh flowers to create a lovely table centerpiece.

Water pours from three levels. Top levels can be removed for smaller fountain arrangement. Lit by intricate lighting system with two bulbs for extra brilliance. Plastic fountain bowl is 9¾ in. diameter. 110-124v. A.C. motor with 65 in. cord. Pumps water electrically. Directions and replacement part information included.
306-P-2599. $79.99 each

All plastic products made in Hong Kong.
Kolor-Flo Fountain made in Germany.

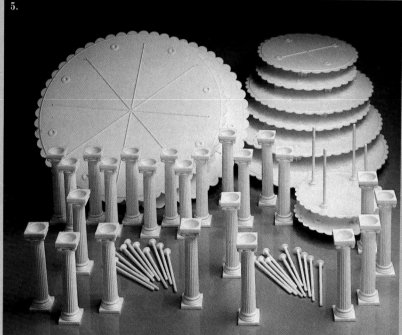

ADD IMPACT AND DRAMA TO YOUR DECORATED CAKES! You'll be pleased with any set you choose. They're all in white plastic designed to add formal elegance to your cake presentation. To protect the surface of your plates, be sure to use Wilton Cake Circles sold on page 162.

1. CLASSIC SEPARATOR PLATE SETS.
Grecian pillars and scalloped edged plate sets in 5 plate diameters and 2 pillar heights. Set includes 2 plates, 4 pillars and 4 pegs.

6 IN. PLATE SET WITH 3 IN. PILLARS.
2103-P-639. $4.99 set

7 IN. PLATE SET WITH 3 IN. PILLARS.
2103-P-925. $5.99 set

8 IN. PLATE SET WITH 5 IN. PILLARS.
2103-P-256. $6.99 set

10 IN. PLATE SET WITH 5 IN. PILLARS.
2103-P-108. $8.99 set

12 IN. PLATE SET WITH 5 IN. PILLARS.
2103-P-124. $10.99 set

2. ANGELIC SERENADE.
Cherub quartet will add just the right note of harmony to your medley of cake and icing. The plates have delicately scalloped edges to add charm and grace to your presentation. 8 in. high, 8 in. diameter plates.
301-P-607. $8.99 each

3. HARVEST CHERUB SEPARATOR SET.
Heavenly foursome adds a touch of enchantment to tiered cakes the year around. Includes four 7 in. Harvest Cherub pillars, two 9 in. separator plates (lower plate has 12 in. overall diameter).
301-P-3517. $9.99 set

4. 30-PC. SQUARE TIER SET.
Features scalloped-edge square plates with 5 inch Grecian Pillars. Includes: 2 each 7, 9 and 11 inch plates; 12 Grecian pillars; and 12 pegs.
301-P-1158. $24.99 set

5. 54-PC. GRECIAN PILLAR AND PLATE SET.
Deluxe collection provides you with round scalloped-edge separator plates and 5 inch pillars. Includes: 2 each 6, 8, 10, 12 and 14 inch plates; 20 Grecian pillars; and 24 pegs.
301-P-8380. $35.99 set

Plastic products made in Hong Kong.

PLEASE NOTE: All prices, certain products and services, reflect the U.S.A. domestic market and do not apply in Australia and Canada.

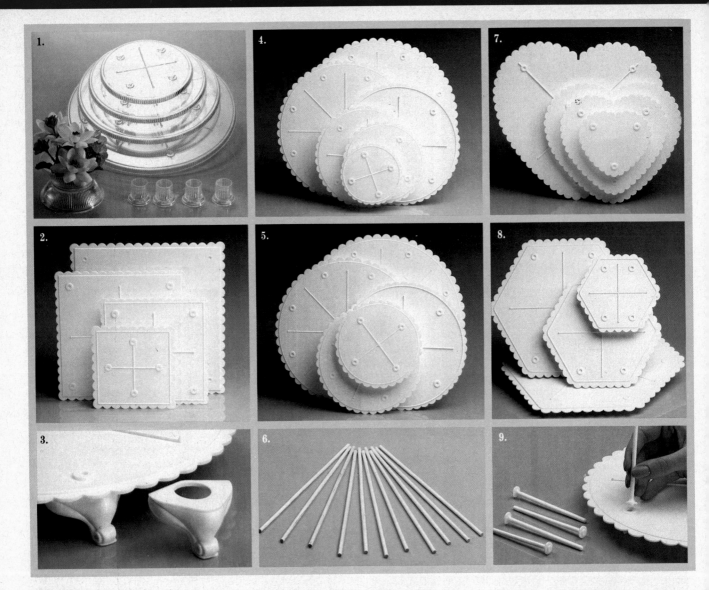

1. CRYSTAL-LOOK PLATES. Cut-glass look edge. Designed for use with our crystal-look pillars on p. 161. Four sizes; 4 in. plastic pegs included.

  7 IN. 302-P-2013. **$1.99 each**
  9 IN. 302-P-2035. **$2.99 each**
  11 IN. 302-P-2051. **$3.99 each**
  13 IN. 302-P-2078. **$4.99 each**

Crystal-Look Feet fit all separator plates. Set of 4.
305-P-613. $1.29 set

Crystal-Look Bowl. 4½ x 1½ in. deep.
205-P-1404. $2.19 each

2. SQUARE SEPARATOR PLATES. Pair up with Square Performance Pans™, p. 167. Edges are gracefully scalloped. 4 in. plastic pegs included.

  7 IN. 302-P-1004. **$2.99 each**
  9 IN. 302-P-1020. **$3.99 each**
  11 IN. 302-P-1047. **$4.99 each**
  13 IN. 302-P-1063. **$5.99 each**

3. SEPARATOR PLATE FEET. Elegant Queen Anne-look feet with scrollwork design are a perfect finishing touch. They'll fit all separator plates. Set of 4.
301-P-1247. $1.29 set

4-5. ROUND SEPARATOR PLATES. Scallop-edged plates in standard and hard-to-find odd sizes. Strongly constructed to last for years. Use with Round Performance Pans,™ page 166. Each includes 4 inch plastic pegs.

4. ROUND SEPARATOR PLATES.
Standard Sizes.
  6 IN. 302-P-67. **$1.79 each**
  8 IN. 302-P-83. **$2.29 each**
  10 IN. 302-P-105. **$3.29 each**
  12 IN. 302-P-120. **$4.29 each**
  14 IN. 302-P-148. **$5.29 each**
  16 IN. 302-P-946. **$7.29 each**

5. ROUND SEPARATOR PLATES.
Hard-to-find odd sizes.
  7 IN. 302-P-1306. **$1.99 each**
  9 IN. 302-P-1322. **$2.79 each**
  11 IN. 302-P-1349. **$3.79 each**
  13 IN. 302-P-1365. **$4.79 each**
  15 IN. 302-P-1403. **$6.29 each**

6. DOWEL RODS. 12 in. long, ¼ in. wide wooden rods. Essential for supporting stacked cakes and tiers. Cut and sharpen with strong shears and knife. (See instructions, p. 86.) Set of 12.
399-P-1009. $1.44 set

7. HEART SEPARATOR PLATES. Match up with heart pans, pages 168 and 181. 4 in. plastic pegs included. Select from four new, improved sizes.

  8 IN. 302-P-2112. **$2.99 each**
  11 IN. 302-P-2114. **$3.99 each**
  14½ IN. 302-P-2116. **$5.99 each**
  16½ IN. 302-P-2118. **$6.99 each**

8. HEXAGON SEPARATOR PLATES. Delicate scallop-edged plates to combine with square, round and hexagon pans, p. 167-169. With 4 in. plastic pegs.

  7 IN. 302-P-1705. **$2.99 each**
  10 IN. 302-P-1748. **$3.99 each**
  13 IN. 302-P-1764. **$5.99 each**
  16 IN. 302-P-1799. **$7.99 each**

9. PLASTIC PEGS. Order extra! 4 in. pegs fit any Wilton Separator plate. Keep tier cake layers in position and securely hold plate in place. Dowel rods must be inserted in cake for support. (See page 86 for how to use.) Set of 12.
399-P-762. $1.44 set

PLEASE NOTE: All prices, certain products and services, reflect the U.S.A. domestic market and do not apply in Australia and Canada.

1.

2.

3.

4.

5.

6.

7.

8.

11.

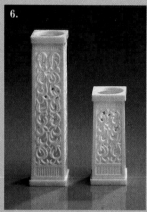

9. NEW!

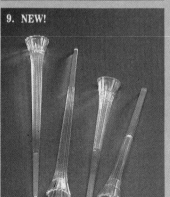

10.

12.

13.

1. CRYSTAL-LOOK PILLARS. Transparent cut-glass look. Use with crystal-look plates, p. 160. Pack of 4.
3 IN. 303-P-2171. $1.99 pack
5 IN. 303-P-2196. $2.99 pack

2. EXPANDABLE PILLARS. Sleek six piece column adjusts from 10" to 3" just by removing sections. Perfect for busy decorators. Pack of 4.
303-P-1777. $8.99 pack

3. GRECIAN PILLARS. Regal pillars with classic scrolls. Add snap-on trims. Pack of 4.
3 IN. 303-P-3605. $2.00 pack
5 IN. 303-P-3702. $3.00 pack

4. CORINTHIAN PILLARS. Resemble authentic Greek columns. An impressive addition. Pack of 4.
5 IN. 303-P-819. $3.59 pack
7 IN. 303-P-800. $4.59 pack

5. ARCHED PILLARS. Grecian pillars with arched support structure. Embossed leaf design. Pack of 4.
4½ IN. 303-P-452. $2.99 pack
6½ IN. 303-P-657. $4.99 pack

6. SQUARE FILIGREE PILLARS. Openwork design. Add color by placing pastel tulle inside. Pack of 4.
3 IN. 303-P-8070. $2.00 pack
5 IN. 303-P-7716. $3.00 pack

7. IRIDESCENT GRECIAN PILLARS. Lustrous styrene plastic columns. 5 in. high. Pack of 4.
303-P-3257. $4.99 pack

8. SWAN PILLARS. Classic pillars are an enchanting combination and an exciting way to hold cake tiers. 4 in. high. Pack of 4.
303-P-7724. $3.00 pack

9. NEW! CRYSTAL-LOOK SPIKED PILLARS. Coordinate with crystal-look plates, p. 160. Plastic spikes snap-on easily. Pierce cake to keep tiers in position. Pack of 4.
7 IN. PILLARS.
303-P-2322. $2.99 pack
9 IN. PILLARS.
303-P-2324. $3.99 pack

10. DANCING CUPID PILLARS. A captivating way to hold cake tiers. 5½ in. high. Pack of 4.
303-P-1210. $7.99 pack

11. SNAP-ON CHERUBS. Accent Corinthian and Grecian pillars with heavenly angels. (Pillars not included.) 3½ in. high. Pack of 4.
305-P-4104. $1.29 pack

12. PLASTIC STUD PLATES. Create separator plates. Glue these studs onto back-to-back cardboard cake circles. Fit Wilton pillars. Pack of 8.
301-P-119. $1.79 pack

13. SNAP-ON FILIGREE. Add a lacy look to Grecian pillars. Pack of 4.
FITS 3 IN. PILLARS.
305-P-389. $1.60 pack
FITS 5 IN. PILLARS.
305-P-397. $2.00 pack

DOILIES, RUFFLES, BOXES...

SERVE AND SUPPORT YOUR CAKES STYLISHLY AND SECURELY. Wilton has the best selection of paper products, cake boards, boxes and cake stands—all designed to add that professional touch!

1. RECTANGLE DOILY. Larger 10 x 14 in. size makes this fancy openwork doily ideal for large sheet cakes and hors d'oeuvres. Use as placemats, too! Pack of 6.
2104-P-1605. $2.49 pack

2. ROUND PARCHMENT DOILIES. Attractive Normandy lace-look pattern.
8 IN. 2104-P-1397. $2.29 pack of 10
10 IN. 2104-P-1532. $2.29 pack of 8
12 IN. 2104-P-1591. $2.29 pack of 6

3. CAKE BOXES. The easy way to store, transport and give your cakes! Sturdy white cardboard boxes (like bakeries use) lie flat for easy storage; fold easily into shape. Pack of 12.

12 IN. SQUARE (5 in. deep).
1912-P-2045. $6.00 pack
14 IN. SQUARE (5 in. deep).
1912-P-2029. $7.00 pack

PLEASE NOTE: All prices, certain products and services, reflect the U.S.A. domestic market and do not apply in Australia and Canada.

4. TUK-N-RUFFLE. Trim your cake with grease-resistant lacy plastic ruffle with tulle overlay. Offset sewn to ruffle best. Attach to serving tray or board with royal icing or tape. Order 60-ft. bolt or by the foot!

COLOR	PER FOOT		60-FT. BOLT	
Green	801-P-1501	35¢	802-P-1504	$11.99
Yellow	801-P-1100	35¢	802-P-1105	$11.99
Pink	801-P-708	35¢	802-P-702	$11.99
Blue	801-P-200	35¢	802-P-206	$11.99
White	801-P-1003	35¢	802-P-1008	$11.99
Silver	801-P-90	45¢	802-P-95	$19.99
Gold	801-P-147	45¢	802-P-44	$19.99

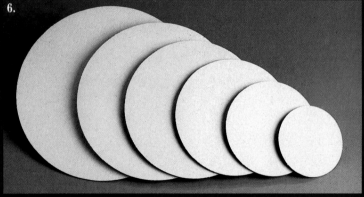

5. RECTANGLE CAKE BOARDS. Large 13 x 19 in. corrugated cardboard sheets are extra versatile—cut to fit most any size cake! Particularly handy for shaped cakes or cakes surrounded by fancy settings. Cover with Fanci-Foil for an attractive serving plate. Pack of 6.
2104-P-552. $3.99 pack

6. ROUND CAKE CIRCLES. Sturdy corrugated cardboard sheets are perfect for tier cakes to protect your separator plates! Cover with foil (sold on facing page) for the prettiest look.

6 IN. 2104-P-64. $1.99 pack of 10
8 IN. 2104-P-80. $2.99 pack of 12
10 IN. 2104-P-102. $3.59 pack of 12
12 IN. 2104-P-129. $3.59 pack of 8
14 IN. 2104-P-145. $3.59 pack of 6
16 IN. 2104-P-160. $4.79 pack of 6

CAKE BOARDS, FOIL & STANDS

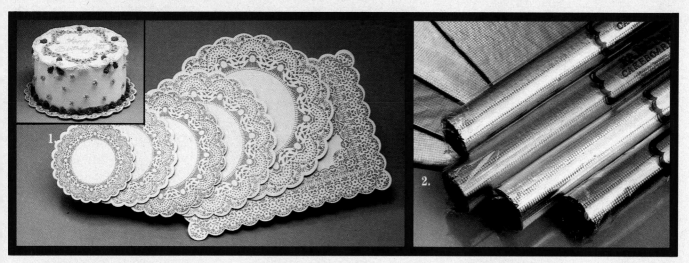

1. SHOW 'N SERVE CAKE SERVING BOARDS. Cardboard cake boards provide support and add a decorative touch with scalloped edge and printed lace pattern. Available in 6 sizes, all protected with grease-resistant coating. Use with tiered cakes to protect your separator plates, add a lacy look, too.

8 IN. 2104-P-1125. **$2.99 pack of 10**
10 IN. 2104-P-1168. **$3.59 pack of 10**
12 IN. 2104-P-1176. **$3.99 pack of 8**
14 IN. 2104-P-1184. **$3.99 pack of 6**
16 IN. 2104-P-1192. **$5.59 pack of 6**
14 x 20-IN. RECTANGLE.
 2104-P-1230. **$5.59 pack of 6**

2. FANCI-FOIL WRAP. Cover cake boards to create inexpensive cake or canape servers. Serving side has a non-toxic grease-resistant surface, safe for food. Continuous roll: 20 in. x 15 ft. **$4.99 each**

ROSE. 804-P-124.   SILVER. 804-P-167.
GOLD. 804-P-183.   BLUE. 804-P-140.
NEW! WHITE. 804-P-191

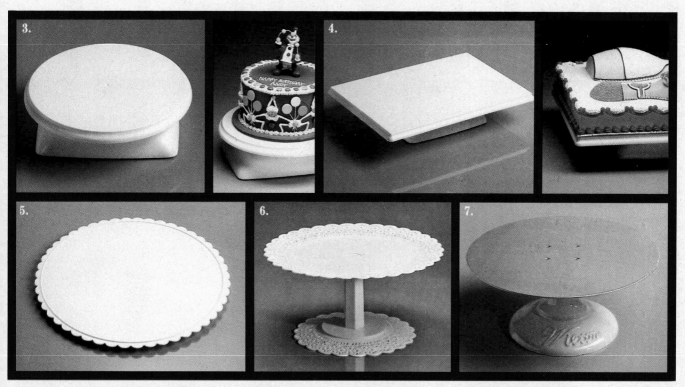

ROTATING CAKE STANDS MAKE DECORATING SO MUCH EASIER! Professional quality cake stands let you turn cake while you decorate for better results with less work.

3. ROUND ROTATING CAKE STAND. Sleek 12 in. turntable accommodates cakes up to 10 in. in diameter. Sturdy white molded plastic cake stand is extra strong with well-balanced 3½ in. high base. (Can also be used with Sheet Plate #4.)
307-P-817. **$13.99 each**

4. SHEET ROTATING CAKE STAND. Large 13 x 9 in. rectangle for decorating shaped, novelty and sheet cakes. White molded plastic with strong base, 3½ in. high.
307-P-833. **$17.99 each**

SHEET PLATE ONLY (fits Stand #3).
307-P-850. **$12.99 each**

5. TRIM 'N TURN CAKE STAND. Hidden ball bearings allow flute-edged 12 in. diameter plate to turn smoothly as you decorate. Compact. White molded plastic stand holds up to 100 lbs.
2103-P-2518. **$7.99 each**

6. LAZY DAISY SERVER. Stationary stand is perfect for decorating, pretty enough to serve and display your cake, cookies, treats! Sturdy white plastic with lace-look scalloped edges, 5½ in. high with 12 in. diameter plate.
307-P-700. **$8.99 each**

7. PROFESSIONAL CAKE STAND. Heavy-duty aluminum stand is 4⅝ in. high with convenient 12 in. diameter rotating plate. Super-strong, stand is perfect for decorating tiered wedding cakes.
307-P-2501. **$34.99 each**

Plastic products made in Hong Kong. Aluminum cake stands made in Korea. Paper products made in U.S.A.

3 IN. DEEP ROUND PANS.

Wilton® Cake Pans For The Professional
OVENCRAFT™

SHEET PANS

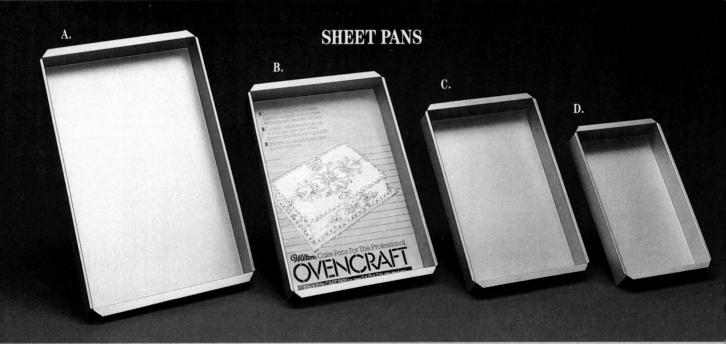

3 IN. DEEP ROUND PANS. Bake cakes to 2-layer height. Excellent choice for busy bakers.
A. 14 x 3 IN. 2105-P-5610. $11.50 each
B. 12 x 3 IN. 2105-P-5609. $10.50 each
C. 10 x 3 IN. 2105-P-5608. $ 8.50 each
D. 8 x 3 IN. 2105-P-5607. $ 6.50 each

D. SHEET PANS. New 2³/₁₆ in. depth for higher, more lavish celebration cakes.
A. 12 x 18 IN. 2105-P-5618. $14.50 each
B. 11 x 15 IN. 2105-P-5617. $11.99 each
C. 9 x 13 IN. 2105-P-5616. $ 9.99 each
D. 7 x 11 IN. 2105-P-5615. $ 6.99 each

QUALITY!

Bakeware comparable to the kind professional bakers use. Expertly crafted to satisfy the most devoted decorator and those who value the very best!
- Specially designed to bake perfect straight-sided cakes.
- Smooth anodized finish aids in cake release.
- Durable, extra-heavy gauge aluminum provides even heating for best baking results.
- Icing recipe, baking hints and cake cutting guide on back of labels.

2 IN. DEEP ROUND PANS.

Featuring These Unique Advantages

 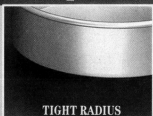 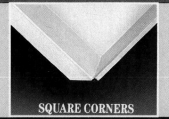 

| ANODIZING | TIGHT RADIUS | SQUARE CORNERS | EXTRA-HEAVY GAUGE |

SQUARE PANS

2 IN. DEEP ROUND PANS. Bake 2 in. high cakes.
A wide choice of sizes—all essential for tiered cakes.
A. 16 IN. 2105-P-5606. $13.50 each
B. 14 IN. 2105-P-5605. $10.50 each
C. 12 IN. 2105-P-5604. $ 8.50 each
D. 10 IN. 2105-P-5603. $ 6.50 each
E. 8 IN. 2105-P-5602. $ 5.50 each
F. 6 IN. 2105-P-5601. $ 4.99 each

SQUARE PANS. New 2³/₁₆ in. depth bakes more
impressive, elegant cakes.
A. 14 IN. 2105-P-5614. $13.99 each
B. 12 IN. 2105-P-5613. $11.50 each
C. 10 IN. 2105-P-5612. $ 8.99 each
D. 8 IN. 2105-P-5611. $ 7.50 each

All pans made in Korea.

PLEASE NOTE: All prices, certain products and services, reflect the U.S.A. domestic market and do not apply in Australia and Canada.

165

PREMIUM BAKEWARE

WILTON ROUND PANS...THE BAKING CLASSICS

2 IN. DEEP

Bake lots of pretty cakes—one, two or even three layers high. You'll get the finest results with Wilton Round Pans. For some suggestions, see pages 7, 18, 42.

A. 10 IN. ROUND.
2105-P-2207. $6.50 each
B. 8 IN. ROUND.
2105-P-2193. $5.50 each
C. 6 IN. ROUND.
2105-P-2185. $4.99 each
D. 16 IN. ROUND.
2105-P-3963. $13.50 each
E. 12 IN. ROUND
2105-P-2215. $8.50 each
F. 14 IN. ROUND.
2105-P-3947. $10.50 each

3 IN. DEEP

For beautiful, high cakes, use one of these bakeware favorites. Ideal for tortes, fruit and pound cakes, and cakes to be covered with fondant icing. See our idea on page 5.

G. 10 IN. ROUND
2105-P-9945. $8.50 each
H. 8 IN. ROUND
2105-P-9104. $6.50 each
I. 12 IN. ROUND.
2105-P-9961. $9.50 each
J. 14 IN. ROUND.
2105-P-9988. $11.50 each

When you shop Wilton for quality you also get a money-back guarantee and quick delivery. Your order will arrive within 10 working days after we receive it! And you can charge your order...VISA and MasterCard are welcome!

All pans made in Korea

PLEASE NOTE: All prices, certain products and services, reflect the U.S.A. domestic market and do not apply in Australia and Canada.

Wilton Performance PANS® PREMIUM BAKEWARE

Whether you're making a traditional round cake or a unique holiday treat, you'll need Wilton Performance Pans Premium Bakeware. It's the line noted for quality, performance and versatility.

All Performance Pans are made of professional quality anodized aluminum; they're durable and dishwasher safe, too.

WILTON SQUARE PANS...THE BAKING VERSATILES

Create basic to breathtaking cakes, delicious meals and exquisite desserts. Perfect for gala celebrations and family dinners. See pages 12, 23, 30, 37 for some ideas.

A. 10 IN. SQUARE.
2105-P-8205. $8.50 each

B. 6 IN. SQUARE.
507-P-2180. $4.99 each

C. 8 IN. SQUARE.
2105-P-8191. $6.50 each

D. 12 IN. SQUARE.
2105-P-8213. $10.50 each

E. 14 IN. SQUARE.
2105-P-8220. $13.50 each

F. 16 IN. SQUARE. (Check oven size when ordering.)
2105-P-8231. $15.99 each

WILTON SHEET PANS...THE BAKE-ALLS

It's easy to make a perfect party cake with a sheet pan. Great for main dish meals, too. For some lovely suggestions, see pages 5, 15, 59, 63.

G. 11 x 15 IN. SHEET.
2105-P-158. $9.50 each

H. 7 x 11 IN. SHEET
2105-P-2304. $5.50 each

I. 9 x 13 IN. SHEET
2105-P-1308. $6.99 each

J. 12 x 18 IN. SHEET.
2105-P-182. $11.50 each

For Your Lavish Tier Creations! Hearts, Rounds, Squares, Hexagons, Petals and Bevels. Make your cake the highlight of any celebration.

1. HEART MINI-TIER SET. Bakes 5, 7½ and 9 in. one-layer cakes with just one cake mix. Set includes three quality aluminum pans, two scallop-edged separator plates, six clear plastic twist legs, complete decorating instructions.
2105-P-409. $10.99 set
HEART MINI-TIER PLATE SET ONLY.
301-P-9728. $2.99 set

2. ROUND MINI-TIER SET. The ideal size tiered cake for small, special gatherings. Includes 5, 6½ and 8 in. diameter pans, 1½ in. deep. With 5½, 7 in. separator plates and 8 clear plastic twist legs. Takes one cake mix. Decorating instructions show you how.
2105-P-98042. $10.99 set
ROUND MINI-TIER PLATE SET ONLY.
301-P-9817. $2.99 set

3. BEVEL PAN SET. Bakes slanted cake edges that can be positioned on top or beneath your cake layers. Ideal for elegant Lambeth Method decorating. Set includes 8, 10, 12 in. tops and 14 and 16 in. bases. Use with coordinating 2 or 3 in. deep pans.
517-P-1200. $25.99 set

4. HEART PAN SET. Bakes the most romantic cakes for showers, birthdays, weddings and more. Set includes 6, 9, 12 and 15 in. diameter aluminum pans. If purchased separately, $27.96.
504-P-207. $24.99 set

6 IN. HEART.	**12 IN. HEART.**
2105-P-4781. $3.99 each	**2105-P-5168. $7.99 each**
9 IN. HEART.	
2105-P-5176. $5.99 each	

5. CLASSIC ROUND PAN SET. Create handsome graduated tiers for formal parties and weddings. Set includes 6, 8, 10 and 12 in. pans. If purchased separately, $25.49.
2105-P-2101. $17.99 set

All pans made in Korea.

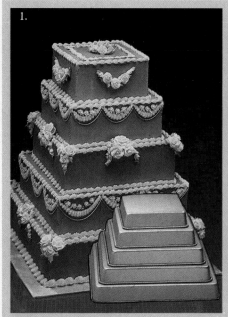

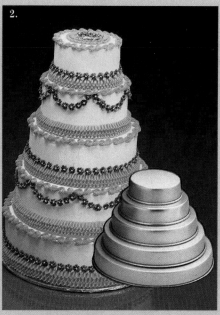

1. 5-PC. SQUARE PAN SET. This basic baking collection consists of 8, 10, 12, 14 and 16 inch pans. 2 in. deep. If purchased separately, $54.99. **505-P-104. $45.99 set**

2. 5-PC. ROUND PAN SET. Create tiered treasures sure to get a round of applause. Set includes 6, 8, 10, 12 and 14 inch diameters. 2 in. deep. If purchased separately, $35.99. **504-P-118. $29.99 set**

3. 3-INCH DEEP ROUND PAN SET. Ideal choice for fondant and marzipan covered wedding cakes. Set includes 8, 10, 12 and 14 inch diameter pans. If purchased separately, $35.99. **2105-P-2932. $29.99 set**

4. 4-PC. HEXAGON PAN SET. See how impressive a hexagon wedding masterpiece can be on page 73. Set includes 6, 9, 12 and 15 inch pans, each 2 inches deep. If purchased separately, $27.96.
2105-P-3572. $24.99 set

6 IN. HEXAGON. 2105-P-5122. $3.99 each
9 IN. HEXAGON. 2105-P-5125. $5.99 each
12 IN. HEXAGON. 2105-P-5133. $7.99 each
15 IN. HEXAGON. 2105-P-5136. $9.99 each

5. 4-PC. PETAL PAN SET. Gala and graceful, whether a few tiers or many high. Set includes 6, 9, 12 and 15 inch diameter pans; 2 inches deep. If purchased separately, $27.87.
2105-P-2134. $24.99 set

6 IN. PETAL. 2105-P-4346. $3.99 each
9 IN. PETAL. 2105-P-5109. $5.99 each
12 IN. PETAL. 2105-P-5117. $7.99 each
15 IN. PETAL. 2105-P-4344. $9.99 each

Wilton.
Performance PANS®
PREMIUM BAKEWARE

1. NEW!

1. NEW! MINI LOAF PAN SET. Eight petite loaves on one pan. Perfect for gift cakes, breads, fruitcakes, molded desserts. Fast way to bake individual treats.
2105-P-3844. $10.99 each

2. NEW!

2. NEW! PETIT FOURS/PASTRY MOLD SET. Eight pretty shapes for popular petit fours. Delightful for dainty desserts, tarts, puddings, pastries.
2105-P-2093. $7.99 set

PLEASE NOTE: All prices, certain products and services, reflect the U.S.A. domestic market and do not apply in Australia and Canada.

3.

4.

3. LONG LOAF PAN. Perfect for party size sandwich loaf and meat loaf, or to create an elegant birthday, anniversary or other party cake. Takes 9 cups batter. Cooling legs attached. 16 x 4 x 4¼-in.
2105-P-1588. $8.99 each

4. LOAF PAN. Bake a pound cake, fruit cake, quick yeast or nut bread. Ideal for main dishes like meat loaf, too. 8¾ x 4½ x 2¾-in.
2105-P-3688. $4.99 each

5.

6.

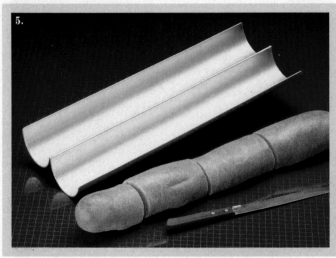

5. TWIN FRENCH BREAD PAN. Bakes two long loaves of crusty, crisp, tender French bread. So handy, you'll use it often. 18-in. long.
2105-P-1268. $5.99 each
All pans made in Korea.

6. 14-IN. PIZZA PAN. Its waffle-textured surface bakes crispier crusts. Ideal size for family pizza. Pizza crust recipe and tasty dessert ideas on back of label.
2105-P-3912. $6.99 each

Traditional and Specialty Pans to help you create superb international recipes. Or, add a special touch to your favorite family desserts with ease and elegance.

1. NEW!

1. NEW! CONTINENTAL FLAN PAN. For the ultimate lusciousness and beauty in dessert cakes. Perfect topped with fruit, custard, ice cream, more. Decorate simply or fancy. All will rate raves. Includes 12-page recipe/idea booklet. 11-in. diameter.
2105-P-2046. **$7.99 each**

2. CHARLOTTE MOLD PAN. Make fabulous desserts easily, including famous Charlotte Cake. Recipe included on label. Great for fruit cakes, molded gelatins, ice cream, other fancy desserts...steamed puddings, too!
2105-P-1270. **$5.99 each**

3. ANGEL FOOD PAN. Perfect for heavenly light and airy angel cake; great for down-to-earth chiffon cakes, fruit cakes, pound cakes and more. Generous-length cooling legs attached. 10-in. diameter. 4¼-in. deep.
2105-P-2525. **$10.99 each**

4. SPRINGFORM PAN. The essential pan for cheesecake. Open springlock and remove for easy serving. Textured bottom for best baking results. 9-in. diameter. 3-in. deep.
2105-P-5354. **$8.99 each**

5. TART PANS. Luscious lunch or dinner quiches and desserts work equally well in these versatile pans. Bottoms lift out for convenient removal of food to serving trays. Three popular sizes.
8-IN. TART PAN. 2105-P-3877. **$4.50 each**
9-IN. TART PAN. 2105-P-3613. **$4.99 each**
10-IN. TART PAN. 2105-P-3267. **$5.50 each**

Wilton. Performance PANS®

PREMIUM BAKEWARE

1.

1. PIE PANS. High quality, durable pans for all types of pies—fruit, custard or no bake; one or two crust. A size for every occasion. All are 1¼-in. deep.
8-IN. PIE PAN. 2105-P-1267. $3.99 each
9-IN. PIE PAN. 2105-P-4030. $4.99 each
10-IN. PIE PAN. 2105-P-1266. $5.99 each

2.

3.

4.

5. NEW!

2. FANCY RING MOLD/PAN. Make pretty cakes, fancy gelatins and special ice cream desserts. Mold cold salads, too. Versatile, quality, anodized aluminum mold is 10-in. diameter. 3-in. deep.
2105-P-5008. $7.99 each

3. POPOVER PAN. Treat your family and guests to light, golden popovers. Delicious with butter and jelly for breakfast; ice cream and fruit for dessert; sauces and gravies for dinner. Popover recipe on label. 6-cup. 9 x 16-in.
2105-P-4992. $12.99 each

4. LITTLE LOAFERS. Bake individual cakes or mini loaves of bread for parties and gifts. Use for molding ice cream and gelatin. Great for individual fruit cakes, too! Set of six, each 4⅜ x 2⅜ x 1½-in. deep. Each takes ½-cup batter.
512-P-1089. $6.49 set

5. NEW! PETITE FANCY RING MOLDS/PAN. Now you can make beautiful individual-serving mini cakes. Perfect for party and school treats. Bake cake, brownies; mold ice cream, gelatin. Ideas on label.
2105-P-2097. $12.99 each

All pans made in Korea.

An exciting selection of specialty pans to help you create international recipes and family favorites. This collection is a must for every home baker.

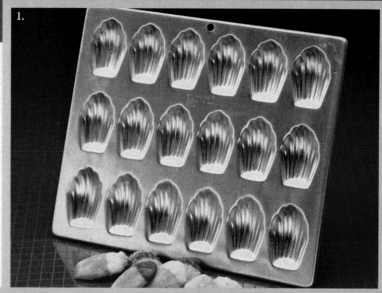

1. MADELEINE PAN. A European favorite. Delicate little cakes perfect for luncheons, buffets or impressive dinners. Recipes included. Make white, chocolate or add a hint of your favorite flavor. Serve alone or with ice cream or fruit. 7¾ x 9½-in.
2105-P-2266. $5.99 each

2. NEW! KUGELHOPF PAN. Bake Kugelhopf, a rich German yeast cake in its traditional shape. Recipe on label. Also ideal for gelatins, ice cream, more.
2105-P-2593. $6.99 each

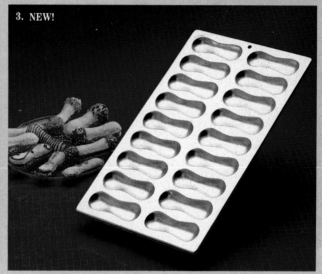

3. NEW! LADYFINGER PAN. Bakes 18 spongecakes. Delicate cakes are perfect for fancy desserts made with gelatins, mousse, fruit, puddings, whipped cream, more. Make tasty snacks, too.
2105-P-1687. $5.99 each

4. TARTLET MOLD SET. Six fluted aluminum molds make individual treats. 3¼ x 2 x ¾-in. deep (Korea).
2105-P-3794. $3.99 each

5. RING MOLDS/PANS. Bake or mold cakes, ice cream, desserts, gelatins or salads in these multi-purpose pans. Two convenient sizes. Each 3-in. deep.
8-IN. RING MOLD/PAN. 2105-P-190. $5.99 each
10½-IN. RING MOLD/PAN. 2105-P-4013. $7.99 each

Wilton
Performance
PANS ®

PREMIUM BAKEWARE

1. NEW! RIBBED LOAF PAN. Ideal for fancy breads, such as cinnamon, raisin, fruit and nut. Use for unusual molded desserts and more! Recipe for Rehrücken on label. Holds one cake mix.
2105-P-2585. **$4.99 each**

2. MINI MUFFIN PAN. Make a dozen dainty muffins, miniature fruit cakes, mini cupcakes and more! Perfect for holiday treats, too! 7¾ x 10 x ¾-in. deep. Takes 2-in. diam. paper cupcake liners.
2105-P-2125. **$5.99 each**

3. TWELVE-CUP MUFFIN PAN. Company for breakfast? Bake a dozen muffins, cupcakes or rolls. Create an original molded party dessert with fruit, ice cream or gelatin, too. 10½ x 13½ x 1-in. deep.
2105-P-2375. **$8.99 each**

4. SIX-CUP MUFFIN PAN. Bake breakfast muffins or rolls for the family. Perfect for party cupcakes or single-serving molded desserts, also. 7⅜ x 10¾ x 1-in. deep.
2105-P-5338. **$6.50 each**

5. SHORTCAKES 'N TREATS PAN. Six individual servings of shortcakes, brownies, ice cream, gelatin and more are a breeze to make with this unique pan. 8 x 12½ x 1-in. deep.
2105-P-5966. **$6.50 each**

1. NEW!

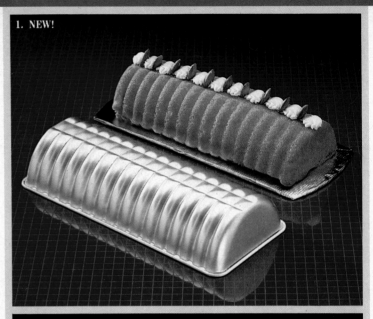

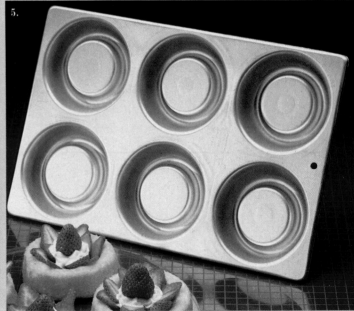

1. NEW!

1. NEW! CLASSIC TUBE PAN. Treat your family and friends to light and airy cakes, soft pull-apart breads, and rich yeast cakes, such as panetone. Anodized finish is perfect for easier release of baked foods. Holds one cake mix.
2105-P-2174. **$7.99 each**

2. JELLY ROLL PAN. Make a delicious jelly roll or ice cream cake roll with this pan. It is the perfect size. Popular jelly roll recipe and baking hints included on back of label. Great for cookies, brownies, biscuits, fancy pastries, too! 10½ x 15½ x 1-in. deep.
2105-P-1269. **$7.50 each**

3. COOKIE PAN. You can bake cookies, bar cookies, brownies, biscuits and fancy pastries with this versatile pan. Super size to bake more at one time. 12 x 18 x 1-in. deep.
2105-P-4854. **$8.50 each**

4. COOKIE SHEETS. Perfect for all pressed, sliced, rolled and drop cookies. No sides for easy slide off. Long grip for easier handling. Two sizes.
10 x 15 COOKIE SHEET. 2105-P-1265. $5.50 each
12½ x 16½ COOKIE SHEET. 2105-P-2975. $6.50 each

All pans made in Korea.
PLEASE NOTE: All prices, certain products and services, reflect the U.S.A. domestic market and do not apply in Australia and Canada.

2.

3.

4.

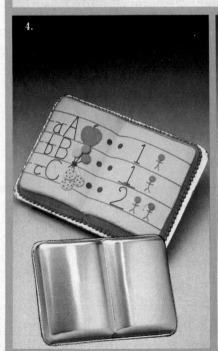

1. MINI FOOTBALL HELMET PAN. The fans will go wild! Imagine the cheers these little cakes will receive at bowl parties, birthdays, tailgate get-togethers. Decorate in your team's colors—alternate ideas and instructions on label. Each well takes ½-cup of batter. Aluminum pan is 13 x 8¾ x 1⅛-in.
2105-P-4308. $7.49 each

2. MINI PUMPKIN PAN. Bake six single-serving cakes. Perfect year 'round party treats—alternate decorating instructions for a clown, bunny and monster. See the funny face Pumpkin Patch on p. 42. Each well takes ½-cup of batter. Aluminum pan is 12¼ x 8 x 1⅜-in.
2105-P-1499. $7.49 each

3. JACK-O-LANTERN PAN. Thrill kids of all ages with a smiling or scary pumpkin face. See the shimmery, smiling gelatin surprise on p. 40. Directions include a harvest pumpkin cake, too. One-mix, aluminum pan is 12¼ x 11⅝ x 2-in.
2105-P-3068. $6.49 each

4. 1-PC. BOOK PAN. Always a novel cake idea. A best seller for birthdays, graduations, holidays and more. It bakes a great greeting card cake, too, see p. 29! Five ways to decorate included. One-mix aluminum pan is 13 x 9½ x 2-in. deep.
2105-P-972. $8.49 each

5. WIZARD PAN. He'll have them under his spell on birthdays, Halloween, holidays and more. Alternate decorating ideas turn this magical treat into a princess, Santa and cowboy. Turn to pages 12 and 41 for two more ways. One-mix aluminum pan is 14½ x 11 x 2-in.
2105-P-2633. $8.49 each

6. MYSTICAL DRAGON PAN. This prehistoric party animal will really get a warm reception at birthdays, Halloween and more. Alternate decorating ideas include a turtle, kangaroo and others. One-mix aluminum pan is 11¾ x 12¾ x 2-in.
2105-P-1750. $8.49 each

1. NEW! BIG FISH PAN. What a catch! This will be a "reel" treat on birthdays, Dad's Day and more. Ideal for molding luncheon salads and gelatin. This pan used for cakes on 22, 40 and 58, too. One-mix aluminum pan is 13 x 12 x 2-in.
2105-P-2763. $8.49 each

2. HAPPY BIRTHDAY PAN. Bake a super-easy-to-decorate celebration cake. The message bakes right in. All you do is outline and cover with one-squeeze stars. Really save time, try the Triple-Star Tip, p. 121. 10-in. diameter, 1½-in. deep aluminum pan takes one cake mix.
2105-P-1073. $8.49 each

3. HORSESHOE PAN. It's a lucky guess that you'll bake lots of super celebration cakes with this one-mix aluminum pan. A winning choice for any happy event the year 'round. 12 x 1¾-in.
2105-P-3254. $8.49 each

4. GUITAR PAN SET. Rock 'em! You'll strike just the right cord with this party cake. Quick-to-decorate...just ice, place plastic trims and add simple icing borders. Strings (not included) can be added for a realistic effect. For more ideas, see p. 6, 48 and 62. Includes plastic neck, bridge and pick guard. One-mix aluminum pan is 17¾ x 8½ x 2-in.
501-P-904. $8.99 set

5. OVAL PAN SET. A classic, pretty shape for any occasion, especially birthdays, Mother's Day and holidays. Each aluminum pan is 9 x 6¾ x 1¾-in. deep. Set takes one cake mix to fill both pans. Birthday and Easter decorating ideas included.
2105-P-1553. $6.49 set

All pans made in Korea.
PLEASE NOTE: All prices, certain products and services, reflect the U.S.A. domestic market and do not apply in Australia and Canada.

1. CANDLELIT TREE PAN SET.
Bakes a beautiful stand-up tree cake centerpiece. You'll need 6 cups of firm-textured batter to fill our 2-piece aluminum pan. Add easy or fancy icing ornaments and garlands. See the clever birthday cake made with this pan on p. 23. Set includes 6 baking clips, heat conducting core and white plastic base/server (candles shown not included). Check oven height, pan is 11-in. high.
2105-P-719. $12.99 set

2. STAND-UP SNOWMAN PAN KIT.
Create two festive favorites! A one-mix cake that lies flat. Or bake two pound cakes, ice backs and position together for a 3-D holiday sensation. For more decorating ideas, see p. 9, 11, 13 and 41. Kit also includes decorating tools, icing colors and instructions. Aluminum pan is 11½ x 6½ x 2¾-in.
2105-P-1394. $8.49 kit

3. SANTA'S SLEIGH PAN.
Everyone's favorite merry man, in old-fashioned sleigh, arrives to wish a Merry Christmas to one and all. Five ways to decorate—holiday and year 'round ideas. Another way to decorate on p. 47. One-mix aluminum pan is 13 x 10⅞ x 2-in.
2105-P-3235. $6.49 each

4. MINI CHRISTMAS TREE PAN.
Bakes six "tree"-mendous holiday cakes. Perfect to serve or give. Add icing boughs, garlands and candy ornaments. Alternate ideas include Santa, pie, bouquet and ice cream cone. Aluminum pan is 13 x 10½ x 1¼-in.
2105-P-1779. $7.49 each

5. MINI SANTA PAN.
Bakes up six jolly faces. Kids will love getting a cake of their own. Alternate ideas for turning Santa into Mrs. Claus, an elf, ornament and child. One 2-layer cake mix yields 12-18 cakes. Aluminum pan is 10½ x 10 x 1⅛-in.
2105-P-4692. $7.49 each

1. NEW! GINGERBREAD BOY CAKE PAN.
"Catch him if you can." This classic favorite will bring back memories and make lots of new ones! He's a joy to bake and decorate. Perfect for birthdays, too! One-mix aluminum pan is 14 x 10½ x 2-in.
2105-P-2072. $6.49 each

2. NEW! SANTA STAND-UP PAN.
Ho. ho, ho, what a jolly, happy cake idea! You can either bake a one-mix cake that lies flat or bake two pound cakes for the stand-up delight. Two-piece aluminum pan, each half is 11¾ x 6½ x 2⅝-in.
2105-P-6007. $10.99 each

3. CHOO CHOO TRAIN PAN.
Create a favorite Christmas toy...add icing and candy trims. On the right track for birthdays, Father's Day, club gatherings, too. Two-part aluminum pan snaps together. Pan sides are each 10 x 6 x 2-in. Takes 6 cups of firm-textured batter. Instructions included.
2105-P-2861. $8.99 each

4. TREELITEFUL PAN.
It's a trim-the-tree party cake. Spruce up with easy icing and candy trims. Decorating ideas include festive trees, a gnome and country church. Also a delicious fruitcake recipe. See the bewitching cake on p. 42, the anniversary cone cake on p. 56. One-mix aluminum pan is 15 x 11 x 1½-in.
2105-P-425. $6.49 each

5. HOLIDAY HOUSE KIT.
Makes a welcoming open-house cake centerpiece. Kit includes icing colors, decorating tools and instructions. For more clever ideas see pages 12, 23, 52 and 53. One-mix aluminum pan is 8⅝ x 9 x 3-in.
2105-P-2282. $8.49 kit

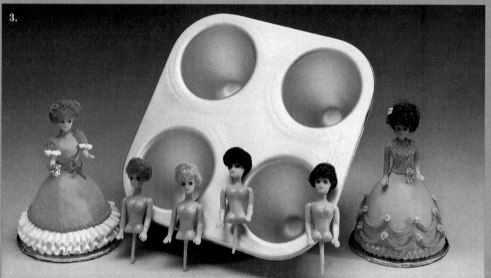

1. PIANO KIT. A grand cake idea for every music lover. Pans take one mix. Kit includes two 1½-in. deep aluminum pans (6¾ x 7¾-in. and 9½ x 7-in.), plastic top, base, 4 snap-on legs, prop stick. 2 candelabras, pedals, bench, music board and keyboard. With instructions. See the wedding shower delight on p. 68.
501-P-8093. $11.99 kit
PIANO ACCESSORY KIT ONLY. 503-P-8084. $6.99 set

2. WONDER MOLD KIT. A living cake doll perfect for birthdays, bridal showers and graduation (see p. 60). Aluminum pan (8½-in. diam., 5½-in. deep), with heat-conducting rod to assure even baking, takes 5½-6 cups of firm-textured batter. Kit contains pan, rod, stand. 7-in. doll pick and instructions.
2105-P-565. $10.99 kit
WONDER MOLD PAN ONLY (without doll pick).
502-P-682. $8.99
TEEN DOLL PICK. 7-in. tall, same as in kit.
2815-P-101. $2.69 each

4. FRECKLE-FACED LITTLE GIRL. For a little girl's cake, choose this cute sweetie. See how adorable she looks on p. 60. 6½-in. tall.
2113-P-2317. $2.69 each

3. PETITE DOLL PAN SET. Doll up your birthdays, wedding showers and more with these cake beauties. Just add icing ruffles, bows and stars. See the clever cakes you can make with this pan on p. 7 and 16. Set includes aluminum pan and four doll picks.
PETITE DOLL PAN ONLY.
508-P-302. $8.49 each
SMALL DOLL PICKS. 4½-in. on pick.
1511-P-1019. $4.99 pack of 4

5. PANDA PAN. What a "panda-tastic" cake. So much fun to bake and decorate for birthdays, baby showers, holidays, Father's Day; 7 more ways to decorate on p. 24, 25 and 27! Two-piece aluminum pan takes 6½ cups of pound cake batter. Includes 6 clips, heat conducting core and instructions. Pan is 9½ x 8⅝-in. tall.
2105-P-603. $12.99 each

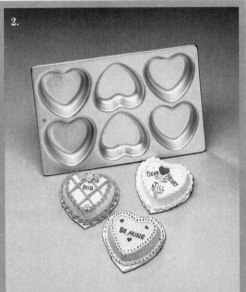

1. DOUBLE TIER HEART PAN.
Bakes a classic heart with a tiered effect. Even the simplest decorating will look impressive on this elegant cake. See p. 30 or 54 for 2 great ideas. Instructions show 4 delightful ways to decorate. One-mix aluminum pan is 11½ x 11 x 2¼-in.
2105-P-1699. $8.49 each

2. HEART MINICAKE PAN.
Bake dainty single-serving cakes or mold gelatin, ice cream or Candy Melts™* (see p. 30) desserts. Six-hearted aluminum pan is 8 x 12⅛-in. Each heart is 3½ x 1¼-in. deep. 1½ cups of batter makes 6 cakes.
2105-P-11044. $7.49 each
*brand confectionery coating.

3. CUPID'S HEART PAN.
It will get your message of love across not just on Valentine's Day, but on Mother's Day, birthdays, anniversaries and wedding showers. Instructions included for decorating pretty and amusing delights sure to win hearts. Don't miss the pretty ideas on p. 20 and 28. One-mix aluminum pan is 13¾ x 10 x 2-in.
2105-P-4911. $6.49 each

4. HEART PAN SET.
Create the most romantic cakes for showers, birthdays, weddings, anniversaries with this complete set. Includes 6, 9, 12 and 15-in. diameter aluminum pans. Retail value, if purchased separately, $27.96.
504-P-207. $24.99 set

5. HAPPINESS HEART PAN SET.
Bakes a show of your affection on any happy occasion. This versatile pan set is a lovely gift idea, especially for bride-to-be. Takes just one cake mix. See the Valentine Pie on p. 28. Each aluminum pan is 9 x 1½-in. deep.
2105-P-956. $6.49 set

6. HEART MINI-TIER SET.
Perfect tiers for small gatherings. This pretty, special cake takes just one cake mix. Set includes 5, 7½ and 9-in. aluminum pans, two scallop-edged white separator plates and six clear plastic twist legs.
2105-P-409. $10.99 set

HEART MINI-TIER PLATE SET ONLY.
301-P-9728. $2.99 set

All pans made in Korea. Plastic trims, doll picks, separator plates and topper made in Hong Kong.

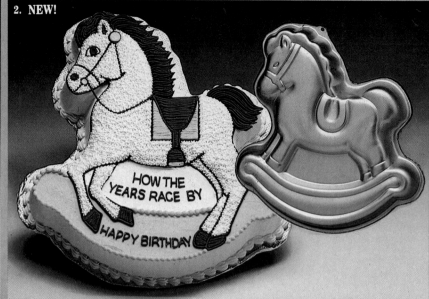

1. NEW!

1. NEW! SHOWER UMBRELLA PAN.
Perfect for showering the mom or
bride-to-be with best wishes.
Instructions and ideas for birthdays
and holidays, too. For more ideas,
look on p. 39, 44, 53 and 68. One-mix
aluminum pan is 12½ x 11¾ x 2-in.
2105-P-2293. $8.49 each

2. NEW! ROCKING HORSE PAN.
You'll gallop through the decorating!
Guests will race to the table to see
this all-time favorite toy cake.
Instructions include birthday and
holiday decorating ideas. See more
delightful designs on p. 47, 54
and 56. One-mix aluminum pan is
13½ x 13½ x 2-in.
2105-P-2388. $8.49 each

3. HUGGABLE TEDDY BEAR PAN.
This best buddy cake will be adored
by young and grown alike. Adorable
for birthdays, baby showers and
school treats. More great ways to
decorate on p. 8 and 17. Aluminum
pan is 13½ x 12¼ x 1⅞-in.
2105-P-4943. $8.49 each

4. GOOD NEWS STORK.
The mom-to-be will beam when this
special delivery cake arrives.
Alternate decorating ideas for
birthdays and travel, too. See the
charming birthday cake on p. 12.
One-mix aluminum pan is
13 x 11¾ x 2-in.
2105-P-4587. $8.49 each

5. MINI CLOWN PANS.
Everyone loves a clown and you'll
love this versatile pan. Bakes 6
individual cakes to decorate with
zippy, zany faces. Complete
instructions and alternate decorating
ideas on label. Each pan well takes
½-cup of batter. Aluminum pan is
12 x 9½ x 1¼-in.
2105-P-5621. $7.49 each

1. BUNNY PAN.
Bakes a cottontail cutie that's always a big favorite. See the clever birthday cake on p. 17. Takes 6 cups of pound cake batter. Two-part, snap-together aluminum pan is 8¾ x 10¼-in. With baking and decorating instructions.
2105-P-2223. $9.99 each

2. LITTLE LAMB PAN.
Creates a lovable 3-D delight for Easter, baby showers and birthdays. Use pound cake batter (6 cups). 2-piece aluminum pan is 10 x 7-in. tall. Easy-to-decorate instructions included.
2105-P-2010. $8.99 each

3. HOLIDAY BUNNY PAN.
The perfect hare for your Easter fare. This "egg-dorable" treat is a joy to decorate. Two-part aluminum pan is 12-in. high and takes 6½ cups of pound cake batter. With step-by-step baking and decorating guide.
2105-P-5885. $10.99 each

All pans made in Korea.

PLEASE NOTE: All prices, certain products and services, reflect the U.S.A. domestic market and do not apply in Australia and Canada.

4. NEW! CHICK•IN•EGG PAN.
Fun's a-hatchin'! Bakes a sunnyside-up cake that's a breeze to decorate! This peep-treat is perfect for baby showers, Mother's Day and birthdays, too. See pages 7, 14, 22, 35, 36 for lots of clever ways to decorate. Instructions include more. One-mix aluminum pan is 14½ x 9 x 2-in.
2105-P-2356. $6.49 each

5. EGG MINICAKE PAN.
Bake up eight party-size cakes. Great for molding ice cream, gelatin and Candy Melts™ brand confectionery coating, too. Half oval wells are 3¼ x 2⅜-in. One cake mix yields about 24 cakes. Decorating guide on label.
2105-P-2118. $7.49 each

6. EGG PAN SET.
Create an egg-traordinary holiday/springtime treat (see p. 33 and 35). Two-piece aluminum pan takes just one cake mix. Each half is 8¾ x 5⅜-in. and has ring base for level baking.
2105-P-700. $9.99 each
EGG PAN RING ONLY.
503-P-954. .99¢

7. CROSS PAN.
A glorious cake idea for Easter, christenings, confirmations—all blessed events. Instructions include a birthday and family reunion cake idea, too. For more lovely designs, see p. 34, 55 and 62. One-mix aluminum pan is 14½ x 11⅛ x 2-in.
2105-P-2509. $6.49 each

SHAPED PANS

1. MINI SHAMROCK PAN.
Irish eyes will be smiling! This one-mix aluminum pan bakes six individual 3 x 4-in. clover-shaped cakes. Alternate decorating ideas on label make it very versatile. Pan: 13¼ x 9¾ x 1¼-in.
2105-P-3459. $7.49 each

2. TRAIL RIDER PAN.
Bake and decorate a cake with lots of get up and go! You'll get a lot of mileage out of this one-mix aluminum pan...perfect for birthdays, Dad's Day, bon voyage and more. Pan: 15¾ x 8½ x 2-in.
2105-P-5583. $8.49 each

3. GOOD CHEER MUG PAN.
Brimming with happy wishes...it's a cake toast to toast the good times. Several clever decorating ideas included make this one-mix aluminum pan a year 'round delight. Pan: 13 x 10½ x 2-in.
2105-P-5496. $8.49 each

4. SAILBOAT PAN.
You'll breeze through decorating this free-spirited cake. It's a sunsational idea for birthdays, Dad's Day, just for fun and more! Instructions include several alternate cake ideas. One-mix aluminum pan: 12⅝ x 10⅜ x 2-in.
2105-P-5532. $8.49 each

All pans made in Korea.

PLEASE NOTE: All prices, certain products and services reflect the U.S.A. domestic market and do not apply in Australia and Canada.

5. BALL PAN.
Round out your decorating talents with this unique pan and have a ball. Make firm textured cakes to stand alone or use half or whole ball cakes atop larger cakes. Set includes two 6-in. diameter half ball pans and two metal baking stands. Each pan section takes 2¼ cups batter.
502-P-3002. $8.49 set

BALL PAN BAKE STAND ONLY.
503-P-881. 99¢ each

6. BOWLING PIN PAN.
Create lots of striking cakes with this 2-part aluminum pan. Make a stand-up cake or lay half cakes atop or along sheet cake (see Pan Index for ideas, p. 192). Set includes two 14-in. pans and two baking racks. Takes one cake mix for 2 halves.
502-P-4424. $8.99 set

BOWLING PIN BAKE RACK ONLY.
503-P-989. $1.99 each

CARE BEARS™ CAKE PANS

1. STAND-UP CARE BEARS™ PAN.
Add new dimension to your next party!
Set includes 2-pc. aluminum shaped
pan, clips and stand to bake a one-piece
bear with firm or pound cake batter.
Pan: 9¼ x 9 x 6-in deep.
2105-P-2350. $12.99 each

2. CARE BEARS™ (Flat) PAN.
This jolly little fellow will make any party
more festive! Instructions show you how
to decorate 4 different Care Bears for
birthdays, fun-times, anytime! One mix
aluminum pan: 14½ x 10¼ x 2-in.
2105-P-1793. $8.99 each
CARE BEARS™ is a registered trademark of
American Greetings Corp. © MCMLXXXIV.
Wilton Enterprises, Inc. Authorized User.

GET ALONG GANG™ PANS

3. DOTTY DOG™ PAN.
Let this lovable character lead the cheers
at birthday parties, sleep-overs and get-
togethers! She'll lead the way to a fun-
time, too. One-mix aluminum pan is fun
to decorate. Pan: 15 x 10 x 2-in.
2105-P-3975. $8.99 each

4. MONTGOMERY "Good News" MOOSE.™
Decorate a cake that's full of fun for your
next children's party! You can count on
this character to be a hit. One-mix
aluminum cake pan is easy to do, too!
Pan: 14½ x 9 x 2-in.
2105-P-1968. $8.99 each
GET ALONG GANG™ and related characters are
registered trademarks of American Greeting Corp.
© MCMLXXXIV. Wilton Enterprises, Inc.
Authorized User.

**NOTE: LICENSED CHARACTER PANS
CANNOT BE SOLD FOR COMMERCIAL USE.**

1. GARFIELD® STAND-UP CAKE PAN SET. Easy to do, even if you've never decorated before! Use 2-pc. shaped aluminum pan, clips and stand to bake a 3-D cake in one step…no cutting or layering needed. Decorating is fast—details are baked right in. Plastic face plate included. Finished cake: 6 x 6 x 9-in. high.
2105-P-3147. $12.99 set
PLASTIC FACEPLATE ONLY.
503-P-3147. $1.99 each
© 1984 GARFIELD. Licensed by United Features Syndicate, Inc.

2. GARFIELD® PAN (Flat). This irrepressible feline is the perfect cake to carry your tongue-in-cheek message for birthdays, Christmas, Valentine's Day and more! Complete instructions for 5 different ideas included. Includes one-mix aluminum cake pan and realistic plastic face plate. Pan: 11½ x 12½ x 2-in.
2105-P-2447. $8.99 set
PLASTIC FACEPLATE ONLY.
503-P-2448. $1.99 each

3. SUPER HEROES PAN. Perfect for birthdays, Dad's Day, promotions and more. Set contains 13 x 13 x 2-in. one-mix aluminum pan, plastic face masks and chest emblems for both SUPERMAN* and BATMAN.*
2105-P-8507. $8.99 set
BATMAN™ EMBLEM AND MASK.
503-P-814. $1.99 set
SUPERMAN™ EMBLEM AND MASK.
503-P-857. $1.99 set
*TRADEMARKS LICENSED BY DC COMICS, INC. © 1978.

4. STRAWBERRY SHORTCAKE™ PAN. She's an adorable sight, sure to delight. Turn her strawberry into a heart, cupcake or gift for any special day. One-mix aluminum pan: 13 x 12¾ x 2-in.
2105-P-4458. $8.99 each
© MCMLXXXII American Greetings Corp.
Pans made in Korea.
Plastic parts and trims made in Hong Kong.
NOTE: LICENSED CHARACTER PANS CANNOT BE SOLD FOR COMMERCIAL USE.

1. NEW! CABBAGE PATCH KIDS® PREEMIE.™
Newest family member is fun for showers, baby's
1st birthday, more! One-mix aluminum pan:
11 x 8 x 2-in.
2105-P-1990. $8.99 each

2. CABBAGE PATCH KIDS® PAN (Flat).
A most welcomed visitor for birthdays, Halloween,
Valentine's Day, Christmas and more—6 ideas in
all. One-mix aluminum pan: 13 x 12½ x 2-in.
2105-P-1984. $8.99 each

3. STAND-UP CABBAGE PATCH KIDS® PAN.
Set includes 2-pc. shaped aluminum pan, clips
and stand to bake a 3-D cake easy as 1-2-3!
Instructions show you 3 ways to decorate this
lovable character. Finished cake: 6 x 7 x 9-in high.
2105-P-1988. $12.99 set

CABBAGE PATCH KIDS® and PREEMIE™ are registered trademarks of and licensed from Original Appalachian Artworks, Inc.
© 1984. All rights reserved.

4. DONALD DUCK PAN. Change his cake into a
drum, gift and more—easy directions tell how.
One-mix aluminum pan: 12 x 14¼ x 1⅞-in.
2105-P-4556. $8.99 each

5. MICKEY MOUSE PAN. Instructions show you
how to change his pencil into flowers, an art brush
and decorating bag. One-mix aluminum pan:
15⅛ x 11½ x 2-in.
2105-P-4358. $8.99 each

Walt Disney's Mickey Mouse and Donald Duck
© Walt Disney Productions.

**PLEASE NOTE: All prices, certain products and services,
reflect the U.S.A. domestic market and do not apply in
Australia and Canada.**

**NOTE: LICENSED CHARACTER PANS CANNOT BE
SOLD FOR COMMERCIAL USE.**

1. RAINBOW BRITE™ PAN. Invite this lovable, adorable little girl to brighten birthdays, holidays, school gatherings and more with her colorful personality! She'll make you a decorating star! Five delightful ways to decorate included. One-mix aluminum pan is 15 x 11 x 2-in.
2105-P-4798. $8.99 each
© 1983 Hallmark Cards, Inc.

2. MINI SMURF™ PAN. Mini cakes are single-serving size—perfect for parties, lunch boxes, school treats! Instructions show you how to decorate the whole Smurf family. 13½ x 9¼ x 1-in. aluminum pan bakes six 4 x 3½-in. cakes.
2105-P-2386. $7.99 each

3. SMURFETTE™ PAN. Golly, what a dolly! Personalize her big balloon or change it into a candy cane, heart or tennis racket—instructions tell you how. One-mix aluminum pan: 16 x 11 x 1⅜-in.
2105-P-5419. $8.99 each
SMURFS™ and related characters. © 1983 Peyo. Licensed by Wallace Berrie & Co., Inc. Woodland Hills, CA. All rights reserved.

4. SMURF™ PAN. This adorable little guy will be the apple of everyone's eye. We'll show you four more smurfing great ways to decorate to make any day special. One-mix aluminum pan: 15¾ x 12 x 1⅞-in.
2105-P-5435. $8.99 each

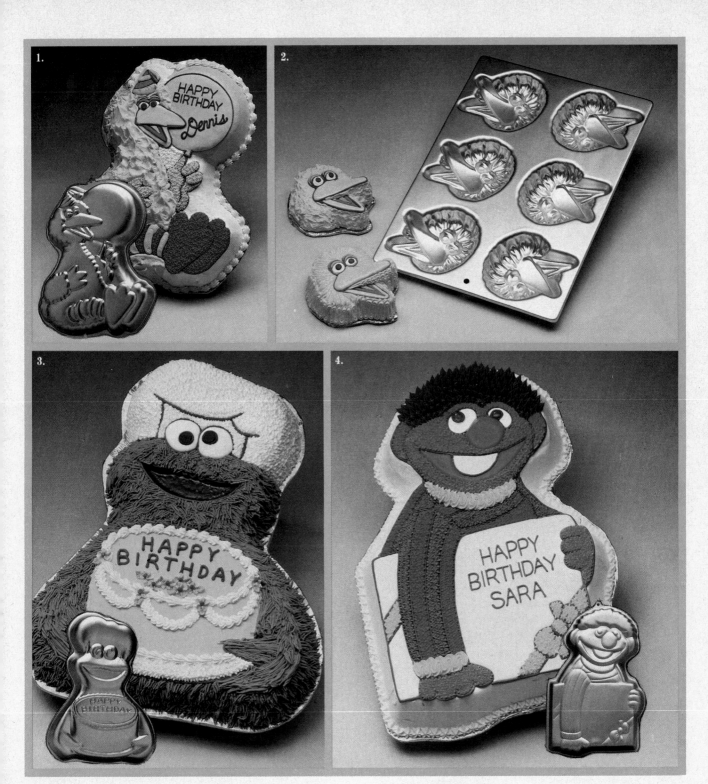

1. BIG BIRD CAKE PAN. What fun! Decorate this lovable Sesame Street™ character with a balloon, clock, umbrella, sunshine or ice cream cone —instructions tell you how. One-mix aluminum pan: 13½ x 10¾ x 1⅞-in. **2105-P-3653. $8.99 each**

2. MINI BIG BIRD PAN. Individual servings are great party treats for birthdays, school, most anytime! Add names and use as "placecards." 13 x 9¼ x 1-in. aluminum pan bakes six 4 x 3½-in. cakes. **2105-P-2384. $7.99 each**

3. COOKIE MONSTER CAKE PAN. He takes the cake! This lovable Sesame Street™ friend should be on hand for birthdays, holidays and more. Fun to do! One-mix aluminum pan: 14½ x 11½ x 1⅞-in. **2105-P-4927. $8.99 each**

4. ERNIE CAKE PAN. This gifted guy stops by to give the birthday boy or girl a big surprise. Turn his gift into 3 other things—instructions included. One-mix aluminum pan: 14½ x 10 x 1⅞-in. **2105-P-3173. $8.99 each**

NOTE: LICENSED CHARACTER PANS CANNOT BE SOLD FOR COMMERCIAL USE.

SUPER SALE!

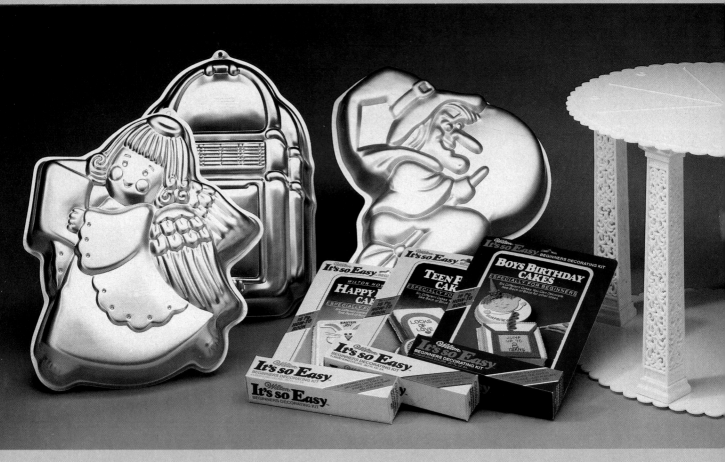

ONE-MIX SHAPED PANS
DARTH VADER™ PAN. (See '84 Yearbook, p. 180.)
2105-P-1278. Was $8.95. **Now $4.00 each**

C-3PO™ PAN. (See '85 Yearbook, p. 180.)
2105-P-1464. Was $8.99. **Now $4.00 each**

BOBA FETT™ PAN. (See '84 Yearbook, p. 180.)
2105-P-1741. Was $8.95. **Now $4.00 each**
™ and © Lucasfilm Ltd. (LFL) 1983. All rights reserved.
Wilton Enterprises Authorized User.

PINK PANTHER™ PAN. (See '84 Yearbook, p. 181.)
2105-P-2576. Was $8.95. **Now $4.00 each**
™ and © 1977 United Artists. All rights reserved.

THE COUNT PAN. (See '83 Yearbook, p. 187.)
2105-P-2673. Was $8.95. **Now $4.00 each**
© 1982 Children's Television Workshop.
© 1982 Muppets, Inc. All rights reserved.

JOYFUL ANGEL PAN. (See '84 Yearbook, p. 169.)
2105-P-2797. Was $5.99. **Now $4.00 each**

YOSEMITE SAM† PAN. (See '84 Yearbook, p. 178.)
2105-P-3207. Was $6.99. **Now $4.00 each**

BUGS BUNNY† PAN. (See '84, '85 Yearbooks,
p. 178 and 191.)
2105-P-3351. Was $8.99. **Now $4.00 each**
†indicates Trademark of Warner Bros., Inc. © 1981

CATHY™ PAN. (See '85 Wilton Yearbook, p. 191.)
2105-P-4641. Was $8.99. **Now $4.00 each**
™ 1983 Universal Press Syndicate.

HIGH FLYIN' WITCH PAN. (See '84 Wilton
Yearbook, p. 167.)
2105-P-4773. Was $5.95. **Now $4.00 each**

ROCKIN' JUKE BOX PAN. (See '85 Yearbook,
p. 166.)
2105-P-5311. Was $7.99. **Now $4.00 each**

**EXCITING SAVINGS ON "IT'S SO EASY"
DECORATING KITS.**
Each includes idea book, decorating tools and
icing colors.

Was $2.99. **Now $1.50 each**

KIT	STOCK NO.	KIT	STOCK NO.
EASTER.	2104-P-1525.	BOY'S	
SPORTS		BIRTHDAYS.	2104-P-3268.
EVENTS.	2104-P-3209.	HAPPY	
GIRL'S		EVENTS.	2104-P-3284.
BIRTHDAYS	2104-P-3241.	ADULT	
TEEN'S	2104-P-3225.	BIRTHDAYS.	2104-P-3314.

QUALITY PLASTIC CAKE TOPS
ANGEL MUSICIANS. (See '83 Yearbook, p. 165.)
1001-P-1800. Was $1.80. **Now 79¢ pk. of 2**

YELLOW SATIN BELL.
1001-P-9195. Was 90¢. **Now 79¢**

SOLDIER BAND. (See '83 Wilton Yearbook,
p. 119.)
2113-P-2198. Was 99¢. **Now 50¢ each**

SKATEBOARD STUNT RIDER. (See '83 Yearbook,
p. 121.)
2113-P-2376. Was $2.50. **Now 50¢ each**

BIKER BOY. (See '85 Wilton Yearbook, p. 134.)
2113-P-2678. Was $2.59. **Now $1.29 each**

SYLVESTER* & TWEETY.* (See '85 Yearbook,
p. 137.)
2113-P-2562. $2.59. **Now $1.29 each**
*indicates trademark of Warner Bros., Inc. © 1979

GRIN 'N BEAR IT CATHY.™ ('85 Yearbook, p. 137.)
2113-P-4085. Was $2.59. **Now $1.29 each**

CATHY™ SAYS. (See '85 Wilton Yearbook, p. 137.)
2113-P-2724. Was $1.59. **Now 99¢ each**
© 1983 Universal Press Syndicate.

BATMAN†. (See '85 Wilton Yearbook, p. 137.)
2113-P-2902. Was $1.99. **Now 99¢ each**
†indicates Trademark of DC Comics, Inc.

PINK PANTHER & INSPECTOR™ SET.
('84 Yearbook, p. 138.)
2113-P-3208. Was $1.50. **Now $1.29 set**
™ & © 1980 United Artists. All rights reserved.

ZIGGY. (See '84 Yearbook, p. 132.)
2113-P-4581. Was $1.25. **Now 99¢ each**
ZIGGY™ by Tom Wilson.
© 1983 Universal Press Syndicate.

SEPARATOR PLATES & SETS
LACY-LOOK SEPARATOR SET. (See '84 Yearbook,
p. 156.) With 16-in. diam. round plates,
12-in. pillars.
301-P-1719. Was $19.95. **Now $13.90 set**

3-IN. CRYSTAL CLEAR GRECIAN PILLARS.
('83 Yearbook, p. 170.)
303-P-1122. Were $2.00. **Now $1.50 pk. of 4**

13-IN. ROUND. (See '82 Yearbook, p. 164.)
302-P-1123. Was $4.25. **Now $3.00 each**

CRYSTAL CLEAR ROUND SEPARATOR PLATES.
(See '83 Yearbook, p. 171.)

Size	Stock No.	Was	Now
9-IN.	302-P-1535.	$2.95	$2.20 each
11-IN.	302-P-1578.	$3.95	$3.00 each
13-IN.	302-P-1594.	$4.95	$3.50 each

PLEASE NOTE: These products are sure to sell super fast! Don't delay—order right away!

CANDY MAKER™ PRODUCTS. (See '83-'85 Yearbooks for more details.)

Mold	No.	Was	Now
CLASSIC MOLDS			
CLASSIC BELL	1001-P-9144	$ .99	$ .50
MUSHROOMS	2114-P-572	1.89	.99
CHESS PCS.	2114-P-602	1.89	.99
COAT OF ARMS	2114-P-688	1.89	.99
STARS/SUNS	2114-P-734	1.89	.99
OVAL	2114-P-971	1.89	.99
NAUTICAL	2114-P-4204	1.89	.99
LOCOMOTIVE/ BALLOON	2114-P-4218	1.89	.99
HAZELNUT/ ALMONDS	2114-P-4240	1.89	.99
GREETING CARD MOLDS			
CONGRATULATIONS	1902-P-910	1.89	.99
CHRISTMAS	1902-P-1339	1.89	.99
NOEL	1902-P-1428	1.89	.99
GET WELL	1902-P-1576	1.89	.79
HAPPY BIRTHDAY	1902-P-1592	1.89	.99
LOVE	1902-P-1606	1.89	.99

CHARACTER MOLDS			
SMURFS I™	2114-P-1617	2.29	.99
SMURFS II™	2114-P-1633	2.29	.99
SMURF™ STAND-UP	2114-P-2036	2.49	.99
BABY SMURF™ STAND-UP	2114-P-2143	2.49	.99

© 1983 Peyo Licensed by Wallace Berrie & Co., Inc. Woodland Hills, CA

CATHY™	2114-P-1706	2.29	.99
CATHY™ (Stand-Up)	2114-P-1722	2.49	.99

™ 1983 Universal Press Syndicate Company.

STAR WARS II	2114-P-1870	2.29	.99
R2-D2 STAND-UP	2114-P-2010	2.49	.99
STAR WARS (HARD CANDY)	2115-P-346	1.99	.99

™ & © Lucasfilm LTD. (LFL) 1983 All rights reserved. Wilton Enterprises Authorized User.

PINK PANTHER	2114-P-3318	2.00	.99

™ & © 1983 United Artists. All rights reserved.

SUPER FLEX HARD CANDY MOLDS			
CHRISTMAS	1910-P-108	$4.00	$2.50
HEART	1910-P-817	2.50	.99
DAISIES	1910-P-876	2.50	.99
LEAVES	1910-P-884	2.00	.99
RUFFLES	1910-P-892	2.00	.99
FLUTES	1910-P-914	2.00	.99
SQUARES	1910-P-930	2.00	.99
OVALS	1910-P-957	2.00	.99
EGGS	1910-P-973	2.00	.99
SUPER FLEX LOLLIPOP MOLDS			
HEART	1910-P-1112	2.50	.99
STAR	1910-P-1155	2.50	.99
FLOWER	1910-P-1198	2.50	.99
ROUND/HEART	1910-P-1228	2.50	.99
ROUND/STAR	1910-P-1244	2.50	.99
VARIOUS SHAPES	1910-P-1287	2.50	.99
VARIETY II	1910-P-1333	2.50	.99
CANDY MAKING ACCESSORIES			
TRUFFLE CUTTER	1902-P-1398	.99	.50
MINT PATTY FUNNEL	1904-P-528	12.95	6.99
VALENTINE CANDY LABELS	1912-P-1936	1.50	.99
STAINLESS STEEL CUTTERS	1901-P-2446	2.00	1.00
CANDY FLAVOR			
LIME	1913-P-454	1.99	1.50
ROOT BEER	1913-P-551	1.99	1.50
SPEARMINT	1913-P-616	1.99	1.50
APRICOT	1913-P-772	1.99	1.50

All pans and stainless steel cutters made in Korea. Plastic products, parts, plates made in Hong Kong.

Decorator's Index

Pan Index

NOTE: Bold face numbers indicate where pan is sold.

For Your Convenience...
Use This

SHOP·AT·HOME
ORDER
FORM

Most of the products in this book are available at your local Wilton dealer. In the event the items you want are not available locally, use this convenient, shop-at-home Order Form. It's easy to use and you'll receive delivery within 10 working days after we receive your order.

Wilton.

Caller Service No. 1604
2240 West 75th Street
Woodridge, IL 60517
(312) 963-7100

(Fill in only if different from Sold To.)

middle initial   last

STATE _____ ZIP _____

ard!

↑ IMPORTANT: This coupon must be detached before ↑
you mail your envelope!

Will Not Be
Delivered
Without
Proper
Postage

Enclose your signed check or money order with Order Form.

Wilton ®

ENTERPRISES, INC.
Caller Service No. 1604
2240 West 75th Street
Woodridge, IL 60517

FROM

Name

Address

City   Apt. No.

State   Zip

If your name and/or address has changed
since you last ordered from Wilton, please
fill in previous address here.

Name

Address

City   Apt. No.

State   Zip

For Office Use Only
Please do not write in spaces

	PRICE OF ONE	TOTAL PRICE	
		Dollars	Cents
ing)	$3.99		
	$5.99		
	$12.99		

For Office Use Only:
- Date
- Cash
- Debit M.
- Credit M.
- Handling Charge
- Air Mail
- Foreign
- Pal/Sam
- Coupon
- Gift Ct.

TAX NOTE
& POSTAGE CHARGE
on chart to the left.

MONEY BACK GUARANTEE
If you are not completely satisfied with your Wilton purchase, return the item for an exchange or refund.

LT

ORDER FORM

① **SOLD TO: (PLEASE PRINT PLAINLY)**

NAME _____
_{first}   middle initial

ADDRESS _____

CITY _____ STATE _____ ZIP _____

AREA CODE _____ DAYTIME PHONE NO. _____

② **CREDIT CARD ORDERS**   VISA   MasterCard

Expiration
Month/Year _____ Sign

③	④			⑤	
PAGE	**STOCK NUMBER**			**HOW MANY**	**DI**
135	1701	P	867		1986 Yearbook
	1607	P	728		Sur
	1607	P	805		Sur

Shipping and Handling Charges (See No. 9)
Orders up to $25.00 .... add $2.50
Orders from $25.01 - $50.00 ..... add $3.00
Orders from $50.01 - $75.00 ..... add $4.00
Orders from $75.01 - $100.00 ... add $5.00
Orders over $100.00 .... add $6.00

Enjoy Quick Delivery!
Your Wilton Order Arrives Within
10 Working Days After We Receive It!

NO C.O.D. ORDERS

⑦ TOTA
⑧ STAT
⑨ ADD
   NOTE
⑩ SPEC
   SUB
⑪ CRED
   TOTA

P**lease Send Cake Decorating/
Candy Making Information to:**

Name _____

Address _____

City _____

State _____ Zip _____

LV

↑ IMPORTANT: This coupon must be detached before ↑
you mail your envelope!

FROM

Name _____

Address _____ Apt. No. _____

City _____

State _____ Zip _____

If your name and/or address has changed
since you last ordered from Wilton, please
fill in previous address here.

Name _____

Address _____ Apt. No. _____

City _____

State _____ Zip _____

Wilton®

ENTERPRISES, INC.
Caller Service No. 1604
2240 West 75th Street
Woodridge, IL 60517

Enclose your signed check or money order with Order Form.

Will Not Be
Delivered
Without
Proper
Postage

Surprise Package

Treat Yourself to Something Special!

Get a super selection of Wilton products at surprising savings. It's an offer made especially for you.

Choose from two special packages. Both contain a variety of products to help you get the most from your baking and decorating. . .and for your money!

Package I contains $12.95 worth of quality products for only

$5.99*

Package II contains $25.00 worth of quality products for only

$12.99*

Order both or just one. Just indicate quantity and total price on the Order Form.

*Products in packages change periodically. Sorry, no returns or substitutions accepted.